ADOPTION NATION

ADOPTION NATION

How the
Adoption Revolution
Is Transforming America

ADAM PERTMAN

BASIC
BOOKS

A Member of the Perseus Books Group

Published by Basic Books,
A Member of the Perseus Books Group

Library of Congress Cataloging-in-Publication Data

Pertman, Adam
  Adoption nation: how the adoption revolution is transforming America /
Adam Pertman.
    p.   cm.
  Includes bibliographical references and index.
  ISBN 0-465-05650-4
  1. Adoption—United States.   I. Title.

HV875.55 .P47 2000
362.73'4'0973—dc21

                                                                00-034297

The paper used in this publication meets the requirements of the American
National Standard for Permanence of Paper for Printed Library Materials
Z39.48–1984.

00 01 02 03 / 10 9 8 7 6 5 4 3 2 1

To Zack and Emmy,
for making my heart beat and my blood flow.

To Judy,
for transforming every moment into a joyous adventure.

To our children's other parents,
for allowing us to share their magnificent creations.

And to my parents, Frieda and Chaim,
for a lifetime of unconditional love and support.

Contents

Foreword by Madelyn Freundlich   *viii*

Prologue   *x*

Part 1

Don't Whisper, Don't Lie—It's Not a Secret Anymore

1   Out of the Shadows, into Our Lives   3

2   A Legal Maze from Coast to Coast   27

3   Joy and Surprises from Abroad   51

Part 2

Sensitive Issues, Lifelong Process

4   Adoptees: The Quest for Identity   77–101   24

5   Birth Parents: A Painful Dilemma   103–128   25

6   Adoptive Parents: Infertility Begets a Family   129–154   25

Part 3

Tough Challenges in a Promising Future

7   Special Needs, Diverse Families   157

8   The Money's the Problem   185

9   Old Lessons for a New World   209

Adoption Resources   233

Notes   237

Acknowledgments   245

Index   249

Foreword

There is no shortage of books on the topic of adoption, from personal accounts by birth parents, adoptees, and adoptive parents to "how-to" manuals on adopting and raising adopted children, to academic research and clinical presentations. But what has been lacking is a comprehensive, up-to-date overview that pulls together and sorts out the often confusing mass of information, and that does so in an engaging and readable way.

In *Adoption Nation*, Adam Pertman, an adoptive father and an award-winning journalist, finally—and admirably—fills this gap. Combining compelling stories with a penetrating and thoughtful analysis of the role of adoption in today's society and its likely future impact, *Adoption Nation* is an indispensable resource for anyone who wants to learn how this crucial issue is shaping lives. As a bonus, it is also provocative, thoughtful, and a delight to read.

Pertman offers a wealth of valuable information and practical advice for people personally or professionally involved in adoption, including critical insights about navigating the turbulent waters of agencies, lawyers and facilitators. What truly distinguishes his book, however, is that he also does far more: He shows how adoption impacts our view of ourselves, our changing families, our metamorphosing communities, and our growing connections to a global world. Since it forces us to confront questions about personal identity, the nature of family, the relationships between racial and ethnic communities, and the role of different societies' perspectives on children and families, adoption has long demanded much wider and deeper attention than it has received. In this book, the subject finally gets its due.

Adoption Nation does not shrink from tough issues, and so it will (and should) spark debate. It probably will even upset some readers who would rather not face up to the flaws in an institution that has served their personal or financial needs. But Pertman's goal is always clearly to improve a process he loves; confronting the truth and advocating for reforms are the wise ways he has chosen to show his affection. Indeed, he tackles every aspect of adoption head-on, with keen observations about its strengths and pitfalls: the thicket of conflicting and often archaic laws and regulations; the twists and turns of both domestic and international adoption; society's ambivalence about adoptees, birth parents, and adoptive families; the controversies engulfing the adoption of children in foster care; the growing cost of adoption; and the swirl of politics that is enveloping adoption on so many fronts.

Every chapter of *Adoption Nation* sheds new light on this multifaceted topic, and every page glows with the presence of real people, whose voices give eloquent testimony to the powerful impact of adoption on their own lives and on the cultural fiber of our country. Written with tremendous authority, and an engaging personal voice rare in a book that is at its core an important sociological study, *Adoption Nation* is must reading for anyone who wants or needs to understand this vital subject and what is a historic revolution in the United States. Perhaps most important, Pertman's is the first book that aspires to inform not only people who know they have direct connections to adoption, but everyone whose life is touched by the process, whether they know it or not. Which is to say, nearly everyone. Those who read *Adoption Nation* will discover just how much they've been missing.

MADELYN FREUNDLICH
Policy Director, Children's Rights, Inc.
Former Executive Director, The Evan B. Donaldson Adoption Institute

Prologue

Seven years ago, when Judy and I discovered we couldn't create a family in the old-fashioned way, we knew as much about adoption as we did about annuities. Which is to say, nearly nothing. Moreover, like most Americans, the little we thought we understood was distorted or misguided or wrong. So we formed opinions about the essential elements in our children's lives—and in our own—that were distorted and misguided and wrong.

Thankfully, we've made enormous progress in a very short time, and so has adoption itself. The hows and whys of the transformation are copious, complex and often subtle; they are the puzzle pieces that I've tried to assemble into this book. But the fact that a seismic cultural shift is occurring is as certain as the growing openness with which adoption, after a painfully long history of secrecy, is finally being practiced.

I was thinking about all this one day when an image popped into my mind. And my friend and colleague at the Boston Globe, the award-winning editorial cartoonist Dan Wasserman, has brought it to life. It's an exaggerated view of reality, to be sure, but it reflects a fundamental truth: The revolution has already radically altered public perceptions of a flawed, frustrating and remarkable institution that answers the prayers and enriches the lives of millions of people every day. I feel blessed to be among them.

what about bmoms & their children? Their lives aren't really enriched. The adopters are -> So, point is, adoption always was for childless couples, not moms or their children. - a bit radical, but true.

"Oh, I'm sorry. . .You couldn't adopt?"

It doesn't take much to start a revolution of thought and spirit. It takes one person and then another and then another. We have to have the willingness to be respectful of each other and not to let differences become obstacles. We have the power to change things.

—Lenny Zakim, human-rights activist and friend (1953–1999)

PART ONE

Don't Whisper, Don't Lie— It's Not a Secret Anymore

1

Out of the Shadows, Into Our Lives

My son was three years old and my daughter had lived on this earth for just two months when I met Sheila Hansen. She's a tall, soft-spoken woman who laughs easily and exudes warmth when she speaks; she has the kind of comfortable self-confidence that immediately makes you think she'd make a loyal friend and a good mother. On that muggy July day, sitting in the conference room of a church in southern New Jersey, she told me a story that chilled me to the bone and forever altered the way I think about my adopted children, about birth parents, and about the country in which I grew up.

In 1961, Sheila was a 21-year-old government clerk in Louisiana when she told her boyfriend she was pregnant. He responded by giving her the name of a doctor who performed abortions. The procedure wasn't legal at the time, but everyone knew you could get one if you wanted to. Sheila didn't want to. As frightened and confused and alone as she felt, the one thing she knew for sure was that she wanted to keep her baby.

Her doctor didn't think it was such a good idea, though. He gave her advice like: "You won't be able to give the child a proper home." And: "This would ruin your life." Her mother was sympathetic but worried about what would happen if Sheila chose to become a parent. "How is a single woman like you going to raise a child?" she asked. "What are people going to think?" Sheila's friends didn't provide much solace either, essentially behaving as though nothing was going on at all. Everywhere she turned, Sheila was reminded that she would bear the unending shame of being an unwed mother, while her "illegitimate" child would be scarred for life with the indelible brand of a bastard.

So, to keep people from seeing her in her "condition," Sheila spent the duration of her pregnancy behind the shuttered doors of her mother's New Orleans home. By the time her delivery date was approaching, she had been tortured into submission by the people who loved her most and by a society that didn't understand her at all. She felt small and helpless, too embarrassed to go to the store much less make a momentous decision that could determine the course of her life.

Her doctor, meanwhile, had found a couple who wanted to adopt a baby. With only her incidental participation, he made all the arrangements for Sheila's hospital stay and for the child to be transferred to the new parents right after birth. To "protect" her from the emotional trauma of the experience, every effort was made to separate Sheila from it: She was registered under an assumed name and was heavily sedated for the delivery, so she would feel and remember as little as possible. The nurses were instructed to refer to her offspring only as "the baby," so that she wouldn't even know its gender.

Not until 8:45 P.M. on November 31, 1995, when her son telephoned her after a determined search, did she learn she'd given life to a boy. "All I did after we hung up was cry," Sheila told me. Based on what she had endured, I expected she would feel only contempt for adoption, but she is wiser than that. While she knows the process is seldom as simple as people would like to believe, she thinks everyone can ultimately benefit if it's done right. Besides, Sheila likes the way her firstborn son turned out (she went on to marry and have another boy), respects his parents, and appreciates the loving home they gave him. "But I'll tell you this," she says, wiping away a tear but faintly smiling at her optimistic conclusion: "The system we had didn't work; thank God it seems to be changing."

After a long period of warning tremors, adoption is "changing" like a simmering volcano changes when it can no longer contain its explosive energy. It erupts. The hot lava flows from its soul, permanently reshaping not only the mountain itself but also every inch of landscape it touches. The new earth becomes more fertile, richer in color. The sensation of watching the transformation, of being a part of it, is an awesome amalgam of anxiety and exhilaration. The metamorphosis itself is breathtaking. Before our eyes, in our homes and schools and media and workplaces, America is forever changing adoption even as adoption is forever changing America.

This is nothing less than a revolution. After a decade of incremental improvements and tinkering at the margins, adoption is reshaping itself to the core. It is shedding its corrosive stigmas and rejecting its secretive past; states are revising their laws and agencies are rewriting their rules even as the Internet is rendering them obsolete, especially by making it simpler for adoptees and birth parents to find each other; single women, multiracial families, and gay men and women are flowing into the parenting mainstream; middle-aged couples are bringing a rainbow of children from abroad into their predominantly white communities; and social service agencies are making it far easier to find homes for hundreds of thousands of children whose short lives have been squandered in the foster-care system.

It's not just that adoption suddenly seems to be appearing everywhere at once, as if revealed by a cosmic sleight-of-hand. Its public image is also exponentially better than it has ever been. The new climate allows birth parents like the comedian Roseanne, the singers Joni Mitchell and David Crosby, along with thousands of men and women unprotected by famous names, to finally ease their torment by disclosing their secrets and meeting their children. It leads celebrities like Steven Spielberg, Tom Cruise, and Rosie O'Donnell to proudly announce the arrival of their adopted children, further raising the profile of the process and accelerating public understanding that it's another normal way of forming a family. And it allows adoptees to learn that they aren't "different" in any negative sense, though they've been treated that way in the past; rather, they're part of a big, successful community whose members range from baseball legend Jim Palmer to former President Gerald Ford to Apple Computer founder Steve Jobs.

Stunningly, marvelously, for the first time in its history, adoption has _huh?_ come into vogue. At a recent dinner party with a half dozen friends, I offhandedly cited a well-known statistic among researchers—that fewer than three percent of American women relinquish their babies for adoption today, a precipitous drop from a few decades ago—to which one woman at the table responded: "Are you sure it isn't much higher? Just about everyone I know with children adopted them." A few weeks later, an acquaintance told me that a classmate of her nine-year-old son, upon learning that he was adopted, sounded downright envious. "That's so cool," the boy said, and none of the other kids huddled around them offered a hint of dissent.

Every historic phenomenon begins with a specific group and then sweeps through the entire population. That's what is happening in America today, complete with the trepidation and triumph that accompany all cultural upheavals. The emerging new realities undeniably are replete with problems and paradoxes. They are raising new issues for families and creating new dilemmas for the country. But they also are more sensible, more humane, and more focused on children's well-being than the realities being left behind.

Adoption is at once a marvel of humanity and a social safety valve. It permits the infertile among us to share the deeply fulfilling, profoundly joyful experience of raising children. It offers a positive option for people who, for moral or economic or personal reasons, believe they can neither undergo an abortion nor parent a child. Most important, whatever it might accomplish for the adults in the picture, it provides a systematic opportunity for children to grow up in stable homes with loving parents.

The revolution was long overdue, and it already is having a penetrating impact. It is advancing the ethnic, racial, and cultural diversity that is a hallmark of twenty-first-century America, and it is contributing to a permanent realignment in the way we think of family structure. It is a revolution reflected in our national and state politics, in our newspapers and on the worldwide web, even in the ads we watch on television. And it promises to help heal one of our most virulent national diseases: the wasting away of children in foster care.

Americans can feel something happening around them, and even to them, but most haven't identified the revolution for what it is. They assume, as we all mistakenly do about so many aspects of life, that only the people directly involved in adoption are affected by it. Americans are too busy or distracted to consider why they hadn't been aware of the "triad" of adoptees, adoptive parents, and birth parents (and certainly wouldn't have talked about it if they had), yet suddenly they see triad members everywhere they turn.

Of course, we were always there. But our existence was carefully cloaked, just as the history of adoption itself has been written, and hidden, in the shadows. Sadly, for too many generations, this wonderful and vexing process diminished nearly everyone in its embrace, even as it enhanced their lives or served their needs.

Too many of adoption's ostensible beneficiaries, adoptive parents, spent decades deceiving those they cherished most; they often didn't reveal their children's origins at all, or insisted they share the truth with no one. The process's most essential participants, birth parents, were dehumanized; they were forced to bury their grief and humiliation within themselves, unable to share their burden with even their closest confidants. And this domestic drama's most vulnerable players, adoptees, the only ones with no say in the decision that defined their existence, were relegated to second-class social and legal status; in perhaps the most insidiously demeaning act of all, even very young adoptees were made to understand that exploring this fundamental aspect of their beings was taboo.

Not a very healthy state of affairs for an institution that was supposed to help people, which adoption most often has done despite its flaws. But now the revolution is upon us. Adoption is emerging into the warm, if sometimes harsh, light of day. It is changing rapidly, radically, and for the better. It's not quite a caterpillar shedding its cocoon, emerging as a flawless, beautiful butterfly. Light reveals imperfections, after all, and sometimes it even causes them. Still, the darkness was a far gloomier place to be, and problems that we see are easier to deal with and resolve than those that remain hidden.

Ironically, one thing we are learning as we realize how widespread adoption has become is that generations of secrecy prevent us from knowing just how widespread it has become. The subject has been considered off-limits for so long, both by individuals and by society as a whole, that until very recently studies have not been devised, census questions have not been asked, surveys have not been conducted. There is no national organization or branch of government that keeps track of adoptions, so determining how many triad members there are—or have been—would require sorting through the individual "finalization" records in every courthouse in every city and town in every state.

What research there is indicates there are five million to six million adoptees in the United States today, about triple the number experts estimated just a few years ago. Add in birth parents, adoptive parents, and biological and adoptive brothers and sisters, and the number of people directly connected to adoption soars into the tens of millions. And many experts expect the reality is even larger because an incalculable percentage of adoptees still don't know they were adopted, while many people on all sides of the triad and within their families continue to mislead anyone who asks, as well as themselves.

The most comprehensive statistics ever compiled on the subject were released in November 1997 by the Evan B. Donaldson Adoption Institute in New York. It is one of a handful of national organizations begun in the last few years to finally explore the topic in detail. The creation of these nonprofit groups, along with a proliferation of academic and legal studies, are further proof that adoption is ending its clandestine phase—even as the research itself hastens the process's emergence into full public view. The Donaldson survey showed that nearly six of every ten Americans have had a "personal experience" with adoption. That means they, a family member, or a close friend were adopted, adopted a child, or placed a child for adoption. And a stunning one-third of those polled said they had "at least somewhat seriously" considered adopting a child themselves.[1]

It's safe to assume those numbers are bare minimums since some respondents don't know the truth about themselves, and since enough of a stigma about adoption still exists to induce some people to respond less than honestly. More to the point, those figures don't include the neighbors, the colleagues and friends, the teachers, the classmates, and all the other people whose lives intertwine with members of the triad and, therefore, whose behavior and attitudes toward adoption can have a profound impact, positive or negative.

Just as the numbers remain tough to calculate, the full scope and depth of the revolution isn't yet totally clear. That's partly because adoption, like any method of forming a family, remains a fundamentally private—as opposed to secretive—concern. Mostly, though, it's simply because the landscape is being altered every day, so it's too early to assemble a complete image out of all the pieces scattered around us: the white parents picking up their yellow or brown or black toddlers at preschool, the TV movies about anguished or triumphant biological and adoptive parents, the movie stars and the people down the street proudly announcing the arrival of their adopted children from Georgia or Guatemala, the news accounts about the soaring rate of foster-care children being adopted or about adoptees clamoring to obtain their own birth certificates.

On a personal level, it's also sometimes hard for people to get a perspective on what's happening around them. To a large extent that's because faulty stereotypes and aberrational horror stories have led us, as a society, to form a distorted picture of adoption. How could anyone's perceptions have remained unaffected, for instance, by the news stories during the 1990s about four-year-old Baby Richard, who cried, "Please let me stay, I promise I'll be good," as authorities in Illinois wrenched him away from his adoptive parents to turn him over to his biological father? But such agonizing tragedies almost never happen, which is why they are big news when they do; and when state laws are subsequently revised to clarify parental rights, which is what has been done across the nation, they receive little attention from the media or the public.

Many Americans also haven't assimilated the changes taking place because so many of them seem counterintuitive, disconcerting, or bewildering. Friends often seem puzzled, for instance, when my wife, Judy, and I explain that we met Zachary's birth mother before we adopted him, and that we hung out for days with Emilia's birth parents before she was born. Some family members also appear addled by our determination to increase our level of contact with the young men and women who gave our children life. When we send the birth parents letters and photos, our relatives ask questions like, "You're not going to send such a flattering picture of Emmy, are you?" Or: "If you really spell out what a great kid Zack is, aren't you afraid they'll want to get him back?" Nearly everyone is surprised, too, when they learn that we, like the overwhelming majority of adoptive parents today, were selected for the privilege by our children's first mothers and fathers.

Better Choices, Enduring Pain

It's already a mercifully different world from the one that brutalized Sheila Hansen and countless thousands of women who suffered through nightmares like hers—though birth mothers still are seen more negatively and have been the beneficiaries of fewer reforms than anyone else involved in adoption. Nevertheless, attitudes and practices are being altered irrevocably for all concerned, and the snapshots from the wedding day of a more recent birth mother provide a vivid picture of the transformation.

Donna Asta, like virtually every bride in every such photo, radiates happiness. Unlike most brides, however, she was thrilled about more than just the fact of her marriage or even the new life she was about to begin. The reason was the pretty little girl in the teal dress posing with the wedding entourage, still clutching the white basket of rose petals she'd carried down the aisle moments earlier. "I can't wait to get home to tell my mom and dad about this," six-year-old Kelly had thought in her excitement.

No one had coerced or pressured or embarrassed Donna into relinquishing her baby for adoption. She was motivated by the same core concern that leads nearly all women, and men when they are involved, to make this excruciating decision today. While they know that physiologically they can become mothers and fathers, they strongly believe they aren't prepared to be parents. The distinction may sound subtle, but it's critical.

Most often, these are women in their late teens to mid–twenties who lack the financial or personal resources to raise a child, or whose lives would be turned inside-out if they tried. Or they suffer from problems they don't want to inflict on a child. Sometimes they're rape victims who can't face the prospect of rearing their attackers' offspring. Increasingly, they're couples who already have one or more children but feel their families would be impossibly strained if they had another mouth to feed. And they are often well-educated. Researchers say women who are younger, or have less schooling, tend to think less about the consequences of their decisions, and therefore are more prone to keep their babies.[2]

Two threads bind these varied participants at the genesis of domestic infant adoption: They do not opt for abortion, even though it often carries less social stigma for biological parents than does placing their children in new homes; and they want good lives for their babies, better than they believe they can provide. The lingering cultural stereotype of birth mothers as uncaring or ignorant young teens who choose adoption to crassly jettison a nettlesome problem is unmitigated and corrosive nonsense.

Donna was lying on a surgical table at an abortion clinic in 1986 when she realized that adoption was the only alternative she could live with. She could barely believe she had walked into this place to begin with; just a few years earlier, after all, she had been president of a Right to Life chapter at her high school. "I was on my back there for what seemed like the longest time, talking to God out loud, asking him, 'What am I doing here?'" she recalls. When the doctor finally approached her, Donna bolted upright and raised her voice: "You will not touch me!"

Donna had fallen in love with "Mr. Wonderful" while she was a 20-year-old junior at the University of Kentucky. Two months later she was pregnant, he was gone, and her sister persuaded her to temporarily move in with her in Nashville, so she would have some support while considering what to do. After she left the abortion clinic, Donna began a process identical to the one many women follow in comparable situations. She opened the Yellow Pages and looked under "attorneys" and "adoption." She was drawn, in the latter category, to a phone number for the local Catholic Charities adoption agency.

In the months that followed, Donna received counseling, read letters, and looked at photos from an array of prospective parents, and was repeatedly given the opportunity to change her mind. She offers only praise for the procedure that preceded her giving birth, but nothing could have prepared her for the emotions that seized her at the end. No matter how sure pregnant women believe they are about parting with their babies, regardless of what impact they think their decisions might have, irrespective of what might seem right or wrong, at least half change their minds once they feel their babies emerging, or hold them, or nurse them or are confronted with the impossible task of forever handing them over to virtual strangers.

The point of sharpest impact for Donna came after she had carried her daughter out of the hospital, which she insisted on doing, and after her counselor had strapped the three-day-old girl into a carrier in the back seat of her Jeep. Donna is a true believer in adoption. For years now, she has worked as a pregnancy and adoption counselor herself for the agency that once helped her. She insists she has no regrets about what she did. But Donna doesn't try to fool herself about the emotions she experienced as she watched the car drive away that day. "It was the most painful moment of my entire life," she says.

During the years that followed, Donna resumed her studies and plowed ahead. She fell in love with her husband-to-be, and they had a baby daughter in 1998. Donna says her healing process, especially early on, was helped considerably by the pictures and letters she regularly received from Kelly's adoptive parents, Carol and Michael Wierzba. Knowing the girl was happy and loved reinforced Donna's feeling that she had done the right thing. Occasionally she daydreamed about seeing Kelly again, but she didn't want to interfere with her upbringing and figured it would be too complicated until the Wierzbas' daughter (as she now thought of her) was much older. So Donna was flabbergasted when, out of nowhere, an employee from the adoption agency called to say that Michael and Carol wanted to take her out to dinner. Kelly was 18 months old, and the Wierzbas wanted to explore the possibility of her birth mother occupying a larger place in her life.

"At first, I told them thanks, but I don't think so. I mean, I just couldn't imagine what they were thinking. I didn't know if I could handle it. I didn't know if Kelly could handle it. The truth is I didn't know what to think, I was so in shock." Donna laughs at the memory. She says it quickly dawned on her that she had nothing to lose in just talking to the Wierzbas, though she feared she'd be so nervous she wouldn't give a good impression. Her voice quivering, she told the agency worker, "Tell them that I said okay." They set a date and a time and hung up. "Only then did I realize what was happening and what was possible. I was bouncing off the walls. All I could think was what a lucky person I am."

And unusual. Arrangements like the one the Wierzbas now share with Donna, in which she is a constant in her daughter's life, are still the exception. They are growing less rare by the day, however, and some degree of regular contact between biological and adoptive families is rapidly becoming commonplace by letter, on the phone, or in person.[3] The main reasons are simple to understand, because they promote honesty and respect, yet difficult to internalize, because they can cause uneasiness and demand selflessness.

First and foremost, social-work and mental-health experts have reached a consensus during the last decade that greater openness offers an array of benefits for adoptees—from ongoing information about family medical issues to fulfillment of their innate desire to know about their genetic histories—even if the expanded relationships themselves prove difficult or uncomfortable for some of the participants.

At the same time, adoption professionals have learned that they lived in a fantasy world for generations and are coming to terms with a hard truth about birth mothers: The vast majority do not "forget and get on with their lives," as though they were machines built to incubate life and give it away. In fact, most of these women sustain emotional and psychic injuries, no matter how good they consider their reasons or how much denial they permit themselves. Overwhelmingly, later in life if not right away, whether they say so out loud or only whisper the truth to themselves in the protective darkness of sleepless nights, they yearn for contact with or knowledge about their children.

Adoption is supposed to help people, not torment them. So, as the consequences of the old ways have become clear, adoption agencies and attorneys who arrange "closed" adoptions have become an endangered species. It's a remarkable reversal from the standard operating procedure of past decades, when all identifying data about birth and adoptive parents were guarded like nuclear secrets—and the very idea of a face-to-face meeting was considered perverse. "What's wrong with her? Why can't she just get on with her life?" social workers asked if a birth mother hinted she'd like to know how her baby was doing. Adoptees and adoptive parents were viewed as ungrateful, perhaps even unstable, if they sought information about the people who made their families possible.

Some birth parents still seek confidentiality, and a small percentage presumably always will because of their personalities or circumstances. But as society and the adoption system permit them to feel less guilt and shame about their decisions, the ranks of the anonymous are dwindling. Most often now, it's the adoptive mothers and fathers who are apprehensive about openness—though, again, in smaller and smaller numbers.

Caution and protectiveness are understandable emotions for anyone with normal instincts and insecurities, but all the more so for most adoptive parents. Our sensitivities about raising a family usually have been heightened by fertility problems that prevented us from producing biological children, then our self-confidence has been further shaken by the emotionally turbulent voyage that adoption invariably entails. As hard as it may be to accept, however, the adoptive parents' gut-level concerns about the consequences of openness are usually exaggerated and often unfounded.

Most reassuring is the fact that there's no clinical or practical evidence to indicate adoptees or birth parents try to disrupt or interfere with adoptions that include sustained contact. To the contrary, many adoptions grow stronger and all three members of the triad become more secure when their relationships cease to be based on fear and fantasy.

In the vast majority of cases, anyway, it's the adoptive parents who are the gatekeepers and decide the extent and timing of any participation (or even knowledge) by their children. While adoptees generally are curious, and ask more and more questions as they get older, they typically don't request detailed information or consider the possibility of in-person meetings until they are into their teens. It's also unusual for adoptees to seek out their biological parents before they are well into their twenties or thirties, ordinarily as planning for their own futures heightens their desire to know more about their pasts.

That's the current, fading snapshot. But, like everything else about adoption, the new picture still hasn't come into focus. Every day, more and more adoptive mothers and fathers are making contact with birth parents while their children are still very small. Adoptees are exploring their roots at younger and younger ages, empowered in part by the extraordinary resources of the Internet, while birth mothers, fathers, siblings, and sometimes whole families are increasingly summoning the courage to search for and develop relationships with their biological sons, daughters, brothers, and sisters.

There undeniably are pitfalls in "open adoption," an imprecise term applied to an array of arrangements in which birth parents stay involved after placing a child. Some problems derive from the specific personalities or situations of those involved, but many are characteristic of various phases of openness, as everyone tries to deal with emotional uncertainty and, if direct contact is included, to determine their boundaries and sort out their evolving roles. In most cases, the long-term gains are considerable nevertheless, and that's why expanding openness is the central characteristic of the adoption revolution.

I'll discuss the pluses and minuses of the new realities throughout this book. The bottom line, though, is that greater openness for adoptees means an upbringing rooted in self-knowledge and truth rather than equivocation or deception; for birth parents, it helps diminish angst and permits grieving, and therefore increases their comfort levels with their decisions; and for adoptive parents, it eases personal insecurities while establishing a steady stream of information for their children and for making critical parenting decisions (based, for example, on the birth family's medical history).

More broadly, the transformation of adoption promises to foster improved attitudes and behavior throughout a society in which nontraditional families are burgeoning. Today, there are children with one parent, two divorced parents, two parents of the same gender, a combination of parents and stepparents; there are girls born by way of donated sperm or eggs or surrogate pregnancy, and boys being raised by their grandmothers or foster parents. There are interracial couples with children who look like a fusion of their characteristics, and there are half brothers and half sisters whose biological siblings have every conceivable combination of skin tone and ethnic background.

As such diverse groupings proliferate, adoption appears less unusual and more like just another way to form a family, which is clearly one reason for its growing acceptance. Indeed, some people find adoption appealing precisely because it usually includes a married couple, and therefore produces something that looks like a conventional nuclear unit. Even as adoption profits from America's broader sociological and demographic shifts, however, it simultaneously is abetting and accelerating them—and not just by adding to the number of multiracial and single-parent households in this country.

Because adoption is the most institutionalized means of forming non-traditional families (other than divorce), and clearly is the one about which most people have the most positive attitudes, it is helping to instigate structural and attitudinal changes that will affect the whole range of complex families. One simple example: Adoption activists, both parents and professionals, are starting to educate teachers about the negative effects of asking their students to draw family trees with stereotypic, genetic-family roots.

This seemingly innocent assignment causes deep confusion and even inner turmoil for many children who only want to be "normal" like their classmates, and are too young to complain or challenge authority. So they feel sullen or angry, and some who "act out" their anxieties are unfairly identified as having developmental or behavioral problems. When the class project evolves into drawing "family orchards," or if the teacher explains that there are all sorts of families and asks the students to depict their own, the educational objectives remain intact with far less risk of unintended emotional shock waves.

Doing good for one group has ripple effects, too. Providing options when teaching about families helps adoptees, but it also benefits the students whose parents are divorced or gay, or who don't know who their fathers are, or who live in unconventional households of every sort. Recall that curb cuts (the slopes at the end of sidewalks leading into roadways) were originally promoted by advocates for the disabled as a means of increasing mobility for people in wheelchairs, and many critics said that amounted to wasteful spending because it targeted such a small segment of the population. Today, every day and in every city and town, millions of bicyclists and parents pushing baby strollers rely on curb cuts and feel frustrated when they encounter streets without them.

Whatever opinions people might have about the multiplicity of parenting situations today, few believe that children should suffer for their elders' decisions. Besides, everyone in a school is better off when constructive attitudes and sensitivity become the norms, just as everyone in a society gains when systemic embarrassment and deceit—two defining characteristics of adoption throughout its history—are replaced by pride and self-respect.

A History of Meeting Needs

Adoption in some manner, with or without the name or laws to formalize it, has been around for millennia. Every Passover, Jews around the world celebrate the ancient Hebrews' exodus from Egypt under the guidance of a young adoptee named Moses. It's a lucky thing for the institution of adoption that children rarely get as upset with their parents as Moses did with Pharaoh. (On the other hand, it's instructive to note how intense an adoptee's drive to find his biological roots can be.) Typically, though, adopted people are more like another famous member of their ranks, Clark Kent, who adores his ma and pa here on earth even as he maintains an emotional bond to his birth parents from Krypton.

Informally, of course, adoption has always existed. Aunts or grandparents, godparents, or even close friends would step in, and most often still do, when mothers and fathers abandon their children, are incapacitated, or die. Through much of recorded history, though, adoption by nonrelatives has been utilized more to meet the needs of adults than to help children. That's still often true today, but it used to be far more blatant. It is believed, for example, that in Rome, China, and other ancient civilizations, many infertile couples and parents who had only daughters formally adopted adult males to serve as heirs, to carry on family names or to participate in religious ceremonies.[4]

English common law, on which America's founders modeled our own legal system, made no reference to adoption at all; in fact, it wasn't until 1926 that England approved its first generalized adoption statute. Scholars believe that nation saw no need for organized adoption because inheritance was dependent solely on bloodlines, and children without relatives to care for them were placed in almshouses, then made apprentices or indentured servants at very young ages. The colonists in this country initially followed those traditions, but adoption in the New World quickly evolved into new forms that reflected the unique nature of a society inventing itself.

For instance, the need for farm labor in the 1700s, especially on large plantations in the South, turned a practice called "informal transfer"[5] of dependent children into a widespread phenomenon. The hardships of the Industrial Revolution, accompanied by a huge influx of immigrants, left so many children homeless in the early nineteenth century that public demand grew for providing improved care. Charitable organizations, invariably led by and affiliated with religious movements, spearheaded this movement to end indentures and systematically place children in permanent homes with families.[6]

At about the same time, adoptive parents began clamoring for laws to give their sons and daughters some of the same rights, such as inheritance, that were automatically granted to biological children. Meanwhile, as a result of rampant poverty and disease, the number of children without parents kept growing. P. C. English, a pediatrician who studied the history of unwanted children, wrote a chilling description in *Pediatrics* magazine in 1984 of the scene in New York City during the middle of the eighteenth century: "The lower East Side of Manhattan was the most crowded area in the world: The population density of 250,000/square mile was twice that of the most crowded areas of London. Waves of immigration, begun by the Irish following the potato famine of 1846, packed a mass of poorly fed humanity into tenements, with unclean water, inadequate sewage and no facilities for preparation and storage of food." Similar scenarios played out all over the country: Squalid, cramped conditions killed so many people that tens of thousands of children, and perhaps many more, were left to wander the streets.

Responding to all those gathering social forces, Massachusetts in 1851 enacted legislation that set out strict procedures for giving children new parents. It was the first U.S. adoption law, and it set several precedents. The most important was that it defined the needs of children as paramount—though that principle hasn't always prevailed in practice during the hundred and fifty years since.

The Massachusetts statute also marked the start of mandatory court approval for adoptions, while presaging that the process would fall under the jurisdiction of the states rather than the federal government. For better and for worse, those were two portentous decisions that every legislature emulated by 1929, and that we all live with to this day. The resulting process has helped to prevent abuses and maintain local standards, but it has also flung open the door to frivolous decision making by individual judges and led to a jumble of state laws that have left adoption underregulated, unconscionably expensive, and unnecessarily difficult, emotionally and logistically, for everyone concerned.

One of the most remarkable chapters in the American adoption story unfolded during the period when the Massachusetts legislature took its groundbreaking legal action. In large cities everywhere, public and private "foundling homes" sprang up in response to the horrendous conditions in which armies of young children were living and dying. These well-intentioned refuges rapidly turned into disease-ridden warehouses where at least as much harm as good was accomplished.

A novel alternative to institutionalization was devised by the Reverend Charles Loring Brace in New York. He founded a benevolent association called the Children's Aid Society, branches of which still exist around the world, and he embarked on an ambitious program of relocating needy children into permanent homes. Reverend Brace believed the optimum circumstances for child rearing existed in rural areas where the spaces were open, the people were honest, and the work was hard. His solution was the orphan train movement, as it came to be called, which continued into the early twentieth century. By the time it stopped running, an estimated 100,000 two- to fourteen-year-olds had been transported from eastern cities to farms in states as far west as Nebraska and Kansas.[7]

News accounts of the time described how the Children's Aid Society announced the impending arrival of orphan trains in communities on its route, and how children were put on display so that locals could choose the ones they wanted. Records indicate few of these de facto adoptees were ever legally made members of the families that took them in, and some were evidently viewed as little more than cheap laborers.[8] Nevertheless, most presumably wound up in homes that were more secure and loving than the ones they left behind—not a hard task considering so many of them left nothing behind at all.

However noble the motives or favorable any outcomes from such efforts, the people who ran the orphan trains typically ignored the wishes of any biological parents who were still around, in a grim antecedent to the condescension experienced by birth mothers like Sheila Hansen. Simultaneously, the children themselves were dealt with less as individuals with rights, desires, or emotions than as possessions that could be taken at will and given away. That attitude still is evident in too many adults' behavior toward young people today and is perpetuated by current adoption law, which essentially treats the transfer of a child from one family to another as a property transaction.

The popular notion is that "everyone wins" in adoption because it allows birth mothers to resolve a problem, satisfies a deep desire for adoptive parents, and places children with families in which they can thrive. It's a wonderful ideal, but it was a myopic vision during the time of the orphan trains and it remains one now. Adoption's glory is that it has fulfilled the dreams of millions over the years, but it has always been an emotionally wrenching and legally complicated process because, by its nature, it must balance the rights and needs of vulnerable people. One of the stark realities of this little-understood institution is that nearly all adoptions are initiated by women and men suffering from heartbreak and loss. For many of these participants, including some who reap enormous benefits from the ensuing process, the wounds never completely heal.

Adoptive parents may love their children absolutely, but many nevertheless feel the ache of their infertility forever—and never stop wondering about the biological baby that never was. And birth parents give up the lives they created, tiny beings who look like them, who gestated inside their mother's wombs and, for nine months, were as much a part of them as their limbs; it's incomprehensible that there are people who believe that a woman, especially, can relinquish a child and then put the experience aside, forget about it, pretend she didn't part with a piece of herself. During the current period of fundamental change, perpetuating the myth of "everybody wins" can impede progress because it trivializes or even ignores the feelings of grief, insecurity, and identity confusion that are integral components of adoption, for adoptees as well as their two sets of parents.

Within the adoption world, such simplistic views can undermine relationships among adoptive relatives, between adoptive and birth families, and between professionals and their clients. They also can lead people inside and outside the triad to unintentionally say and do things that inflict emotional pain on relatives, friends, and acquaintances who are tied to adoption. Children tend to get hurt the most, and the most often. Even during the revolution, we live in a nation in which "You're adopted!" is sometimes a taunt, "What kind of woman would give away her baby?" is still considered a reasonable question, and "I'm sorry you couldn't have real children" is still meant as an empathetic remark.

Discovering a New World

One of the unequivocal benefits of the growing candor about and openness within adoption is that people feel increasingly comfortable confronting and trying to remedy their problems. As a result, just as civil rights activists over the past few decades have sensitized Americans about their language and conduct toward minorities and women, adoption activists are finally helping people understand that adoptees and their various parents have hot buttons, too.

Naturally, some of those buttons differ within the many distinct types of adoption being practiced. Adoptees from foster care typically are older and have lived with their birth mothers, for example; their sensibilities and sensitivities therefore can differ markedly from those, say, of children adopted as infants from abroad or those adopted domestically at any age who don't share the skin color or cultural backgrounds of their adoptive parents. It would be unreasonable to expect everyone to understand such subtleties and complexities overnight, but it's easier for people to excuse the occasional slip of the tongue or behavioral slight if they feel they are generally treated with respect.

Members of minority groups seldom believe they have achieved that goal, while people outside those groups often have trouble fully grasping the gravity of the problem. (How many generations has it taken for people to "get" that racist and sexist jokes, even if they strike some listeners as funny, hurt people's feelings and perpetuate negative stereotypes?) Here are two examples to illustrate the point as it pertains to adoption:

- On May 28, 1998, newspapers around the country published a "Herman" cartoon—actually a reprint from years earlier, syndicated that day because the cartoonist was on vacation—that showed a bratty-looking boy holding a pair of shears, which he'd just used to cut down one end of a hammock. A hawk-nosed man lay on the ground between two trees, telling his son: "Tomorrow, I'm having you adopted."
- A few years ago, the American Greetings company issued a Valentine's Day card with a cat on the front saying, "SIS, even if you were adopted, I'd still love you . . . " Inside, the thought continued: "not that you are, of course. At least I don't think so. But, come to think of it, you don't really look like Mom or Dad. Gee, maybe you should get a DNA test or something. Oh well, don't worry about it. We all love you, even if your real parents don't. Happy Valentine's Day!"

Is it political correctness to label those attempts at humor as thoughtless and destructive? The people who wrote them didn't intend to hurt anyone, and perhaps they wouldn't if birth parents ceased feeling pain as soon as they relinquished their children, but they don't. Or if adoptive parents were perfectly secure about their children's emotional development, but they aren't. Or if a seven-year-old boy, looking for a card for his sister on Valentine's Day, understood that his birth mother gave him a new home as an act of love and sacrifice. But he hasn't internalized that difficult concept, at least not yet, so the "joke" just inflames his sense of rejection and fuels his resentment at being different.

Adoption operated so clandestinely for so long that most people have learned very little about it, which has led even the smartest and best-intentioned among us to accept erroneous stereotypes, draw unfair conclusions, and act without realizing that our actions can inadvertently inflict pain on a family member or a friend. That's not to say America has been a breeding ground for generations of emotionally damaged or dysfunctional residents because of adoption. Whatever issues the process may raise, it has given the vast majority of its participants joy and has enriched us as a nation. After all, everyone faces hurdles in life, and most of us figure out how to get around the ones we can't get over. As Roseanne Roseannadanna used to say on *Saturday Night Live*, "It's always something." For some of us it's adoption, for others it's racism or divorce or Uncle Charlie, who promised two years ago that he would move in for only six weeks. Most important, unlike many other complexities of life, adoption is seldom an oppressive or minute-to-minute concern. And, in most cases and for most people, the upside is huge.

That's why some couples are willing to deplete their savings, borrow from relatives, or even take out bank loans to pay the $15,000 to $35,000 it typically takes to adopt a white baby in this country or a child from abroad. It's an outrageous sum of money that locks out far too many would-be parents—and that's hardly the only way in which the mighty dollar has come to play a corrupting role in adoption. What's clear, nevertheless, is that neither cost nor any of the other myriad obstacles that line its road have prevented the process from becoming an increasingly prevalent means of creating a family.

"After we discovered our fertility problem, we resigned ourselves to not having children," says Susan Correia. Her husband, Russell, shakes his head in agreement as he puts their smiling Chinese daughter into her baby seat. "We never thought we'd adopt, that's for sure," he explains. "We thought from the beginning that we didn't want to get onto that roller coaster." Even without doing much research, they knew the procedure could be bureaucratic and anxiety-producing. They'd heard the heart-wrenching stories about prospective parents who thought they had "their" babies, only to learn that the mothers had changed their minds. And they believed the costs might be prohibitive.

"We didn't have a whole lot of information, but there are so many potential pitfalls, and the fear of the unknown may be worst of all. It was our sense of things that it could turn out to be a nightmare," Susan recalls. Then, one day, a friend told her that infant girls in China were being abandoned and, she says, "It went straight through my heart." She decided to talk to her husband about the possibility of adoption.

Infertile couples seldom fully accept the notion that they'll never have children. Often they try sophisticated and expensive medical interventions, sometimes they turn to sperm or egg donors (a misnomer, since both the men and women "donors" are usually paid), occasionally they employ a surrogate mother. Invariably, they fantasize about somehow defying physiological reality and becoming pregnant.

The Correias are both social workers who live in a modest house in Portland, Maine. They didn't consider any of the costly modern methods available for appealing nature's ruling that they would not produce offspring. Still, after deciding that they wanted to adopt an infant from China, they had to find a way to pay the adoption agency, to pay for the airline tickets to travel halfway around the world, to pay for the hotels and all the other expenses they would incur. They took out a home-equity loan.

Eighteen months and $18,000 later, the Correias came home with Hope. In every way. She was ten and a half months old and weighed just ten pounds when her new parents first took her into their arms. That was about two hours after they arrived at the well-kept, two-room brick building, a couple of hours' drive from Beijing, where forty-eight infant girls were unknowingly awaiting their turns to become someone's daughter again.

Susan and Russell stayed away from domestic adoption largely because they didn't want to be disappointed or hurt. But having children is always a gamble, whether the risk is miscarriage or a stillbirth, a frustrating bureaucracy or a pregnant woman's change of mind about keeping her baby. Adoptive mothers and fathers invariably have tales to tell, and sometimes they're unnerving. They inevitably end with a common conclusion, however: The parents would go through it all again in a heartbeat to get the child they found at the end of their journey.

When the Correias arrived at the orphanage in Gao Ming, they saw a couple of attendants carrying a baby out the door. It was Hope. She was being rushed to the hospital, where she had spent much of the previous week being treated for bronchitis and pneumonia. "They told us she was very sick," says Susan. "I'm not religious, but I thought, God's not going to send us this far for something horrible to happen."

It didn't. The hospital prescribed antibiotics for Hope, an English translation of the name she had been given at the orphanage, and soon released her to the Correias. They took the child to a private clinic, where they paid a doctor to examine her again, and he pronounced her ready for travel. In another week, after all their final paperwork was completed and processed—China operates one of the safest, most efficient adoption programs in the world—Russell and Susan took their daughter back to Portland.

For primarily cultural reasons, though finances also are a frequent factor, more than ninety percent of all the people who adopt infants outside the public-welfare system are white, like the Correias. Blacks, Latinos, and Asians historically have cared for needy children within their extended families, adopting them formally or informally, but seldom taking in unrelated babies. For the most part, the white prospective parents who seek to adopt want infants of their own color, though that is changing with a sharp rise in foreign adoptions, the growth of intermarriage across ethnic lines, and a steady shift in social attitudes as the population of our country becomes increasingly diverse.

Ironically, some of the same factors that have coalesced to improve both adoption's image and reality also have reduced the number of available white infants. The stigma attached to unwed mothers, for example, led more than eighty percent of them to give up their babies into the middle of the twentieth century. Researchers estimate that figure fell to under twenty percent by the early 1970s, and today most experts believe it has plummeted to less than three percent.[9] Again, those numbers describe white women; the rate of relinquishment among other races has remained below two percent throughout the history of U.S. adoptions.

Whatever the absolute number, it's nowhere near large enough to satisfy the desires of infertile, late-parenting baby boomers and members of the generation that followed, many of whom are now starting families of their own. The laws of supply and demand (along with their frequent companions, greed and graft) are largely responsible for the escalating costs of adoption; they are also among the key reasons so many Americans have come to rely on other nations to complete their families.

A small number of international adoptions took place after the two World Wars, when Americans took in orphaned children from Europe. But the practice didn't become systematic, and didn't start regularly crossing color lines, until Americans began adopting the mixed-race children whom G.I.s had fathered during the Korean War.[10] South Korea remained the major source of young adoptees until the 1990s, when China opened its doors to the adoption of little girls, who are viewed as less important than boys there. The Soviet Union's breakup further accelerated the pace of adoptions abroad, particularly since many of the orphans were white Europeans. By the end of the twentieth century, Russia over-took China as the largest source of adopted children.[11]

Turmoil in other nations, whether political as in Russia or social as in much of Latin America, has contributed mightily to the adoption revolu-tion in this country. That's true because it has placed little Asian girls and Latino boys in previously all-white schoolyards in small towns from coast to coast. This reality forces teachers, fellow students, other parents, and members of the communities at large to deal with issues that have long been commonplace in larger, already diverse cities and towns. And it's true by virtue of the sheer numbers involved, which invigorate the process itself, raise its public profile and—because so many of the kids are different colors from their parents—thrust adoption into the open simply because no one can pretend the caramel kid and his sunflower sister look very much like their freckled Irish mom or olive Italian dad.

Unlike its domestic counterpart, for which no records are kept, interna-tional adoption is precisely tracked because legal documents for everyone who enters the United States must be filled out for the Immigration and Naturalization Service. Just under 1,700 children came into this country for adoption in 1964, the first year for which the INS statistics office could provide me with data. Within twenty years, the number had climbed to almost 9,500. By 1998, the last year for which figures were available before publication of this book, it had nearly doubled to 15,724—and the trend line looks like an upward slope for the foreseeable future.[12]

Nationalists in Russia and some other nations are critical of cross-bor-der adoption, arguing that Americans are capitalizing on the misfortunes of other societies by taking their children, and then are depriving those children of their heritage by raising them in a foreign land. It's an argu-ment with direct parallels to transracial domestic adoption; for instance, detractors maintain that African-American culture generally and black children individually lose out in adoptions by whites.

The confounding dilemma in the adoption world is that there are prob-ably more than enough needy children in the United States to fill the homes of everyone considering adoption. There's a big obstacle in the doorway, though: They're rarely perfectly healthy white babies. Instead, they're older boys and girls of every race, many with emotional and be-havioral problems. There are perceptual obstructions, too: Some Americans believe they'd have to cut through exasperating bureaucracies to secure one of these children, and they're too often right. Many also think the older child they adopt from abroad will have fewer problems than the one they'd get from foster care, and they're too often wrong.

The good news is that the revolution is shaking the public system to its core, with potentially huge consequences for adoption and for our nation. More than half a million children were mired in temporary living situations toward the end of the last century, draining the public's energies and tax dollars with little promise of growing up to be productive citizens. But today, state after state is radically revising its standard for the placement of children under its supervision. For decades, the defining principle in the public welfare system had been "family reunification" at almost any cost, a wonderful ideal that entailed putting kids in foster homes while their mothers (and fathers, when they were around) received help to deal with their violence, alcohol, drugs, or other issues. Unfortunately, far too often, the children were shuttled back and forth between foster and biological parents for years. They grew up amid instability and worse, so a lopsided majority developed emotional and behavioral problems that hurt them personally and made them less appealing prospects if and when they became eligible for adoption.

Studies underscore this point, which is intuitively evident anyway: The younger the child, the more likely he or she is to be adopted. They also indicate a direct correlation between the age of a child and the long-term stability of an adoption (the earlier, the better[13]), while virtually every piece of current research agrees that stability and love during children's youngest years play critical, lifelong roles in their psychological development, their emotional well-being, and their ability to learn.

So there's no mystery about the goal. Educate prospective parents so they know they can choose not to spend tens of thousands of dollars for an adoption, because they can use the public system for little or no money. And reform the government bureaucracies so they're less intimidating to enter and easier to navigate. For a variety of reasons, not everyone would pick this option, and it probably will never provide enough newborns for all the people who want them and can afford to adopt them elsewhere. Many more people would use the public system, however, if the children were younger and less challenging, and if the procedures for adopting them weren't so wrapped in red tape.

It's quite a dream, but not a fantasy. Nationwide, in response to inducements ranging from budget crunches to altruism to court orders, the "best interests of the child" is finally being interpreted as "permanency." So after a specified period of time that can be as short as several months, state officials must now either determine that children will live with their birth families—which is usually the case, and should be—or take legal action to terminate parental rights and open the door for adoption.

This approach has been accelerated by federal financial incentives enacted during the Clinton Administration, and it has already led to stunning increases in public-sector adoptions. From 1995 to 1998, as permanency became the primary objective, the number of these adoptions soared to more than 36,000 children nationwide—an increase of about forty percent. And the jump was even higher in some individual states.[14] "It's been a horror show until now," says Jeffrey Katz, former executive director of the Rhode Island Adoption Exchange, a private organization that promotes adoption of children in state care. "It's finally changing, though, and it's changing very fast."

If done well and sustained as a matter of policy, this overhaul of foster care could have a pervasive positive impact, even beyond helping the millions of children and adults who will be directly affected. First, assuming the number of people turning to public care continues to grow, monetary considerations would abate from a higher percentage of all adoptions. At the same time, the balance could gradually shift toward the supply side, thereby applying pressure on private agencies and lawyers to become more competitive.

Be prepared for horror stories, too. Revolutions produce victims, and in this one there inevitably will be birth parents who don't get sufficient opportunities to keep their children, adoptive parents who won't receive enough counseling to cope with their new families, adoptees who will be trouble and troubled. But the new approach in foster care was meant to make kids the number one priority, and they should be the big winners in the long run, whatever the short-term difficulties.

Obviously, the overarching benefit for children is the chance to grow up in a secure environment. They will also gain, however, if money becomes less of a factor in adoption. Children are concrete thinkers who have trouble grasping a conceptual distinction like the one between paying for services required to adopt a child, and buying the child. A five-year-old might not talk about it or even consciously consider the implications, but imagine the potential psychological effects of seeing a television program on which it's mentioned that the adoption of some child from her home nation "cost only $18,000." Or if she overhears someone, maybe her grandmother or her father's fishing buddy, asking, "How did you find the $25,000 to get your daughter?"

The problems abound, yet the adoption community is teeming with enthusiasm and optimism. A world in flux can be a disconcerting place in which to live, yet adoption is helping make America a more exciting, vital nation rather than a more unsettled one.

I remember the moment it dawned on me that we all might be in the midst of a phenomenon bigger than just a sociological blip caused by aging, infertile baby boomers seeking alternative ways of forming families. As West Coast bureau chief for the *Boston Globe*, I was covering the O. J. Simpson murder trial at the time. Dozens of us reporters sat shoulder to shoulder in a small press room on the twelfth floor of the Los Angeles courthouse. I was typing my daily story, right on deadline, when the interruption came.

"This is awful," said Diana, a computer specialist and the only non-journalist in the room. She was standing right behind me, rustling a newspaper and pointing to a story in it. I turned around and asked what was wrong. Diana showed me the offending article. It was about the Baby Richard case, in which an Illinois man won custody of his biological son from the adoptive parents with whom the four-year-old boy had lived nearly all his life.

"Imagine how I feel," I replied. "I have an adopted son." (We hadn't adopted our daughter yet.)

"Really?" said the *Chicago Tribune* reporter sitting at my left elbow. "I've got two adopted kids."

The *Time* magazine correspondent to his left looked amazed. "I've got two adopted kids, too," he said.

Diana, wide-eyed with disbelief, whispered: "I'm adopted."

I was surrounded, and so are we all. Suddenly, or at least it feels sudden, adoption is being transformed from a quiet, lonely trip along America's back roads to a bustling journey on a coast-to-coast superhighway. The infrastructure has become so extensive that it has made all of us—not just adoptees, birth parents, and adoptive parents—into fellow travelers. We should do all we can to make this a smooth ride.

2

A Legal Maze
from Coast to
Coast

If you watched one of the following scenarios unfold on a television show, you'd think that the writer had suffered from an overly vivid imagination. If you read either of them in the newspaper, you'd shake your head in disbelief and hope this kind of thing doesn't happen too often. But if you were part of the American adoption community, you'd probably be mesmerized by the TV program and stunned that journalists were finally covering issues of such direct relevance to you.

Story number one: At the age of seventy-two, Mary Insulman discovered she was adopted. A cousin mentioned it in passing at the funeral of a family member, and Mary was flabbergasted. What else had her parents lied to her about? Her mother and father had been wonderful people who adored her, so perhaps they'd had their reasons. Still, she felt hurt and indignant. Then, as Mary's resentment abated, her curiosity grew. She surprised herself by how intensely she wanted to learn about her roots, and she figured she didn't have a lot of time for digging.

Adoptees are the only U.S. citizens who don't automatically have the right to obtain the records relating to their births. But Mary learned that Oregon, where she lived, permitted adopted persons to seek copies of their documents in court. So, three times over the following three years, she pleaded with a judge to let her have a copy of her original birth certificate. She assumed it would include the name of her birth mother, at least, and maybe of her birth father. She thought that knowledge itself would fill an internal void and, if she was lucky, it might enable her to find a biological relative to chat with.

The judge denied her requests every time. She interpreted the law as permitting her to provide access to records only if an adoptee demonstrated a compelling need—say, for example, if there was a medical emergency that required a sibling's organ donation. "Mere curiosity," said the judge, could not override the biological mother's presumed desire to hide her identity at the time she placed her baby for adoption.

"It's really beyond belief. I've never been political, but this just makes me crazy. . . . It makes me want to go out and do something," says Mary. "There's no way that judge or anybody else can possibly know whether my mother wanted to remain anonymous forever when she gave me up, and there's surely no way to know if she felt that way later in her life. Besides, the whole thing's absolutely ridiculous. There's no way my mother's even alive. So who is being protected, and from what?"

Story number two: Harold and Melissa Frederick had tried everything from fertility drugs to herbal therapy. They were exhausted, exasperated, and disappointed. They had talked about adoption on-and-off for most of the three years in which they'd tried to have a child, and now they decided it was finally time to act. They were both in their late thirties, and they didn't like the idea of simultaneously planning parties for their own retirements from work and for their kids' graduations from high school.

He was a producer for a small radio station in Massachusetts at the time, six years ago; she was a grade school teacher. Together, they made a comfortable middle-class salary, but they were taken aback when their counselor at a local adoption agency estimated they would have to pay between $12,000 and $16,000 in fees and expenses. And that didn't include the money they used to hire an attorney to help them navigate through a procedural maze that they found confusing and bureaucratic.

"There were so many possibilities—should we adopt from the foster-care system, privately through a lawyer, or through an agency or from abroad? We went to meetings, read a lot, talked to friends. We finally agreed that we wanted to adopt a newborn in the United States, but even then it was still confusing how exactly to proceed," Harold explains. "It seemed like every state had its own, different laws about everything, and we just didn't have the time or the knowledge to work our way through it all, and we certainly didn't want to make any mistakes. That's why we got a lawyer."

It's a good thing they did. By the time they completed their little girl's adoption a year later, they had to contract with four adoption agencies in three different states. They had to circumvent a judge who said she would never finalize the Fredericks' adoption because they had engaged in an enterprise that amounted to "baby-selling." And they wound up spending more than $33,000. "It wiped us out," says Harold. Aware that his experience could sound like a cautionary tale against adoption, he smiles the fulfilled smile of fatherhood and adds that he and his wife "would do it all again in a second."

Of the 130,000 to 150,000 adoptions approved in U.S. courts every year—only about 30,000 to 40,000 of which involve babies and very young children[1]—a minuscule number wind up entangled in high drama or trauma. But all types of adoptions, even those that begin with people believing they've ensured a calm, smooth ride by paying tens of thousands of dollars, travel a course replete with complexity and intensity.

Almost everyone I know who has adopted a child, or has relinquished one, or is an adoptee older than seven or eight, has poignant tales to tell. My wife and I, for instance, were about to board a flight to pick up "our" baby several years ago when I decided to make one last call to South Dakota, just to say we were on our way. There was no reason for concern, since we'd been in telephone contact with the expectant mother for months, and the social worker had told us a day earlier that all was well. But this time I could hear the sorrow in her voice as soon as she picked up the phone. "Don't come," she said. "Betty's mother promised she'd help bring up the child. She's going to keep him."

The airline had to delay the flight to get back our suitcases. They were crammed with baby toys, an adorable pair of pants and matching shirt in which we were going to dress our son for his journey home, and a silver box for Betty with a slot inside its cover for a photo of her child. We had it engraved with a message of eternal gratitude.

Judy and I were zombies for the next couple of weeks. When we allowed ourselves to feel anything, we cried. Then we discussed whether we really wanted to take the risk of going through something like this again. Ironically, another tragedy gave us the perspective and the strength to do so: I learned that the wife of a colleague at work had endured a stillbirth. Nine months of anticipation and joy had ended in death and grief. That got us thinking about the family members and friends we knew who had lost their babies to miscarriage. We finally arrived at a healthier place, internalizing the fact that adoption is no more perilous than carrying a baby. In a way, a pregnant woman changing her mind is the adoptive parent's version of miscarriage, but with a decidedly happier ending: The child is alive, and he's in the arms of someone who loves him.

Such experiences don't make the lives of triad members better or worse, but they certainly make them different. And that understanding highlights one of the most profound alterations that adoption is undergoing, both in how it is practiced and how it is viewed: It's not just becoming a mainstream way to form a family; it's also rapidly being recognized as a unique process with distinct patterns and characteristics. Unfortunately, as the stories at the beginning of this chapter illustrate, the nation's laws, regulations, and attitudes haven't caught up with the fast-evolving reality on the ground.

Nevertheless, given how far we've come in a relatively short period of time, there's good reason for optimism. As late as the 1960s, the conventional wisdom among practitioners and participants in the adoption community was that children should be "matched" to parents with whom they shared physical and personality traits—and even intellectual capabilities, as best as they could be determined. The resulting families were supposed to proceed as though nothing unusual had happened, as if they were identical in every way to their biologically formed counterparts. They could pass as "real" families.

This standard operating procedure assured a central role for secrecy, the institutionalization of which began with the Minnesota Act of 1917, the first statute to seal adoption records.[2] The cultural camouflage continued until the process went almost completely undercover by the end of World War II, as American conformity was embraced and promoted in everything from cookie-cutter homes (with white picket fences, of course) to how many children a family should have (2.2, if at all possible). Married couples who couldn't produce offspring felt inadequate and embarrassed, so the wives would sometimes stuff pillows under their blouses and then go visit aunts in faraway states during the final stages of their "pregnancies"—while, in fact, they were waiting to adopt. Social workers often brought their babies in the dead of night.

It was a mirror reflection of the sham in which countless tens of thousands of single, pregnant women were compelled to participate. Ashamed and confused, they told everyone they were visiting far-away relatives, too, but they went to homes for unwed mothers instead. In those cloistered settings, they were assigned fictitious names, given wedding rings to wear outside, and cajoled by employees to formulate adoption plans "just in case" they decided not to "ruin their lives" by parenting their babies.

Most of the people involved probably meant what they said and meant well. The prevailing theory among social workers at the time held that illegitimate children (and their mothers) stood the best chance of success if they weren't stigmatized by a birth out of wedlock. Simultaneously, the conventional wisdom among behavioral specialists was that heredity played such a small role in human development that there was no need for anyone to know about, much less stay in touch with, their blood relatives.

Those precepts shaped public opinion about adoption and led professionals to devise "best practices." As a result, for example, states in the 1920s began sealing adoption records and birth certificates—which were regularly stamped with the word "illegitimate"—to protect children and their biological parents from being disgraced by a birth outside of marriage. The intent was to prevent the public, not the parties to an adoption, from seeing the damning information. By the 1940s, however, expert opinion solidified that adoptive families stood their best chance of thriving if they locked out all reminders of how they were formed, so nearly every state amended its statutes to require a court order for anyone to obtain documents containing identifying information about an adoption's participants. Furthermore, it became common practice to create new "original" birth certificates, with the children listed as having been born to their adoptive parents.

Some adoption workers still comply with adoptive parents' requests for children of a given gender or physical description, and a handful of states permit matching by religion, but such selectivity in any form is now rejected in the vast majority of cases. While many Americans don't like the fact that single women now account for one-third of all babies born in the United States,[3] neither those mothers nor their children usually suffer from systemic shame or ostracism. And, although there are still those who believe child-rearing is all nurture and no nature, most people understand that heredity plays a vital role in virtually every aspect of human development.

Yet fraudulent birth certificates are still produced when adoptions are finalized every day, and adoptees have to petition judges in order to look at their own records, regardless of whether they're merely curious or they need to locate a genetic relative for a life-saving medical procedure. Those unaltered realities are both deep flaws in the new, improved version of adoption and potent symbols of how difficult fundamental change can be to achieve. Like the other indignities that have undermined adoption's integrity, this one also is on its way to becoming a discredited relic. But not without a struggle.

Progressive advocacy groups like the American Adoption Congress, the largest national organization representing all sides of the triad, have lobbied for decades to allow adoptees (but not the general public) to obtain their own documents. Still, as of this writing, only six states provide nearly unfettered access: Kansas and Alaska, neither of which ever closed its records; Delaware, whose politicians ended most closure in 1998 with barely a word of protest from anyone; Tennessee, which in 1999 won a four-year legal battle to amend its laws; Alabama, where only two legislators voted against unsealing records in May 2000; and Oregon, whose Supreme Court—also in May—spurned an appeal by critics who wanted to overturn an open-records law approved by voters more than a year earlier.

It was during Oregon's election campaign that Mary Insulman surprised herself by becoming a revolutionary at the age of seventy-six, appearing on news programs and campaigning zealously for "my basic human right." Like its counterpart in Oregon, the Tennessee statute—which is now in effect, with no evidence that it has disrupted anyone's life—had been put on hold by lawsuits arguing that adoptees' seeing their birth certificates would shatter the anonymity that birth mothers purportedly sought when they relinquished their babies.

Those two court cases were initiated by a well-organized minority within the adoption world who strongly oppose openness. Mostly they are religious conservatives who say birth mothers might get abortions if they fear eventual exposure, along with businesspeople concerned that fewer prospective clients might adopt if they worry that their children might one day seek out their birth parents. As both the Oregon and Tennessee outcomes demonstrate, the proponents of closure are fighting losing battles. Nearly all adoptive and birth parents in domestic adoptions today can learn each other's identities, even if they don't decide on ongoing relationships, while nearly all research shows the nation's abortion rates steadily declining.[4] At the same time, the Internet is making it increasingly easier for adoptees to explore their backgrounds, and find their birth parents if they want to, with or without access to their original birth certificates.

Notwithstanding the vision-blurring power of the dollar, ignorance and not malice has been the primary reason adoption laws and practices have developed so randomly, so seemingly immune at times from reasonable standards of rationality and decency. The birth certificate issue is an easy example. The desire to know about and connect with one's genetic ancestry has long been accepted as a normal instinct, perhaps even a basic component of human nature. That's what the newscasters and sociologists said in explaining the extraordinary popularity of the book and TV movie *Roots* more than two decades ago; it's why drawing family trees has been a routine teaching technique for as long as anyone can remember; and it's the reason the current genealogy craze in this country is being characterized on television, in books and magazines, and especially on the World Wide Web, as a fun hobby and a fulfilling activity for people of all ages.

Except for adoptees. Just a few decades ago, adoption agencies told them that even asking questions about their origins indicated something might be wrong with them. Many adoptive parents, usually inadvertently, still make their children feel ungrateful or guilty when they ask about their birth parents or, worse, consider contacting them. And judges continue to treat adults like Mary Insulman as if they are children. Some even demand adoptive parents' consent in requests for identifying documents, regardless of the applicant's age, as if the adoptees were asking for something other than information that scam artists, murderers, and everybody else in the United States can obtain as a birthright.

"Openness Gets a Lot of Credit"

While it may appear that the incidence of adoptions in this country is soaring, particularly of babies and infants, that's not the case. It's the candor in public discussions of the process, the entry of adoption into mainstream culture with popular movies like Mike Leigh's *Secrets and Lies*, and the visual reminders provided by a growing percentage of children who look nothing like their parents, that lead us to think a seismic numerical shift is taking place.

In fact, the trend line of single women choosing to raise their offspring started heading upward decades ago, and studies show a growing percentage of single fathers are now deciding to do likewise. At the same time, abortion became legal and readily available, while contraceptive use became routine. As a consequence, fewer newborns became available for adoption.[5] In turn, the lower supply has contributed to both the steep escalation of adoption costs and the explosion of interest in adoptions from abroad.

It is also a major reason that adoption is being transformed at such stunning speed. The change was coming anyway, but its pace is being accelerated by birth mothers who, in fact, don't want anonymity. Quite the opposite: It is their understanding that they will always know their children are in loving families, and may even remain part of their lives, that provides many with the impetus and the strength to proceed with their adoption plans. In a dramatic turnaround from the impotence they felt in the past, these women are now being empowered to pick their babies' new parents and to help shape their adoption arrangements. Because they possess something that other Americans badly want.

"Just a few years ago, the flood of domestic adoptions I was doing stalled to a drip because the birth mothers just weren't coming in," says Jim Savely, the owner of Small World Adoptions in Nashville. There's no mistaking his ideological or professional views. Christian religious icons decorate his office walls, and his agency was a plaintiff in the lawsuit that attempted to reverse Tennessee's unsealing of birth certificates. Jim is also a businessman and a realist, though, so he responded to the decline in pregnant women's interest by instituting new policies that chipped away at decades of secrecy, and even encouraged contact between adoptive couples and birth parents.

"It was like somebody just turned the tap back on," he says, shaking his head in wonder. "And I guess I have to admit the openness gets a lot of the credit for that. It sort of lets these women come out of the shadows and makes them feel better about themselves and what they're doing. It's been very, very hard for me to catch up with the openness idea because I've been so opposed to it for so long, but I've got to admit that most of the people I see here do seem to be able to assimilate the truth from the untruth and deal with it." When people like Jim Savely are climbing on board, along with the conservative and religious clients they attract, the imposing assertion that adoption is changing America even as America is changing adoption sounds like an understatement.

During the 1950s, the number of people seeking to adopt babies roughly equaled that of women placing their children.[6] Today, about six would-be parents apply for every available (usually white) baby.[7] And far more want infants but don't try to adopt because they perceive the process as too daunting and the costs as too high. This chasm isn't the consequence solely of the radical public shift toward acceptance of un-married parents. The same baby boomers who waged the culture wars of the 1960s and '70s also chose to marry at later ages and, especially as un-precedented numbers of women pursued careers, many couples put off family formation until they were in their thirties or forties.

Then they discovered they couldn't produce children, even with the help of the highest-tech of medical interventions, so they flocked to adopt. They were more receptive to the process, too, because their gener-ation as a group was more philosophically liberal, less concerned with adhering to social norms, and often personally repelled by the kinds of stigmas that had tainted adoption. The late-blooming boomers infused the institution with those same attitudes, thereby contributing to a reformation that had already begun.

My wife was forty-three and I was forty-two when we adopted Zack, and we were all three years older when we got Emmy. For a year, Judy and I used drug therapies, numerous cycles of in-vitro fertilization, even a couple of tries with donor eggs. All to no avail. Like the overwhelming majority of adults who decide to adopt in America today, we did so because we were infertile. I don't look forward to explaining this to our kids, but there's no sugar-coating the bottom line: Adoption was our second choice.

The mistake many people make with that knowledge is concluding that second choice means second best. We adoptive parents know better. To love my son and daughter any more than I do, I would have to grow a second heart. The children we all wind up with are randomly selected anyway, whether they're the result of a broken condom, a third try after two miscarriages, an adoption after failed infertility treatments, or another pregnancy to ease the lingering pain of having relinquished a child years earlier. There have been several stories in the news during the last few years about babies who were unintentionally switched in the hospital. In each case, when the error was discovered, the parents anguished about giving up the child they had taken home and fallen in love with; some insisted on regular visitation. The lesson about parent-child bonding isn't subtle.

My twin brother and I were born in postwar Poland, at a time when my parents—both Holocaust survivors whose families were decimated by the Nazis—felt neither emotionally nor financially capable of raising more than the two children they already had. But my mother became pregnant and a doctor told her an abortion might kill her, so here I am. Knowing why I was born has never made me feel insecure or unwanted. My life is filled with blessings and difficulties like everybody else's, and I have two devoted parents who would move mountains for me. Just as I would for my adopted children.

Onward to Cyberspace

The annual number of court finalizations taking place today is thought to far exceed the 50,000 in 1944, which was well before the adoption explosions in both the public and private sectors. But it's considerably lower than the estimated 175,000 in 1970, when society was about to accept legal abortions and single motherhood. We have a more concrete idea about past than present numbers because Washington used to collect voluntary data from the states, first sporadically between 1944 and 1957 through an agency called the Children's Bureau, and then annually from 1957 to 1975 through the now-defunct National Center for Social Statistics. Most states usually didn't respond to the federal inquiries, presumably because of the stigma surrounding adoption and because obtaining such specific data from scores of individual courts was a laborious task, especially before computers. So today's figures are guesstimates, and they're undoubtedly on the low side, but they're the closest thing adoption researchers have to comprehensive statistics.

It's important to point out, too, that many if not most of the adoptees in these counts are not infants placed by American women (and men when they participate) or children adopted from foster care or from abroad. In fact, about half of all U.S. adoptions are by stepmothers, stepfathers, and other relatives assuming legal guardianship.[8] The people in those relationships deal with their own adjustment periods and persistent issues, some unique to their particular situations and some endemic to adoption. But the laws and regulations governing adoption by family members have always been more consistent and less demanding than those pertaining to unrelated adults. It's people in the latter category who experience the most controversies and difficulties, and who therefore are the primary beneficiaries, the test subjects, and the revolutionaries in adoption today.

"It's very exciting. I think it's a cause for hope and optimism for most people in the triad and the country as a whole," says Madelyn Freundlich, former executive director of the Evan B. Donaldson Adoption Institute and one of America's foremost adoption experts. "But everything is changing so fast and on so many tracks, especially toward openness, that I think it's confusing or unsettling for some people. . . . I think we see the transformation in many ways, including the fact that people have very quickly, viewed in a historical context, even changed the types of children they adopt and the ways they adopt."

Freundlich's last comment refers to an array of changes, including one away from the adoption of older children through public agencies and toward the "independent adoption" of infants. Those are arranged, usually for a considerable fee, by nonprofit or for-profit private agencies, lawyers and "facilitators," a new breed of adoption entrepreneurs who specialize in finding pregnant women for prospective parents. As many as two-thirds of all newborns adopted in this country are now placed independently.[9]

Yet the fastest-growing segment in this realm is not among professionals or businesspeople, though agencies and/or lawyers are brought in to help with procedures and legalities. Instead, the biggest boom is at the grass-roots, where there has been a huge increase in adoptions being arranged by the parental participants themselves. This portentous shift applies mainly to what is called domestic infant adoption—that is, of healthy newborns and infants, most of them white, usually sought by white couples.

Lots of cultural and historical currents converged to get us to this point, including spiraling costs. But the main catalyst of the do-most-of-it-yourself phenomenon is the Internet, which is altering nearly all adoption practices as thoroughly as it is other aspects of our society. By definition, the people involved in a computer match must communicate and invariably meet in order to consummate their agreement, so the Net is providing jet fuel for the openness movement. It also is raising important questions, which it's too soon to answer definitively, about whether the participants are sufficiently aware of their legal obligations or, more important, whether they are getting enough (or any) counseling about the emotional and developmental issues they and their children will face.

Federal and state officials are moving to regulate some cyberspace activity, for example dealing with pornography and commerce, but adoption isn't on their list. Politicians have always shied away from the nuts and bolts of the process, arguing that they shouldn't meddle in family life. In practice, though, they have sometimes chosen to step in, and like judges, they have been strikingly inconsistent when they have done so.

For instance, motivated as much by financial as human considerations, federal and state lawmakers in the mid-twentieth century decided the foster-care system, including its adoption component, needed supervision. Not so, however, for the adoptions of domestically born babies, whether the arrangements are made by private attorneys, agencies, or individuals. There are more regulations relating to the adoption of children from abroad, but they mainly consist of operational and citizenship standards set by the U.S. Immigration and Naturalization Service, rather than efforts designed to ensure that adoptions are conducted ethically or that the people involved are fairly treated.

So, outside of the public arena, the procedures by which children receive new families in this country are guided by a cherished American principle: laissez-faire capitalism. There are no mandates for birth parents to receive counseling or to protect them from coercion, no safeguards to prevent adoptive parents from being emotionally or financially manipulated. As for the children, they are subject to the same economic forces as automobiles or toasters. Supply and demand. Whatever the market will bear.

Money is the mad bomber of the revolution. At a time of serious improvement in virtually every other area, adoption's unregulated growth into a big business threatens to succeed secrecy as the institution's own worst enemy. When it regularly costs tens of thousands of dollars for an adoption, it does more than just erect another towering barrier between our nation's haves and have-nots, or raise troubling concerns about the social and psychological implications of treating children as commodities. It also serves as a powerful incentive for profiteers to find new ways to pressure pregnant women, to lie to adoptive parents, even to steal babies or con their mothers into giving them up.

That's what two Long Island women were charged with doing when they were arrested in June 1999, along with a Mexican lawyer who worked with them; they pleaded guilty a few months later to arranging at least seventeen illegal transfers of children by tricking or bribing their mothers. American couples, who didn't know or didn't want to know how their sons and daughters were obtained, paid up to $22,000 for each of them.[10]

Big money threatens to undermine the confidence that prospective parents and the general public must have if adoption is to fit comfortably into America's cultural mosaic, without people developing a new set of negative views about the process. When the sums involved are so large, they also can blur the vision—and raise questions about the motives—of well-intentioned professionals. For instance, some adoption agencies offer college scholarships and other programs to help birth mothers get on their feet after they place their children for adoption. Is that a wonderful idea conceived from the heart, or a subtle inducement to get wavering women to give up their children? Or both?

It's essential to stress that the overwhelming majority of adoption practitioners strive to do so legally and ethically. Neither birth mothers nor adoptive parents should take this critique as anything other than a red flag signaling them to find out as much as possible about the people they are dealing with. But reform organizations, along with many social workers and researchers, see the warning signs of a major problem.

It has happened before. High demand for infants by infertile couples prompted incidents of baby-selling around the country from the 1920s through the 1960s, including some extensive and highly profitable black-market operations. One of the most infamous was run by Georgia Tann, who headed the Tennessee Children's Home Society for twenty-five years and was considered one of the finest adoption specialists of her time. A state investigation into her activities, begun just after she died of cancer in 1950, concluded that she and a friend who was a judge had colluded in the theft of at least one thousand babies from unmarried and poor women who were drugged, duped, and lied to. Tann sold the children to wealthy out-of-state couples for about $750 each.[11]

A similar operation took place in the small Georgia town of McCaysville for more than a decade ending in 1965. There, a doctor named Thomas Jugarthy Hicks capitalized on the disgrace young women felt about carrying a fetus without wearing a wedding ring. They came to him to give birth or to ask for an abortion; he took their babies. He reportedly sold about two hundred of them to couples in at least eight states, who paid from $250 to $1,000 each. And they knew exactly what was going on: They would drive home from McCaysville hiding the children on the floor or in the trunk of their cars.

Baby-selling became enough of a concern to prompt some state legislatures and U.S. congressional committees to hold hearings on the subject in the 1950s and again in the late 1970s. Those led to a tightening of laws governing the interstate transportation of children and to restrictions on what payments adoptive parents may make. States now prohibit anyone from accepting money for "finding babies" or "placing children," but they allow widely variable "reasonable fees" for services. Those include paying lawyers, social workers, and birth mother expenses such as medical care during pregnancy.

Today, as those "reasonable" fees skyrocket, the conditions are ripe for abuse again. Outside the public system, it's hard to complete any adoption for less than $15,000, and there are private attorneys and agencies charging as much as $50,000. In some other countries, meanwhile, there's no way to determine how well-paid "facilitators" obtain the children whose adoptions they arrange for American parents. A high-stakes game is being played out there, and nobody's watching for cheaters.

State and federal officials, whose newfound enthusiasm for adoption has already resulted in a wave of activism that includes $5,000 federal tax credits for adoptive parents and accelerated placement of foster-care children into permanent homes, need to get involved. The government didn't stand by when Bill Gates allegedly engaged in dubious business practices a few years ago, and the concern then was only software. Even during an age when computers seem so vital to everyone's lives, the laws relating to them shouldn't demand more accountability than those pertaining to our children.

It's tough to see the big picture, of course, when your emotions are running high and your few functional brain cells are able to think only about what might happen next in your own life; that's what it feels like when desperate pregnant women and adoptive parents are contemplating adoption. It's hard to attain perspective, too, because most of our preconceived notions about adoption still differ markedly from reality.

Even the savviest prospective parents start the process innocently, even ignorantly, because—whatever else people have thought about adoption—we have viewed it as a self-contained, neatly packaged solution to persistent societal problems. Many of us cling to the reassuring stereotypes: There are people who can't procreate, and there are pregnant women who can't parent. Their needs intersect, so they do the right thing and move on. Then the adopted kids get to live lives identical to those of their nonadopted friends. Everybody gets to write a new autobiography on blank pages.

It's a wonderfully American notion, this idea that there's a quick and easy fix for everything, always a way to leave the past behind and start from scratch again. Yet we know that the reality is a tangled continuum of pleasure and pain, fulfillment and frustration. Among the most glorious aspects of adoption is that it does indeed offer the promise of new beginnings, that it does bring happiness and hope. But it's not a magic elixir that somehow heals all wounds or induces amnesia in those who use it.

As long as it remained underground, we could pretend it was whatever we wanted it to be. Now, however, we can see adoption for what it is: not a one-time curative event but a process that forever remains a part of its participants' lives—to varying degrees, of course, sometimes publicly but usually privately. More broadly, as evidenced by the stories at the start of this chapter and others that make the nightly news, we now know that adoption is a huge institution replete with complicated issues involving individual liberties (do adoptees have a "right" to their birth certificates?), racial tensions (should white parents teach their black or Asian children about their cultures?), and economic disparities (are rising costs locking out all but the rich?).

Adoption is both a product of our grand, imperfect culture and an integral component of it. Given how haphazardly it has developed—with almost no effort among states, attorneys, and agencies to unify or coordinate statutes, practices, and regulations—it's a minor miracle that it has evolved into as efficient and productive a process as it is today. At the same time, it's no surprise that the resulting hodgepodge includes so many flaws, inconsistencies, and opportunities for financial and emotional abuse.

Even within states, the laws and rules often are inconsistently administered and hard to understand. Moreover, they vary from municipality to municipality, court to court, judge to judge. And there is no system to help people get through the labyrinth, resolve conflicting standards, or simplify the often unnerving trek. All these factors combine to make the process more cumbersome and expensive than it needs to be, while frequently forcing adoptive and birth parents to endure unnecessary grief and frustration.

Few triad members have as harrowing a time completing a domestic infant adoption as Harold and Melissa Frederick did, but their experience graphically illustrates the pervasive problems many people encounter. In 1994, the Fredericks (not their real name) were living in Massachusetts, one of only four states—with Colorado, Delaware, and Connecticut—that permit adoptions only by a licensed agency that must adhere to specified standards.[12] The idea is to ensure that all parties receive adequate counseling, as well as to minimize the possibility of other service providers operating as though they are merely running a business in which the product happens to be children.

Whether and how much agency participation should be required is a glaring inconsistency nationwide. A few states impose detailed rules to protect all parties, even when no agency is involved and when the parents make their own arrangements. Some establish concise regulations for agencies but vague ones for independent adoptions, while others monitor the latter because they believe the absence of professionals increases the risks of coercion, price-gouging, and other unscrupulous behavior.[13]

While agencies exist nationwide, fewer and fewer states mandate their use in any way. Rather, the politicians who make laws and policy have accepted the argument—put forth mainly by attorneys who offer adoption services, but also by prospective parents anxious to get children more quickly—that agencies often move too slowly and bureaucratically (which can be true), and that opening the field to competition helps hold down costs (a ridiculous, self-serving assertion belied by today's soaring prices).

After doing considerable homework, the Fredericks contracted with an agency near their home, but they also decided to get additional help to expedite the process. Herbert Friedman, a well-respected Boston lawyer with a long history of adoption work, suggested that the Fredericks improve their odds by signing on with a second agency in another state. Since every state sets its own time limit for biological mothers to reconsider their decision after a baby's birth, Harold and Melissa asked for recommendations of states in which this difficult waiting period was shortest.

Americans may adopt across state lines, so many participants seek the states with statutes that they view as most accommodating to their own needs or desires. Payment for a child per se is prohibited everywhere, for instance, but some prospective birth mothers gravitate toward states that permit a majority, if not all, of their medical and living costs to be covered during pregnancy.[14] Many adoptive parents, on the other hand, look for states in which they can take custody of a baby within hours, if not immediately after birth.[15]

The Fredericks' attorney suggested six states where the waiting periods were only a few days. The couple narrowed their choices down to Texas and Florida, then wound up selecting an agency outside Miami because it was a relatively short and inexpensive plane ride away. Soon, based on phone conversations, letters and photos, a Ft. Lauderdale–area woman in her second month of pregnancy chose Harold and Melissa to adopt her baby. The three adults developed a friendly, trusting relationship over the telephone and, a few months later, the excited parents-to-be arranged to fly down to meet Linda and her mother. John Lennon once wrote that life is what happens while you're making plans. Well, the day before they were to leave, Melissa learned she was pregnant.

They immediately called Herb to ask if that posed a problem. It did. He advised them that their Massachusetts agency accepted only clients who could not procreate, so they had to find another agency with different rules. After that, they headed for Florida and asked Linda if their new circumstances affected her decision. To their relief, she found their honesty made them even more appealing. Besides, she said, she was thrilled that her baby would grow up with a sibling so close in age that they could be friends.

A few months later, fate added another detour to the Fredericks' nerve-wracking ride: Harold was offered a better job in Pennsylvania. Herb advised the couple to drop their latest Massachusetts agency and find one in their new state to complete all the necessary arrangements, including their "home study." That is a procedure in which a social worker visits the residence of would-be parents, observes their interaction and interviews them, then assesses whether there are problems like alcoholism or severe spousal disputes that should prevent them from adopting. A few states require only a post-placement evaluation of that sort, while most mandate several visits beforehand and at least one more afterward, along with a criminal background check, to assess whether the environment is safe for the child.[16] The cost of home studies, which are paid by the people seeking to adopt, ranges from several hundred dollars to a couple of thousand dollars, depending on the agency, the location, and the income of the applicants.

One of the responsibilities of the Fredericks' latest agency, in Pennsylvania, was to coordinate the adoption's legal finalization. As it happens, only one judge was assigned that duty in the area to which the couple were moving, and she had previously overseen only public adoptions in which money rarely changed hands. When the judge reviewed the Fredericks' file, she saw that one state's residents had hired an agency in another state and had already spent about $15,000. She fumed that the "transaction" was "immoral." She told the agency: "As far as I'm concerned, this is about the same as baby-selling. If this adoption comes before me, I will not approve it under any circumstances."

In the end, a combination of good legal advice, clever maneuvering, and a bit of luck bailed the couple out. Though Harold had already relocated, he was living in a temporary apartment while searching for a house big enough for a four-member family. Melissa was still in Massachusetts, where she was tying up the loose ends at her own job, packing their belongings, and dealing with the sale of their home.

Herb advised them to sign up again with their last Massachusetts agency, which then completed their adoption while they were still technically residents of that state. The Pennsylvania agency conducted the home study, transferred the results to Massachusetts, and took care of assorted other details that didn't require a judge's consent. The Florida agency provided counseling for Linda, obtained her formal relinquishment, and handled the legalities of her baby's interstate placement. All three agencies coordinated their efforts to comply with each other's state laws. The Fredericks were especially lucky on this count, since the Interstate Compact on the Placement of Children—which governs cross-border adoptions throughout the country—is so bureaucratically and inconsistently administered that it often hinders rather than expedites the process.

Inconsistency for All

The list of disparate, confusing, and conflicting adoption statutes and regulations runs from coast to coast.

About half the states, for example, prohibit pregnant women from formally agreeing to an adoption until after a baby's birth, but don't specify how long after delivery they can sign relinquishment papers. Some of these same states, and most others, impose a waiting period after the birth during which the mother is not permitted to sign the papers, so that she can reflect on her decision. These periods range from twelve hours in Kansas to three days in Kentucky to fifteen days in Rhode Island.[17]

Attorneys and agencies often advise prospective parents, if they live somewhere with a short waiting period, to ask a birth mother if she will travel to their state for the final stages of pregnancy and delivery. It sounds like a great idea at the time, and most people nervously awaiting a child snap at it even though it can greatly increase their costs (airline tickets, room, board and medical expenses). But it's a dubious practice that is gradually being abandoned by responsible practitioners as they recognize its potential downside: For women unsure of their decisions, moving to a foreign environment, away from friends or family, and being financially supported by nice people who desperately want a child, can amount to unfair pressure to give up their babies.

State laws also deviate widely in how much time they give birth parents to revoke their consent, and under what circumstances. In West Virginia, they may change their minds for up to twenty days without a court order but for six months or longer if they claim an irregularity took place. In Alabama, it's five days or two weeks, depending on a court's judgment about the best interests of the child.[18]

There are comparable differences on most other important issues, ranging from advertising for pregnant women, to the ways adoptees and biological parents may seek contact with each other, to the rights of birth fathers. Several states regard the men who sire babies as full partners in all decision making, a few treat them as sperm donors who deserve little consideration, while most fall somewhere in between.

Nearly half the states, some in response to heartbreaks like the Baby Richard case, have established "putative father registries" that men must sign if they want a say about an adoption. But the rules about when men must sign up and under what circumstances—soon after sexual intercourse, sometime before or after a birth, even within a specified period after an adoption—are all over the lot.[19] Almost no one knows the registries exist anyway. "I'm no fan of biological fathers coming out of nowhere to claim paternity, but I do think it's an unrealistic expectation for a man to send a postcard to the Secretary of State after he has sex," says Joan Hollinger, a University of California law school professor whose longtime specialty has been adoption.

Other processes, designed to help adoptees obtain information about themselves or locate their biological parents, are equally obscure and inconsistent. After a request is submitted in a "search and consent" state, an adoption agency or a court-appointed intermediary usually looks for the birth parents and, with their approval, either gives the adoptee the requested data or facilitates a reunion. In states with "mutual consent" registries, people can list their names at a central location; if both the seeker and the person being sought enroll, then the desired records are released. Some states have both systems, while a handful permit access to identifying documents only if the applicant proves "good cause" in court.[20]

In states where people besides adoptees are allowed to use registries, they are increasingly being employed by adoptive parents to find their children's biological mothers and fathers, and by birth parents to locate the children they relinquished. That is, to the extent these registries are used at all. Again, they are rarely publicized, and they come in so many different forms that they're hardly user-friendly.[21] Most significantly, the Internet is turning them into bureaucratic irrelevancies.

The same is true for statutes relating to advertising for women considering adoption for their babies. Many states permit unrestricted advertising, some regulate its placement and content, and a few make it a criminal offense. All these laws are dinosaurs, since they were enacted with only newspapers and magazines in mind. Today, along with home pages recounting the jubilant or painful tales of reunions between adoptees and their birth parents; beside the how-to guides for foreign and domestic adoption; amid the multiple directories of triad members searching for their biological mothers and fathers, sons and daughters, sisters and brothers, cyberspace is brimming with ads written by individuals, agencies, lawyers, and facilitators, some wanting to do good and others striving to make a buck, but all looking for pregnant women who don't plan to become parents. Anyone with access to a computer can place an advertisement or respond to one, regardless of where they live or what the laws are.

Ironically, it was the foundling homes of the late nineteenth century, often decrepit places where orphaned children received little attention but lots of diseases, that made infant adoption possible. Health-care experts pressed for the placement of children in families, but there were hardly enough wet nurses available to keep the youngest of them adequately fed in the institutions, much less with individuals. In response, a few of the foundling homes in New York funded research to develop a formula for infants derived from cow's milk. Once that was done, anyone could nourish a baby.[22]

Still, the phenomenon of modern adoption didn't develop for several more generations. Many Americans, including some who cared for abandoned and illegitimate children in foster homes, orphanages and other institutions, believed these boys and girls might be genetically inferior, bad seeds with poor prospects for growing up successful.[23] Older children were sometimes adopted by people outside their biological families, but until World War I babies who needed new homes were typically taken in by friends and relatives. There was nothing surreptitious about the process or about the identity of the birth parents, and contact between them and their offspring was commonplace.

The flow of professional research, and then public opinion, shifted heavily from nature to nurture over the following decades. At the same time, it became acceptable, and even trendy, for mothers to use bottled formula exclusively or to augment their nursing. Those two factors combined to persuade more and more infertile couples that it was not only all right to adopt babies, but that they could then raise their children without publicly revealing that they were "different."

Nearly all adults who grew up knowing they were adopted will now tell you that they were curious about their backgrounds, a little or a lot, occasionally or constantly. They'll tell you they used to daydream about their birth parents, fantasize about what they looked like, wonder why they parted with their babies. Even those who say they never had much curiosity will tell you they used to glance around new places—and sometimes still do—on the off chance that there might be a man or a woman there of a certain age, maybe just a few years younger than their adoptive parents, whose voice or facial features or even body type might resemble their own.

During the 1950s, perhaps coincidentally as adoption became more visible with the arrival of Korean war orphans into the United States, some adult adoptees began asking for more information about themselves. Behavioral researchers, meanwhile, had started suggesting that greater honesty helped adopted children develop trust in their parents and generally abetted their development. Increasingly, adoptive parents told their children that they were adopted. But few entertained questions or had answers, even fewer allowed the topic to become public, and virtually none conceived of taking the long leap of meeting the birth parents, much less establishing a relationship with them.

In 1974, after years of studying the effects of the adoption system on all its participants, three California researchers and social workers—Annette Baran, Reuben Pannor, and Arthur D. Sorosky—published a seminal adoption book called *The Adoption Triangle: The Effects of the Sealed Record on Adoptees, Birth Parents, and Adoptive Parents*. In it, they not only argued that birth certificates and other documents should become accessible, but also proposed an experiment in which triad members in some adoptions, under specific circumstances, might benefit from knowing each other. Nine years later, after a small number of Americans successfully tried the concept, the authors recommended that something called "open adoption" should become the norm.

It has taken decades, but a lopsided consensus is now mounting in favor of adopting that idea broadly. But there's less agreement about the details. It's far too soon, for instance, to even consider formulating guidelines about what degree of contact among the various parties might be best in any given situation. That decision will always depend on the specific circumstances and personalities anyway, so in most cases it should probably be left to the wisdom and instincts of the people involved.

In at least eight states, virtually unpublicized experiments are being conducted that could lead to answers to some of these thorny questions, or at least help establish criteria to steer the system and its participants in positive directions. These experiments are cooperative adoption agreements,[24] legal documents whose very existence underscores how radically adoption practices are changing. The parties to an open adoption use them to spell out rights such as visitation by interested parties—mainly birth parents, but sometimes grandparents, siblings, or other relatives—along with various people's responsibilities, such as sending pictures or initiating phone calls.

These documents typically can be amended as relationships evolve, particularly as the adoptee grows older. Like prenuptial agreements, they seem to work for a minority of people in specific circumstances, and will never be for everybody. They initially make some adoptive parents most nervous, because they fear that failure to adhere to the written terms could somehow jeopardize their adoptions. On that count, at least, they should rest easy. While cooperative adoption agreements were created partly because many promises to birth parents had been broken in the past, courts have already ruled that violating the pacts cannot be used as the basis for undoing an adoption.

Whatever the uncertainties about greater openness, some distinct patterns are emerging that can serve as guideposts for anyone considering an adoption and for people, like Judy and me, who are trying to figure out the future of connections we've already made. A steadily growing body of research and personal experiences also provides insights into how this new incarnation of adoption is likely to evolve, and helps explain why it's proliferating among Americans of every description even though, not long ago, it was considered a strange trip that might appeal only to a few aging West Coast hippies.

The earlier extended relationships are formed, the easier the adjustment and the greater the benefits.[25] For most people, it seems, the process may be best started after a period of exclusive bonding between adoptive parents and their children. That may sound self-evident, but many psychologists, social workers, and triad members had wondered, reasonably, whether any advantages of contact might be outweighed by confusion or even divided loyalties by adoptees, heightened insecurity and looser bonding by the adoptive parents, and less opportunity for birth mothers to get distance and heal.

But those theoretical concerns don't seem to manifest themselves in practice, at least not dramatically or frequently. The only consistent caveat offered by participants in open adoptions is that adoptive and birth parents should get counseling, especially before they begin their interactions, to diminish the potential for friction by teaching everyone what to expect and how to respond to any problems that do arise. Whether the help comes from an adoption agency, independent professionals, or triad support groups, it enhances the prospects for long-term success while minimizing any discomfort along the way.

The participants in open adoptions generally report they are happy with them, even if they have to deal with periodic personality conflicts.[26] In fact, many adoptive parents surprise themselves by wanting more contact as they learn that their primary roles with their children, emotionally and functionally, aren't undermined by the occasional presence of a birth mother and/or father; that their ability to answer their children's questions (and their own) is enhanced; and, maybe most important, that the birth parents aren't there to try to win their children back.

In a study of 720 triad members over five years, Dr. Ruth McRoy of the University of Texas in Austin and Dr. Harold Grotevant of the University of Minnesota found that adoptive parents in open arrangements are more secure about their adoption's stability and more at ease discussing adoption in general. Several studies, including this one, have also found that children in open adoptions exhibit fewer behavior problems than their counterparts in closed adoptions.[27]

Adoptive and birth parents in ongoing relationships discover another simple but essential truth: Open adoption is not co-parenting. Members of the triad should repeat that like a mantra, and explain it to their friends and relatives, because its acceptance will not only alleviate some of their own stresses but also will help everyone in our society feel more comfortable about this curious concept as it takes hold and grows more visible.

"There are just so many concerns, so many fears and insecurities that go through your mind. . . . I never, never thought we'd do more than write letters," says Carol Wierzba, who, along with her husband, Michael, initiated a relationship with their daughter's birth mother, Donna Asta. "Our friends and relatives just thought we were crazy or something. Sometimes, I still can't quite believe what we're doing, and I know most people don't think they could ever conceive of doing anything like this, but it's right for us . . . and we know that it's good for Kelly."

The Wierzbas don't fit anyone's stereotype of radical reformers. They are accountants who live in a middle-class suburb of Memphis. They're soft-spoken, religious, and conservative. They approached their decision to invite Donna into their extended family slowly, cautiously, but as the trust built among them, it picked up speed and soon ceased to feel awkward or extraordinary. Certainly there are examples of bumpier rides, and many participants in open adoptions will never want interactions as close as this one. What's more, in practice, most open adoptions go through intervals of more and less contact, depending on the needs of the child, the chemistry among the parents, and the other unpredictable elements of life. Some people become friends, others grow estranged. It's a time of flux, of uncertainty, of assessing boundaries in our families and within ourselves.

Just like in the rest of the nation, where stepbrothers and half-sisters live during the week with dad and his new wife, then spend weekends with their respective moms and their live-in boyfriends. Or girlfriends. Make up a scenario and it's probably happening somewhere. However it all shakes out, though, this much already seems certain: When hundreds of thousands of people like the Wierzbas are embracing openness in adoption so comfortably and extensively, they are collectively rewriting the American definition of the term "extended family." It's another blazing neon sign proclaiming that the old order is being overthrown, and a new future is being created.

3

Joy
and Surprises
from Abroad

It's no accident that Americans adopt more children internationally than do the inhabitants of the rest of the planet combined. After all, nearly every one of us came to this extraordinary country from somewhere else. We don't always find it easy to accept new waves of immigrants, but we invariably succeed in weaving their facial structures, their skin tones, and their heritages into our cultural tapestry. Throughout its history, this nation has opened its doors to people who, for more reasons than anyone can count, have needed new homes. It has taken us in, given us new lives. Adopted us.

What it has not done is force us to sever our emotional, spiritual, or physical ties to our forebears or our ancestral lands. Rather, one of the genuinely noble, enriching aspects of the American sensibility—notwithstanding the intolerance of some narrow-minded people and political movements—is its celebration of people's connections to their past. We marvel at the beauty of an African-print dress, revel in the music at a Latino festival or an Irish step dance, savor the delights of Asian restaurants, incorporate the expressive words of other languages into our own.

In many essential ways, adoption is a metaphor for the society in which it is coming of age, and in which it plays an increasingly active and visible role. More and more of the parallels are revealing themselves as the domestic branch of the institution emerges from the shadows, but they have been evident for half a century to anyone who has paid attention to or participated in the adoption of children from overseas.

The white couples who took in Korean War orphans knew that stuffing pillows under the wives' blouses wouldn't fool anybody. They couldn't even consider deceiving their sons and daughters into thinking they hadn't been adopted. And they repeatedly learned that, no matter how hard they tried to become Ozzie and Harriet, their parenting experience would be shaped by their decisions to raise children of races and cultures different than their own, children who would come home crying when classmates or teachers hurt them with racial taunts, children whose curiosity about their backgrounds was aroused each time they passed a mirror and couldn't detect a hint of their parents' features in their reflections. Or children who avoided looking at themselves altogether.

"I have Korean friends now who used to stand in front of the mirror and try to make their eyes bigger and rounder, or wore blond wigs or even dyed their hair blond. Ridiculous things like that. My way of dealing with it was to not look in the mirror much, I guess because I knew I wouldn't like what I saw," says Crystal Lee Hyun Joo Chappell, whose white adoptive parents raised her and three other Korean children in the small town of Dimondale, Michigan, starting in the 1960s. Apart from her siblings, Crystal was the lone Korean in her elementary school; her parents' friends were white, as were their neighbors, their friends, the shoppers at their local stores. And the adoption agency had counseled her parents not to dwell on their children's past, but to immerse them in their new realities so they would "assimilate" quickly and thoroughly.

As is still the case in many adoptions by Caucasian parents of children from other races and cultures, whether born in the United States or in other nations, the absorption process sometimes works too well. "I was brought up 110 percent American," says Hyun Joo, who has used the first name given to her at birth, along with her adoptive last name, since reuniting with her biological mother in Korea several years ago. Asked what it meant to be "110 percent American," she replies: "I really thought I was white."

So she was unprepared, even shocked, when some older boys pummeled her with profanities and racial slurs on the school bus during her sixth-grade year. The little kids in the supermarket were even more cruel: They just stared. "There were constant reminders of who I was and what I really looked like, but I learned to ignore them, deny them, pretend they weren't there. It was a matter of self-preservation, I guess. But it was pretty horrible to see an infant surprised by your face, looking at you like you're an alien. You can't fault a baby because a baby's so innocent, but at the same time you feel inhuman."

This notion of coming from another planet permeates the self-descriptions of adoptees of all types and ages, most pointedly those who feel disconnected from their personal histories. That doesn't mean, as a group, that they yearn for one specific piece of their puzzle—though most want basic data about their birth parents, at a minimum, at some point in their lives. But a lopsided majority, including those who profess little interest in their genealogies, will say they feel more grounded and secure when their adoptive parents infuse their upbringings with the cultures from which they came, routinely give them information about their backgrounds and, when physical differences are apparent, expose them to other people who look like them.

Some studies, and some adoptees themselves, suggest that their inner turmoil—especially if they are deprived of background information—can lead to behavioral or ego problems. Most research, however, indicates they grow up with the same kinds of formative issues, and achieve at the same levels, as their counterparts raised in birth families. Adoption doesn't typically define adoptees' day-to-day existence, but it can play an important role in how they perceive themselves at various stages of their lives. To the extent that parents can help their children form positive self-images, giving them the resources and support to feel like earthlings simply seems like the right thing to do, even when it might be emotionally or logistically difficult to accomplish.

One of the defining characteristics of the adoption revolution is the realization of that truth. As a result, a growing number of agencies and social workers are abandoning the fantasy of blind assimilation and doing a 180-degree turn: They advise prospective parents to incorporate their children's heritage into daily life. When someone white considers forming a family with children of another race, for example, whether from foster care or through a private adoption, the professionals recommend establishing role models and making friends of that race, perhaps even moving to a new neighborhood so their sons and daughters can mature among peers who look like them. And so they know their parents are comfortable with, and respect, people who share their children's traits.

Prospective parents who adopt from other nations regularly receive such guidance today. Indeed, because the majority of intercountry adoptions involve social workers and other specialists employed by agencies—people educated to understand these issues as opposed to private practitioners or untrained individuals, no matter how competent, making their own arrangements—the integration of other nations' customs and histories into American families, into our social fabric, is progressing rapidly.

There's no small dose of irony in this trend, since many Americans choose to adopt abroad expressly because they believe (sometimes correctly, often not) that it will allow them to avoid dealing with a fundamental aspect of their children's past: the birth parents. Yet the adoptive mothers and fathers are most often willing, even eager, to learn their children's native language, take them to cultural festivals, and engage in a host of other activities to ensure a sense of connection and to enhance self-worth, generally including trips back to the city or village from which they were adopted.

Some children in other countries, as in the United States, are placed for adoption because their parents are unable or unwilling to care for them. The vast majority, though, are the victims of much larger domestic tragedies, from civil strife in Central America and Africa to overpopulation in India to the devaluation of girls in China. This is the way it has been from the start, since the first measurable wave of adoptees arrived on our shores in the wake of World War II.

From 1948 to 1953, Americans adopted 5,814 children from Germany, Greece and, to lesser extents, the other battle-ravaged nations of Europe; nearly everyone adopting was white, and most of the children were very young. Infertile couples, along with some who wanted to provide homes for war orphans, also began reaching across color lines. During this same six-year period, they adopted 2,418 Asian children, about two thirds of them Japanese.[1]

As Japan and the nations of Western Europe restored their economies, they also slammed their doors to adoption by foreigners, and they have mainly remained shut since. For good reasons and bad, ranging from reflexive nationalism to personal pride to the need for sustaining human resources, countries don't like to give up their children any more than parents do. When things are going well, very little cross-border adoption takes place; when the outflow increases, it's a pretty strong hint that something's gone wrong.

Something's always going wrong somewhere, of course, so the interlacing of other cultures into our own will continue for the indefinite future. Inevitably, it will also accelerate the time when we acknowledge that the central metaphor for our country's development, that of a melting pot that takes all comers and produces a homogeneous human called an American, might never have been more than a lofty ideal. It's becoming very clear, with the help of adoption but as a result of myriad other demographic trends as well, that we've spent the last 225 years stitching together a stunning patchwork quilt, one rife with imperfections and in constant need of maintenance, to be sure, but a marvel of creativity and craftsmanship nevertheless.

While thousands of Americans had already adopted children from abroad, usually on their own or with minimal government help, it was a wealthy Oregon farmer-businessman named Harry Holt who began the institution now called intercountry adoption. In 1955 he saw a newsreel depicting the wretched existence of Korean War orphans, nearly all of whom were the biracial offspring of American soldiers. He and his wife were so moved by the children's plight that they sold some of their holdings, used the proceeds to lobby Congress (successfully) to institute the first U.S. laws spelling out uniform procedures for adopting from other countries, then established an orphanage in Korea. At the ages of fifty-one and fifty, respectively, Harry and Bertha Holt, who had already raised seven biological children, adopted eight homeless Amerasians from Korea.

Since those early days, Holt International has grown into a huge organization, maintaining its deep roots in Korea while branching out into many of the other nations whose domestic problems have left millions of children without families worldwide. It has been joined by more agencies and attorneys every decade, most motivated principally by compassion and altruism, but a steadily escalating number in recent years wanting to cash in on the misery of destitute children and infertile adults. At the dawn of the twenty-first century, several hundred licensed U.S. agencies were involved in intercountry adoption, along with an unknown number of lawyers and facilitators.

Korea remained the primary "sending country" for four decades, until China and Russia—for very different reasons—decided to allow foreigners to adopt their children. The government in Beijing did so because its population-control policy, which permitted parents to have only one child, led to the abandonment of newborn daughters on such a massive scale that orphanages overflowed. Almost simultaneously, the shredding of the Iron Curtain revealed that hundreds of thousands of Eastern European children, perhaps millions, were being warehoused in dilapidated institutions because their parents were too poor, too alcohol-dependent, and/or too emotionally impaired to care for them.

Romania was the first Communist country to unseal its borders, after the revolution in December 1989 that deposed its longtime dictator, Nicolae Ceausescu. After thirty-four years of despotic rule, during which he created one of the most hermetic and rigidly controlled societies on earth, Ceausescu was overthrown in a popular uprising. He was so reviled that, after he was executed by firing squad, the national radio station announced: "The Antichrist is dead." The events of the following few years, most notably the breakup of the Soviet Union, changed the course of modern history. On a smaller scale, they also altered the direction of adoption, domestic and international, and in so doing exposed the highs and lows of its motivations, mechanics, and consequences.

At first, when the Western media reported as many as 200,000 sickly children were institutionalized or wandering the streets in Romania, the world's reaction was as heartening as it was telling. People everywhere, particularly Americans, swooped in to help, many by donating money and some by offering to adopt. Without a doubt, nearly everyone was driven by a desire to do good. But it's also undeniable that adoption practitioners and would-be parents, particularly those frustrated or intimidated by the procedures of adopting a baby within the United States, were excited by the prospect of an immense new source of Caucasian children. That wasn't an expression of bigotry. People of every nationality and color generally find it less complicated and more comfortable, at least initially, to raise children who resemble them.

Still, adoption is inculcating our society with more and more children who don't look like their parents, and by doing so, it is playing a small but important role in alleviating bias on a personal level. There are innumerable white grandparents, uncles, aunts, and cousins, for example, who have surprised themselves with the unconditional love they feel for their new black or Asian or Hispanic relatives, and who have learned critical lessons as a result. Adoption is helping to crack the walls of prejudice and intolerance on a broader scale, too: Just one family of Korean children starkly demonstrated to the white majority of Dimondale, every day, that people with different appearances could be kind, smart, accomplished, and easy to live with.

That scenario was unusual when Hyun Joo was growing up in Michigan in the 1970s, but today it is being duplicated nationwide at an escalating rate. In 1998, the last year for which statistics were available, Americans adopted almost 16,000 children from abroad, more than 10,000 of them from Asia, Central and South America, Africa, and the Caribbean. The comparable figures a decade earlier were about 8,000 total, 7,800 of whom were born in nations where the dominant skin tones and facial features aren't white-European.[2]

These statistics reveal unmistakable trends: First, the tide of Americans adopting overseas is rising, both in sheer numbers and as a proportion of all adoptions outside the children's own families; by the latter measure, foreign adoption is up from less than 10 percent a decade ago to perhaps

20 percent today. Meanwhile, due almost entirely to the opening of Eastern Europe, an escalating number of the internationally adopted children are Caucasian; it's hard to nail down precisely how many because the former Soviet states include residents who are Asian or of mixed descent.

Some equally important, but less evident, underlying shifts are also evident from the Immigration and Naturalization Service visa counts. One is the rapid growth, on a percentage basis, of children adopted from Central America as the people there cope with endemic poverty, natural disasters, and the aftermath of devastating civil wars. From 1989 to 1998, the official annual total of adoptions from the region jumped from 595 to 976; of those, amid alarming indications that a lack of regulation had led to baby snatchings and black marketeering, Guatemala's share leaped from 202 to 911.

An even more consequential change—a revolutionary chapter in international adoption history—was unfolding at the same time, half a world away. During this ten-year period, annual adoptions from Asia rose by more than 50 percent, from 5,112 to 7,827. That explosion was significant on its own, but it wasn't the lead of the story. This was: During the final decade of the twentieth century, the number of children adopted annually from mainland China skyrocketed from thirty-three to 4,206.

Across the United States today, it's getting increasingly difficult to find a playground without at least one little girl from China, being watched lovingly by a white mother or father. Support and educational groups for adoptive families with Chinese children are proliferating, and their members are becoming vocal advocates for adoption-conscious reforms and ethnic sensitivity in schools, medical facilities, and other social institutions. For the most part, the parents also seem to be ensuring the continuous, long-term infusion of Chinese culture into our country by teaching their children about their homeland, its customs, and its traditions from the time they are infants.

"It's not that previous groups of adoptees weren't readily identifiable by the country they came from, or that the parents didn't organize and promote their interests. Those things have been true in most other groups, too—Korean adoptions for a long time, and certainly many of the parents of children from Romania, Russia, and the rest of Eastern Europe today are very proactive and very involved," says Maureen Evans, the former executive director of the Joint Council on International Children's Services, an umbrella organization of licensed, nonprofit American adoption agencies.

"But, as a group, the parents of the Chinese girls have been more educated and more sharply focused about their children's heritage from the start. . . . And there are differences in the children themselves: We never had so many come from a single place in such a compressed period of time before, all of them very young and healthy, and all of them girls. It's the Chinese children, in their numbers and their gender, all about the same age, who have changed and will continue to change the face of adoption."

And, in the process, the face of America. Demographers already estimate that our country's population will consist of nearly as many minorities, meaning people with black, Asian, non-white Hispanic, and American Indian heritages, as Caucasians by the middle of the twenty-first century.[3] The population specialists rarely take adoption into account when they make their calculations, however, so the pace of change will certainly be somewhat quicker and the multicultural nature of our evolving nation will be even greater because adoptees, from China and elsewhere, will integrate the traditions and customs of the places they were born with those of their adoptive nation.

Russell and Susan Correia started their multiethnic parenting the minute they brought their ten-month-old daughter home to Portland, Maine, dressing her in clothes they had bought in China and decorating her room with artwork from her homeland. They also speak enthusiastically about maintaining her ties to and associations with her roots. Their main regret is that, because Hope was abandoned, she'll never be able to meet members of her birth family or even obtain information about them.

"We'll take her back to where she was born when she's old enough to understand it all," says Susan. "We want her to know who she is and to know we're proud of that. It's something we'll celebrate and honor for her and with her." Russell nods in agreement. He says some people don't understand why he and Susan are learning Chinese, why they belong to an organization of families with Chinese children, why it's so important to keep their daughter connected with her culture. But he feels fortunate, not put-upon.

"We've become, unwittingly, educators in adoption and tolerance, so maybe we're part of something bigger that's making America a better place, I don't know. It's certainly not why we adopted to begin with. . . . But we've also got to remember that this kind of thing has been going on a long, long time, so we're not doing something that's so unique," he adds. "My grandparents came over from Portugal two generations ago; they passed on their heritage into our country, and now, through Hope, we'll pass on both the Portuguese and the Chinese heritages. That's a good thing, isn't it?"

Testing the Limits

The unhappy reality is that many governments can't care for all their people, but that doesn't excuse the exploitation that takes place in the name of adoption. Unregulated, unscrupulous facilitators coerce or bribe poor and single women around the world to part with their babies, then charge tens of thousands of dollars to American agencies and lawyers for their "services." Agents for some U.S. adoption businesses dole out bribes to foreign judges, orphanage administrators, and other authorities to accelerate the process, to alter or create documents, even to arrange infants' adoptions over their parents' objections.

There is an extent to which, in countries like Vietnam and Russia that have functioned with underground economies for decades, payoffs are an inescapable part of doing business of any sort. Children aren't merchandise, though, and they should never be treated as such. So it's reassuring to know that only a small segment of practitioners surrender to their baser instincts. Still, there is no organized oversight of international adoption, just as there is almost none within the United States, so there are villains out there, feeling unconstrained about testing the legal and moral limits of their operations.

Sally Gillman, a senior employee at a nonprofit adoption agency in California, warns would-be parents who come to her that "everything you can imagine happens out there on Planet Adoption—the good, the bad, the exquisitely beautiful and the grotesquely ugly." Sally, not her real name, recalls a trip she took recently to Guatemala to meet with her agency's representative about an Oklahoma couple's adoption:

"Everything essentially had been done already. The home study, the visa documents, the paperwork in Guatemala City, the whole ball of wax. This couple was ready; they'd gone through years of infertility treatments, had a couple of domestic adoptions fall through when the birth mothers changed their minds, had a really hard time emotionally and spent a whole lot of money. They'd been trying to have a child, one way or another, as I recall, for nearly four years. . . .

"I told them before I left that I thought it would take just a few more days before they could fly down to see their son, a seven-month-old boy they named Tommy, and then they could take him home a couple of weeks later or so. Well, I met our guy for coffee . . . and he told me, flat out, that he'd gone to another agency and told them he had this baby ready to go, and told them how much his costs were and they'd said yes. They paid him something like $5,000 more than we'd agreed to. I don't know if they knew what he was up to or just thought it's what this facilitator charges. Maybe he was lying, just trying to get me to up my price. I don't know. I was just revolted and walked out.

"We've obviously never used him again, but this couple I was dealing with was incredibly, absolutely devastated. It caused terrible stress between the two of them. The wife wanted to try again; the husband said he couldn't take any more disappointment. I recommended they receive counseling, which they did. I believe they finally decided to give up on having children. The whole thing was just horrible. . . . I don't even want to think about where the guy got the baby, knowing what I do about his ethics. I mean, it was bald, outright baby-selling." Asked how many children her agency had placed in the past through this same representative, Sally sighs her response: "Two. Two too many."

Sally informed the other American agency (which had agreed to pay more money) about what had happened, and received assurances that it would also cease using this facilitator. She says she did not report the man to Guatemalan authorities for the same reason that she doesn't want to be identified by name: because he was a prominent lawyer who "had friends high up in the government." She's afraid that nothing would happen to him if she filed a complaint, but future adoptions by her agency in Guatemala could be jeopardized.

The majority of professionals avoid dilemmas of this sort by dealing only with established institutions, whatever their problems, rather than with individuals. Many concede they cut corners here and there, however, and some undoubtedly avert their eyes so they can later deny they knew about shady activities conducted on their behalf. An indeterminable number, sometimes knowingly and sometimes not, also commit errors in judgment that yield grim consequences: They don't provide parents-to-be with sufficient information, emphatically enough, about the problems and risks they might face.

Studies have shown for decades that institutionalization, by depriving children of close emotional relationships, can badly impair their capacity to make personal connections throughout their lives. It can slow their intellectual and emotional maturation, and can erode their ability to make transitions from one developmental stage to the next. Sometimes the children's psychic disorders are so severe that, when their adoptive parents simply touch them to show affection, they scream.

In some countries, institutionalized children also have been sexually abused, beaten, shaken, and routinely handled so roughly that they sustain internal damage of every physical and psychological sort. To make matters worse, their medical records are often shoddy or deliberately falsified to camouflage the treatment they've received. And, as if all that's not complicated enough to unravel, many orphanage officials and doctors routinely report children as suffering from serious conditions that they don't really have, because their countries don't permit healthy children to be adopted by foreigners.

Most often, even the children with serious problems can be successfully dealt with through medical intervention, counseling, and other therapies. Indeed, long-term research into the lives of Romanian adoptees, who endured particularly horrid conditions, shows most making enormous strides.[4] But many of their parents are irate that they weren't told more from the start about a host of issues—the specific environments in which their children lived, the documented repercussions of institutionalization, the warning signals of various developmental problems, the best strategies for raising children with their particular difficulties, and the resources available to help them. Some people, given that kind of input, would not have adopted; others would have been spared serious disappointments. Most would have proceeded, but with better information with which to raise their sons and daughters.

The combination of abysmal conditions in orphanages and questionable behavior by practitioners can produce excruciating outcomes. Consequently, the last several years have seen an explosion in "wrongful adoption" lawsuits, in which adoptive parents claim their agency, attorney, or facilitator lied or willfully withheld information about the mental or physical health of adoptees and/or their birth parents. The plaintiffs typically seek sizable financial settlements to compensate for the suffering they endured or to help them deal with their children's expensive medical treatments.

Wrongful adoption suits were first filed in the 1980s by Americans who adopted domestically years earlier, then discovered their children had problems their agencies had been aware of, could have determined, or should have suspected given the birth parents' medical histories. Most professionals at the time had acted in good conscience, since the accepted practice was to provide only "positive" background. In fact, it was widely believed that disclosures about mental illness or other maladies would unfairly brand the child and cause undue anxiety for adoptive parents.

A series of very costly judgments helped to change their minds, or at least their policies. One of the most influential was rendered in Massachusetts in 1995, when the state's highest court unanimously upheld a jury award of $3.8 million to a couple that had adopted from the public system twenty years earlier. The justices ruled that the state was liable because its employees had not disclosed that the girl about to be adopted was mentally retarded and that her birth mother was a chronic schizophrenic.

Coupled with the simultaneous trend toward more openness, expensive verdicts like that one induced adoption practitioners to keep better records, obtain more extensive information from birth parents, and become more forthcoming with adoptive parents. The incidence of domestic wrongful-adoption suits has since declined, though they're still filed regularly. The number in the international arena, meanwhile, is steadily climbing. A couple of examples provide a glimpse into the kinds of complaints that exist:

- In March 1991, Gary and Joan Mancinelli of Wilmington, Delaware, adopted two-and-a-half-year-old Romanian twins. They say they were repeatedly assured that the girl was healthy and that the boy's hepatitis B could be easily treated. Once they got home, however, their son's disease was found to be in a very active stage; doctors said his condition was degenerative and terminal. The Mancinellis sued their agency for $200,000 in compensatory damages and $1 million in punitive damages, plus attorney's fees.
- Jerald and Rhea Lastick of Wayne, Pennsylvania, told their Maryland adoption agency that they wanted a child without serious special needs, but would accept one with problems that could readily be corrected. They were matched with a boy listed as having serious ailments, but were assured that it was "standard procedure" in Estonia to lie about children's conditions in order to fool the government into releasing them for adoption.

  When they went to see their son in September 1995, the Lasticks learned he had been born dead and then revived, had severe pneumonia in utero, had a brain hemorrhage, and was paralyzed from the waist down. The Lasticks maintain they were promised they could halt their process once in Estonia, but were told after they arrived that the adoption had been finalized. The couple hired a local attorney, who succeeded in getting the adoption nullified on grounds of fraud. They sued their agency for $200,000 in compensatory damages, an undisclosed sum in punitive damages, plus attorney's fees.

The outcomes of these cases haven't been disclosed, but agencies typically win such suits because adoptive parents' contracts explicitly state that they're aware of the risks going in. In any event, such dire scenarios constitute a tiny fraction of all adoptions abroad. But they dramatically illustrate the frightening results that institutionalization can produce, and they highlight how starkly clear professionals have to be in executing their responsibilities. The good news is that more and more countries, including those in Eastern Europe, are taking steps to revise their laws and clean up their orphanages.

At the same time, whatever faults adoption practitioners may have, on the whole they are promoting higher standards and making significant contributions to the welfare of homeless children. Nonprofit organizations in particular—but also some money-making agencies, attorneys, and facilitators—are furnishing financial and logistical support to orphanages as part of their missions. Scores of others are building new orphanages, providing their own staffing, and assisting in the training of local personnel. Their actions not only benefit the residents of the facilities receiving direct assistance, but also act as models for and apply pressure on other institutions in their areas.

The very existence of intercountry adoption serves several similarly constructive purposes. Nations that allow foreigners to assume custody of their children almost by definition invite examination by social-work and medical professionals, the media, and human-rights groups. The resulting advice can have a profound impact in places where the leaders want to do the right thing. And even minimal reporting about and monitoring in authoritarian countries like China have provoked reforms, if for no other reason than to prevent embarrassment for institution administrators and government officials.

Perhaps most pointedly, whatever its problems, intercountry adoption puts into practice the paramount principle that professionals almost universally agree should guide the process in all its forms: to provide parents for children who need them, not the other way around. That goal sometimes gets obscured or lost, particularly in the world of domestic infant adoption, where Americans yearn for the fulfillment that their fertile friends can achieve by simply tossing away their condoms or birth control pills.

Do the U.S. adoption practitioners helping other countries care for their children have a vested interest in their work, so that their well-paying clients will get continued access to younger and healthier adoptees? Sure, but only an uninformed cynic could believe that's typically their principal motivation. Nor do most people believe these countries' problems will be significantly alleviated by the adoptive parents who provide new families to a tiny proportion of their youngest, neediest citizens.

But it's crucial to stay focused on the children, and with few exceptions, the ones who are adopted will live better lives than they could have received, institutionalized, in their homelands. At the same time, the surge in adoptions abroad has prompted some of the affected nations to improve their laws, their orphanages, and the treatment of their own children. The progress has been painfully slow and remains wildly erratic, but it's real. In this way, at least, the American adoption revolution is being felt around the globe.

The Only Constant: Change

Institutions are the rougher international equivalent of America's public-care system, and disparate (or nonexistent) statutes around the world constitute a larger version of the state-to-state labyrinth that prospective parents must negotiate when they decide to adopt a child domestically. Guatemala's legislature recently drafted a new law allowing only married couples to adopt its children, for instance, while China—which allows single people to adopt—lowered its minimum age from 35 to 30.

Nations obviously must make judgments based on their own values and needs, but other factors sometimes come into play as well. In particular, many of the countries coping with adoption issues face excruciating economic difficulties and/or are in states of political flux; as a result, some change their rules frequently and with little notice in response to shifting perceptions, political pressures, and even personal views.

The nation of Georgia is a vivid example. The number of children from that former Soviet republic adopted by Americans had steadily risen from just two in 1992 to ninety in 1996. But the following year, President Eduard Shevardnadze's wife, Nanuli, announced that Georgia's gene pool was being "depleted" by unscrupulous agencies. She launched a crusade against all further adoptions. Government authorities informed dozens of Americans—some of whom had already held the babies they expected to adopt, filled out all the necessary forms, and were just waiting in local hotels for final details to be completed—that their cases were being placed on hold. Some returned home as parents, most didn't. Twenty-one children were adopted from Georgia in 1997, six in 1998, and none in 1999.

In much the same way that a minority of black activists and social workers in the United States fear their culture is being diluted by white adoption of African-American children, some officials in developing countries worry they are losing their future human resources to wealthy nations exploiting their poverty and internal strife. Most people involved in adoption, including those who prefer to keep children within their racial or national groups, see things differently. Asserting that the children's current welfare takes precedence, they argue that until there are enough homes in their own communities for all those in need, placing them in other nurturing families is infinitely healthier, for them and their societies, than letting them languish in foster care or institutions.

Perspectives that seem so straightforward in principle can be tough to maintain in practice, however. Adoption is the subject of debate in every country with orphans, and other factors besides the children's conditions at the moment invariably come into play. They periodically lead to temporary disruptions of adoptions and, occasionally, they redraw the map altogether. The seismic shifts in international geopolitics in the 1990s starkly make the point. In 1989, Americans adopted just thirty-three children from China and none from Russia. By 1995, the People's Republic had become the largest foreign source of U.S. adoptees (2,049) while Russia rushed ahead of Korea (1,684 to 1,570). In 1998, the onetime superpower attained the dubious distinction of sending more children to be raised abroad than any other country, 4,491 to China's 4,206.[5]

It's not an achievement that filled most Russians with pride. Moreover, a growing concern about corruption led President Vladimir Putin to impose a moratorium in May 2000 on the adoption of Russian orphans by foreigners until reforms are instituted. As of this writing, his order was being followed sporadically in various regions of the coutnry, but American agencies were working to comply with the new rules. Whatever happens, the tumultuous events in Moscow underscore the fragile and unnerving nature of the process.

Scares like this have happened before. In November 1997, in a statement that echoed Nanuli Shevardnadze's comments in Georgia, the chairwoman of the Russian parliament's Committee on Women, Family, and Youth Affairs declared that adoption by foreigners amounted to "cultural genocide." She introduced legislation, which did not receive majority support, that would have effectively stopped adoptions until Moscow and Washington approved a treaty mandating better supervision, procedures, and safeguards for the rights of everyone concerned.

Unlike in Georgia, where officials are making good on their vow to care for their children, this was a subterfuge meant to exhibit compassion without having to produce results. Putin's action appears more genuinely intended to foster positive change—but only procedurally. The Russians could implement unilateral improvements for the nearly 600,000 children under state care, but they've shown minimal inclination to do so and have limited resources to expend in any event. Neither reality seems likely to change as a result of Putin's reforms or during the years it would take to negotiate a treaty, assuming one could be finally signed. And the population of Russia's orphanages would continue to grow in the interim.

Besides, a treaty already has been drafted that seeks to accomplish everything the Kremlin critics said they wanted. But Russia's lawmakers haven't ratified the Convention on Protection of Children in Respect of Intercountry Adoption, written in the Hague in 1993, indicating that they prefer to retain the issue for political gamesmanship. The U.S. Congress has been considering the pact during the writing of this book. If it is approved by the United States, which adopts far more children from other countries than any other nation, the Hague Convention promises to foment a revolution in international adoptions as pervasive and far-reaching as the one already playing out domestically.

The treaty mandates that each of its adherents create a Central Authority to deal with a broad array of adoption-related matters, from breaking down bureaucratic and legal barriers between nations, to preventing practitioners from exploiting birth parents or making improper financial gains, to protecting the rights of children. The Central Authorities would coordinate their efforts to achieve smooth procedures, and signatory countries would be obliged to toughen many of their laws and regulations. For instance, they would have to register agencies that wanted to operate in other Hague nations, and would set rigorous standards by which those agencies would have to abide.

No doubt, the Hague Convention would be imperfectly implemented, inconsistently interpreted, and frequently circumvented. It's a breathtakingly ambitious undertaking nevertheless, and it sets a far more serious starting point for systemic improvements than any nation-by-nation or issue-by-issue piecemeal approach could establish. Equally important, simply by ratifying the treaty, the governments of the world will be effectively sanctioning adoption as a routine, normal way of building families—simultaneously reflecting how far the process has come and thrusting it another giant step forward.

Representatives from fifty-five capitals, including Washington, participated in drafting the Hague Convention and signed it in 1993, signaling their support for its goals and implicitly promising to secure its ratification back home. At least thirty-five governments have formally approved the pact since then, but they don't yet include the biggest sending and receiving nations: China, Russia, South Korea, and the United States.

America, given its paramount position in the adoption world, should take the lead in ensuring that the treaty is widely endorsed and implemented. To the extent that it is, this historic document will have a profound, long-term impact on millions of children and their parents. Its ripple effects should also prove significant within its member nations; perhaps, by insisting on standards of conduct, registration requirements for practitioners, and consistency across global borders, it could serve as a prototype for straightening out the virtually unregulated maze that characterizes adoption within our own country.

Ultimately, the ongoing changes in domestic and intercountry adoption have to be coordinated if the institution's positive image and smooth integration into our society are to continue. There's a limit to how many horror stories politicians and ordinary citizens can hear before they begin forming new stereotypes and building new cultural walls to separate adoption from what they view as normal life. Furthermore, reforms in the two branches of adoption need to be connected simply because they sometimes intersect.

For instance: A small but indeterminable number of adoption practitioners bring women from other nations to the United States on tourist visas for the final stages of their pregnancies. That way, they can give birth here, sign their relinquishment papers, and fly back home. It's a relatively quick and easy routine, especially compared to either the typical international or domestic adoption experience. The adoptive parents, usually higher-income Americans who can afford the $25,000 to $50,000 in costs, are thrilled to get a baby with so few hassles; the people putting together the arrangements make a tidy profit; and the birth mothers return to their homelands with anywhere from a thousand to several thousand dollars to compensate them, ostensibly, for "medical and living expenses."

Putting the monetary issues briefly aside, the ethics of this sort of enterprise may be arguable in those instances where the women freely and genuinely agree to part with their children. But it's unclear (and certainly unmonitored) whether anyone on either side of the ocean seriously tries to make that determination. The arrangement itself is also probably illegal, or at least legally questionable, in many if not most other countries, which have their own adoption statutes that their citizens are obliged to follow.

A majority of the birth mothers involved in these operations are poor and/or unmarried women from Russia and other former Soviet states. They are usually recruited by middlemen who are paid $10,000 to $20,000 by their American employers for each pregnant client they send to the United States. There's no way to know what financial or personal inducements these brokers may offer. And the women, living in a foreign environment with no support system other than the adoption workers caring for their daily needs, can feel compelled to sign their relinquishments even if, once they get to this country or after childbirth, they're no longer sure they want to part with their babies.

U.S. implementation of the Hague Convention, and the changes in domestic law that would be required, would make it far more difficult to
carry out such murky transnational adoptions. It would also, for the first
time, impose standards on an obscure category of adoption that almost
no one knows anything about, much less monitors or regulates—that is,
the adoption of American children by people in other nations.

Most of the estimated two hundred to three hundred boys and girls affected annually are of mixed race, suffer from handicaps, or otherwise
have special needs. They aren't the easiest to find homes for, so it's wonderful that people abroad, mostly in Canada but also in other nations,
want to give them families. But some small number—there are no statistics, just anecdotal accounts—are healthy white babies placed by U.S.
practitioners with wealthy Western Europeans. These are people who, for
whatever reasons, don't want to or can't adopt infants in their own countries and, consequently, are willing to pay as much as $50,000 to $100,000
for a white child from the United States.

It isn't just unscrupulous entrepreneurs who are taking advantage of
the almost-nobody's-watching, almost-anything-goes international atmosphere, nor is it just the well-intentioned professionals who are avail-
ing themselves of the loopholes. Some perfectly ethical prospective
parents discover for themselves that there are back doors, side windows,
and other unorthodox entry points through which they can adopt.

Steve and Linda Balinalik, both dance teachers in Washington, D.C.,
had intended to go the conventional route, through a large and reputable
adoption agency in their area. In July 1998, they submitted their paperwork, along with a $1,000 application fee, and initiated a home study.
They'd read news reports about problems with children from Russian orphanages, but they'd also been told that the process there could be
wrapped up relatively quickly. They'd already endured years of infertility treatments and were now in their forties. They wanted to start a family, and they couldn't bear much more waiting.

"I prayed a lot, to tell you the truth. I prayed we both had the strength
to do this and had the strength to take on whatever child we got," says
Linda, who handled most of the logistics of the couple's adoption. "I
wanted a kid yesterday, so I knew what we would have to do is close our
eyes and take the leap . . . rather than just wringing our hands until we
were ninety years old. At some point you have to let go of all these fears
that you've got and have faith, in God or whatever you believe in, and
take the leap."

One day soon after making their decision, Linda shared her excitement
and apprehensions with a friend, a woman who had emigrated from

Moscow herself just a few years earlier. "You don't want to do this," Anastasia cautioned. The birth mothers are almost all alcoholics or drug addicts, she explained, while the children suffer from malnutrition and other serious problems developed while living in miserable institutions. Linda was shaken but resolute, believing Anastasia's opinions had been skewed by unfair stereotypes and personal resentments. An hour later, the Russian émigrée called to say she had indeed been exaggerating, and felt terrible about having upset Linda.

As if to assuage her guilt, Anastasia volunteered to help. "I have a friend in Russia who does adoptions," she said, "and I can telephone her to do something for you." Linda talked the offer over with her husband that night, and they decided they'd make the call themselves. The woman in Moscow, named Maria, spoke fairly good English, but they decided to use Anastasia as a translator to minimize the possibility of any misunderstandings. The Balinaliks found Maria to be friendly and honest; she asked appropriate questions about home studies, immigration procedures, and other legal matters, and her responses to their questions seemed clear and forthright.

The couple was tempted to proceed. They figured they could cut months off the process and save thousands of dollars by forgoing their agency. Still, they didn't want to skirt any laws, do anything unethical, or wind up getting fleeced. So, after a second conversation with Maria, they asked for a meeting with their adoption agency's attorney. As they sat in his Virginia office, he called the facilitator in Moscow, interviewed her at length, and told his clients afterward: "I think it's going to be fine, go ahead. You'll probably save $4,000 or $5,000. Put it toward the kid's college education."

Within a couple of months, after Federal Expressing legal documents back and forth, Linda received an envelope that she was told would contain the photographs and biographies of four children. When Steve got home that night, they sat together in their bedroom, held hands, and prayed before opening it. Two photos were of girls, two of boys; their ages ranged from four months to almost three years.

Linda recalls the experience as "frightening and painful." It felt too much like they were shopping. But it also felt like they were finally going to realize their dream of having a family. "They're all cute, we can't go wrong," Steve told his wife. She was drawn to the youngest child, a blond, blue-eyed boy from an orphanage 260 miles northeast of Moscow. His biography included numerous physical ailments, all described in clinical terms, but they'd been warned to expect phony problems, so they weren't overly concerned. They called Maria to ask for a videotape of the boy. It arrived by overnight mail a week later, and the couple took it to a pediatrician in Washington who specializes in children adopted from Russia. At 3 o'clock the next day, a Sunday afternoon in March 1997, the doctor called to say that Sergei looked perfectly fit.

The Balinaliks went to meet their son the following month. His orphanage was old and sparsely decorated, but clean. It smelled of ammonia. Sweat saturated their necks as they waited in a small room adjoining the spacious nursery in which about forty children were resting, two lying kitty-corner in each oversized crib. After a few very long minutes, a nurse brought in a small, nicely dressed boy. He smiled a lot.

Linda and Steve were allowed to hold him, feed him, play with him. They felt simultaneously frightened and exhilarated. Linda was so overcome with the feeling that she was finally becoming a mother that she began to cry. "Please stop," the nurse advised her. "The baby will see it and think something is wrong." After about an hour, they were asked to leave, but were told they could return the next day. After that, they were to go home and return in two weeks to formalize the adoption.

To this day, neither Linda nor Steve can quite believe the adventure they experienced next. They had taken out a second mortgage on their home and now needed to tap into it. They had already given Maria's colleague, Dmitri, $2,000 in small bills to pay expenses and grease their path (they didn't ask how) during their first visit. This time, Maria had told them in a fax to bring $10,000 in cash and indicated they were to reveal the money's existence to no one. They called the agency lawyer to ask if it was all right to follow those directions. "That's the way it's done," he answered.

Two days before their scheduled departure, Dmitri called, breathless and apologetic. He said that May Day celebrations in the area of their son's orphanage had been officially extended, so they needed to postpone their arrival for another week. He also said a new judge had been assigned to their case, and she wanted to meet both prospective parents. They had previously been told that just one of them could make the long journey to pick up their child; now Steve had to scramble to buy a second airline ticket and beseech coworkers to fill in for him on very short notice.

By coincidence, a baby shower had been scheduled for the evening before their departure, so they asked a banker-friend to bring their $10,000 to the party. "We went upstairs and I counted it," says Linda. "I felt like we were a couple of drug dealers or something." Later that evening, as they were filling their suitcases with baby clothes and toys—a few for their son, now called Andrew, and more for the orphanage—the couple realized they'd overlooked an important detail: They hadn't bought a money belt or other device to conceal the stack of crisp, new $100 bills they needed to carry with them.

Linda pulled an old knee sock out of her dresser drawer and stashed "the wad," as she calls it, inside. The next morning, she stuffed the surprisingly thin package into her right sock, along her shin, then slid on a pair of blue jeans. She was nervous, but she wasn't about to let that anxiety deter her from her mission: "I just kept telling myself that this is what I have to do to adopt my son, that's all there was to it." They cleared customs without incident. Then the airline lost their luggage. "I guess the bright side is that the money wasn't packed away, but we weren't thinking about any bright side. We were tired, frazzled, and very upset. And we didn't want to think that this was an omen," says Linda.

After a sleepless overnight train ride to the town where their son's orphanage was located, Dmitri met them at the station and took them to an open-air market to buy fresh clothes for their morning meeting with the orphanage director. They'd been traveling for twenty-six hours and were exhausted. At the orphanage that Sunday, they were told everything was proceeding well, but they had to appear before the judge the following day and couldn't see their son again until they picked him up Tuesday for the trip home.

The driver who took them from their dilapidated hotel to court was a man they'd never seen before. He said Dmitri was busy—bringing the judge from her home. The "court" turned out to be an aging schoolhouse; the judge was a tall, elegant woman who sat at the teacher's desk in a onetime classroom. She asked a few questions, like: "Is this your house?" as she held up a photo. When they answered "Yes," she said: "You're very lucky." Ten minutes later, they were done. They didn't leave for another hour, though. Dmitri had to give the judge a ride home first, and she hadn't completed her daily duties yet; he also had to drop the judge's teenage daughter off at her boyfriend's house.

The Balinaliks went to get Andrew the following day. This time, he was wearing nothing at all, not even a diaper; the orphanage was too poor to part with anything that other children could use. The couple, meanwhile, began doling out their cash. Dmitri had advised them to give the institution's director $1,000, in addition to a blood-pressure kit and some other medical equipment he'd asked for himself. Their luggage also finally arrived that morning, so they were able to deliver a cache of toys and clothing.

They gave Dmitri $2,000 (he said he'd cut his price by $1,000 to compensate for the extra airline ticket they hadn't expected to buy) and they counted out another $3,000 for Maria upon their return to Moscow. She handed them an itemized bill. They examined it carefully, then destroyed it. Including the money they'd initially paid to their agency, the price of the home study, the immigration and visa fees, travel expenses and all the other costs they'd incurred, they figured they'd spent less than $15,000 altogether on Andrew's adoption. The next day, they took their son home.

Lessons from Romania

It's an intuitive truth that children mature and function better within stable, caring families than in any environment where they receive little individual attention or little sustained affection. That's why kids who bounce back and forth between their biological parents and temporary homes—no matter how nurturing or compassionate their foster parents may be—usually wind up troubled. It's also a major reason the United States and most other Western nations decided more than a half century ago that a family setting was nearly always preferable to almost any form of institutionalization.[6]

Group facilities remain the housing of last resort for deserted children in the developing world, however, with tremendous variations in the quality of their personnel, infrastructures, and the quality of care they provide. As far as anyone can determine, though, no country any longer tolerates conditions as horrendous as the ones discovered in Romania in December 1989. Ceausescu and his wife, Elana, who served as his chief deputy and was executed along with her husband, believed that increasing their country's population would somehow help to alleviate its indigence. They imposed policies promoting childbirth, forbidding abortion and contraception, and financially penalizing couples who didn't produce children. The two leaders, meanwhile, were looting the nation's treasury. The predictable result was a nightmarish nation in which people lived in desperation and fear, in which poverty grew pervasive, and in which families became increasingly less able to care for their children. So they were routinely abandoned.

The institutions into which they were then placed reflected the grim realities of their society at large. Children were tied onto beds. Some were found lying in their own excrement. In winter, many froze to death; the rest of the year, they atrophied away or died of malnutrition. Diseases went untreated, physical and emotional abuse seemed to be officially tolerated, and affection apparently was an emotion that these children's pathetic caretakers were too exhausted or socially brutalized to exhibit.

After Ceausescu's successor lifted a decades-old ban on entry visas and the legal prohibition on speaking to foreigners, aid agencies from the

United States and Europe poured money and resources into the country. Within a short time, in response to news accounts about the plight of institutionalized children, individual Americans and other Westerners also traveled to Romania, where they picked children to adopt. The fees involved, most of which went to orphanage executives, totaled about $2,000.

Just two such adoptions by Americans were recorded in 1989; it's a bit surprising there were any, given that the revolution didn't culminate until Christmas. The following year, the number jumped to ninety, after which all hell broke loose. Hordes of facilitators, lawyers, and agencies, seeing the immense demand by white prospective parents, figured they'd discovered a human gold mine. Rather than finding homes for the kids from institutions—who were generally older and in need of help—the entrepreneurs, along with some ordinary Americans making their own arrangements, turned to local "baby brokers" for higher-priced but relatively healthy babies and toddlers.

In 1991, Americans adopted 2,594 children from Romania. A black market in babies, often bought or coerced from vulnerable families, boomed. For one year, for the first time in more than three decades, Korea was supplanted as the primary source for U.S. adoptions abroad.[7] But the illicit enterprise in Romania was too flagrant to remain secret, and it quickly ignited an international furor.

By the middle of the year, the new leaders in Bucharest felt compelled to shut down all adoptions. They rewrote their laws to improve protections for birth parents and to give only licensed agencies in the United States and elsewhere the authority to deal directly with Romania's government on adoptions. The outflow of children from that nation's institutions into American adoptive homes fell to a few hundred annually until in June 2000, the government said corruption had again infiltrated the system—and imposed a three-month moratorium to clean it up.

Romania's experience warrants special attention not only because it represents a particularly wrenching chapter in adoption history, but also because it teaches such an explicit, unambiguous lesson about the venomous effect of money in transactions that involve human beings. The lure of big bucks draws in people who have no credentials or understanding of the sensitive issues at stake, and absent tight regulations or monitoring, it can insidiously poison the judgment of even well-meaning professionals. In Romania's case, some agencies clearly believed they were rescuing children from miserable lives and early deaths, regardless of how or from where they were obtained. But the participation by "serious" organizations fueled an inexcusable operation, provided cover for the worst offenders, and contributed to its lasting longer than it otherwise might have.

When money spawns such high-profile scandals, it damages adoption itself in a comprehensive way: by undermining many Americans' confidence in a process they tend to hear about only through horror stories. Such episodes mislead some people into believing that adoption is an intrinsically dubious way to have children. And, along with sporadic, gut-wrenching tugs-of-war like the one over Baby Richard in Illinois, the specter of baby-selling contributes to a nebulous sense that something's somehow "wrong" with adoption—and, by subconscious implication, with its participants.

Fortunately, in practice, the positive aspects soar above the negative. Tens of thousands of Americans, the great preponderance of those who adopt from overseas each year, do so with barely a hitch. And the vast majority of their children were unambiguously homeless, genuinely needy, and truly lucky to be adopted. Most of them, as a sort of cosmic payback, become unwitting revolutionaries simply by growing up proud of their origins and comfortable with their place in the world, as adoptees.

PART TWO

Sensitive Issues,
Lifelong Process

4

Adoptees:
The Quest
for Identity

G. William Troxler wants to assure everyone that there's nothing to worry about. He is not interested in humiliating the woman who gave him life. Nor does he want her to become his mother; he's already got one he loves and doesn't need another at his age. But Dr. Troxler, who is the president of Capitol College in Laurel, Maryland, would like to meet Marianne at least once, if she's still alive, if for no other reason than to understand the circumstances that led to his adoption fifty-three years ago.

"I want to tell Marianne, first, that whatever trauma she suffered in giving me up, it turned out okay. I want her to know I've had a great life, I have a great family, and I'm okay about the decision she made, whatever her reasons. To whatever extent she has been tormented because she didn't know what had come of her child . . . or has suffered from wondering what I think of her, I want to alleviate that pain, at least," says Dr. Troxler.

"Then, if she were willing, I'd ask her what she could fill in about my biological family information—her own and my father's. Is he around? Do I have any siblings? Is there anything I should know, historically or medically, that I could share with my son? Basically, I want to deliver any information about myself that she thinks is important, and then we'll figure out where to go from there. I'm not looking to terrorize anyone or invade her privacy. I'm not even looking for a relationship. . . . I just want information about myself that most people take for granted. That's all."

The search for identity is an essential, inescapable part of life. As children, we ask our parents questions about where we came from, who we look like, why we're short or blond or freckled. Our teenage years are typically characterized by angst, anger, and a panoply of other inflamed emotions because our insides are burning impatiently with the need to discover who we are. Then, as the embers cool, some of us travel to our ancestral homelands, many of us sort through photos of deceased relatives whom we resemble more by the day, and a steadily growing number of us while away the hours scouring the Internet in search of grandfathers or great-aunts to add to our family trees.

For generations, most adoptees were told—or assumed, if they were told nothing at all—that they should view their adoptive parents' backgrounds as their own. They did that, and for the most part they still do; it feels good and right to embrace every aspect of the family in which we grow up. But the adoptees always knew that they had a second background, too, the one that explained their appearance, that accounted for some of their talents and traits. They knew there were people out there from whom they'd inherited their strong chins or weak hearts, with whom they had shared at least nine months of early life and hundreds of years of history. Some adoptees cared deeply about all this, while others seldom gave it a second thought. But they all knew.

Today, the most overt and passionate adoption revolutionaries are the triad members who believe they have the right to obtain all the pieces of their personal puzzles. These people come in all ages, colors, and religions. They are conservatives, moderates, and liberals who disagree on just about everything else, including many other issues relating to adoption. On this one subject, though, their feelings converge along a high-voltage pathway. They bristle at the well-intentioned explanations and hushed excuses of the past; they're livid that America's laws still single them out for treatment they consider demeaning; and they're determined to overthrow the status quo.

On its face, the change these tens of thousands of adoptee-activists have chosen to focus most sharply upon—gaining access to their original birth certificates and other documents that could contain the names of their biological parents—may seem more self-centered and less socially consequential than the reforms being pursued elsewhere. It's certainly true that other facets of adoption are mutating more quickly: The movement of foster children to permanent homes is advancing so rapidly that even its promoters can't predict the long-term impact. And some facets appear more revolutionary: The shift toward greater openness is altering the way millions of people think and live every day.

Yet obtaining identifying information is the issue that is radicalizing and galvanizing more of the adoption community than any single concern ever has. It is provoking activism of a type and at a level unprecedented in the history of the institution. As these efforts succeed and escalate, they are ensuring that adoption not only grows more honest from within, but also that it attains an increasingly high-profile presence in the media of our country and in the consciousness of its citizens.

In Oregon, for instance, adoption became front-page news throughout the late 1990s and into 2000 because an adoptee named Helen Hill decided she'd heard enough excuses from politicians about why triad members needed to be protected from each other. She thought that, if all her state's residents learned about the issues involved, they'd agree it was time to scrap antiquated laws and make sweeping reforms.

A revolution succeeds only when its leaders can persuade the masses of the rightness (and righteousness) of their cause. Helen and her comrades did just that. They collected signatures, fought off legal challenges, produced commercials. When voters got the chance to participate in the first referendum in history on an adoption question, a solid majority said "yes." Opponents blocked the measure's implementation with appeals and legal ploys, but they lost every time. On May 30, 2000, a U.S. Supreme Court justice denied a final appeal from opponents, effectively upholding a state Supreme Court decision of two weeks earlier. Today, thousands of adult adoptees in Oregon have already received their birth certificates—and activists have vowed to fight again and again until they win from coast to coast.

The most vocal promoters of this unorthodox approach, circumventing a state legislature and going right to the voters, are members of Bastard Nation, a radical adoptee-rights movement. Its name is deliberately provocative, designed to shock people to attention and mock the derogatory term applied for generations to all children born outside of marriage. Helen Hill belongs to the group, which was essentially created through e-mails on the Internet in 1996.

Bastard Nation's tone is reminiscent of ACT-Up, the gay-rights organization of the 1980s that used harsh language and confrontational tactics to raise awareness of AIDS at a time when neither government nor private researchers were devoting much attention to combating the disease. The bastards, as they call themselves, are already making their mark with successes like the one in Oregon and, perhaps more important in the long run, by burning up the Web with information promoting their legislative objectives and providing resources that anyone can use to search for birth relatives.

The Internet is a vital player in the adoption revolution. It is the place where some changes are launched, others are accelerated, and all are discussed by anyone who wants to join in a chat room or send an e-mail. Nearly every adoption agency, lawyer, and facilitator has at least one cyberspace address; prospective parents establish sites to seek out pregnant women considering whether they want to parent their babies; public-welfare groups post photos of children in need of homes; researchers collect data and report their findings. Type the word "adoption" into a search engine, and thousands of sites appear, containing poignant experiences, registries for triad members who want to reunite, and a wealth of wisdom about every conceivable topic related to adoption.

Specifically, the activists are focusing on obtaining two things: their original birth certificates and the right to find blood relatives with no ifs, ands, or buts attached. Most states offer reunion mechanisms, but with conditions. They generally require either "mutual consent," meaning both parties must register before either can contact the other; or "search and consent," in which the sought-after party may tell an intermediary that she wants to be left alone.[1] Those sorts of caveats are opposed by serious reform organizations like the Adoptees Liberty Movement Association, which was formed almost forty years ago by a pioneer of the adoptee-rights crusade, Florence Fisher; the twenty-two-year-old American Adoption Congress; and the upstart Bastard Nation.

While it may sound reasonable to prevent communication unless both sides agree to it first, enshrining the prohibition in law is ludicrous. No other adults in America are treated in this way, and singling out adoptees marks them as lesser citizens entitled to fewer rights. There are other problems with state-run registries, too. A glaring one to make the point: Requiring mutual consent means that once a birth mother dies, even if she wanted a relationship with the child she relinquished, no legal mechanism remains by which the adoptee can learn about his past or trace other biological family members.

Moreover, the registries are so poorly publicized that they have become a ruse by which opponents of openness can say they are willing to offer contact, while providing a means they know will minimize the possibility of success. To be fair, some proponents of search-and-consent procedures and mutual-consent registries really believe birth mothers were guaranteed confidentiality. But it's a factual myth, a false impression that might occasionally have been reassuringly conveyed by adoption professionals or desired by some distraught pregnant women, but never put in legal form. Good intentions notwithstanding, it's also selective logic to assert that a birth mother's "right" to anonymity has to be upheld, even though it's not specified anywhere that such a right exists, but that adoptees have no "right" to see their birth certificates or to contact their relatives, even though everyone else in America can freely do so.

Whatever their motivations, the purveyors of this reasoning have used it to win battles in state after state, usually to prevent access to birth certificates and sometimes to impose strict rules making searches more difficult. But now they're losing the war. The appeals court in Oregon, whose judgment was affirmed by the state's Supreme Court, explicitly rejected the constitutionality of their arguments.[2] Moreover, there are no caveats, no strings attached in cyberspace. On-line reunion registries, volunteer searchers, professional detectives, and entrepreneurs promising that "we can find anyone" are proliferating, even as adoptees, birth parents, and biological siblings use the extraordinary resources of the Web to conduct their own searches and arrange their own reunions.

The growing ease of computerized searches, combined with burgeoning voluntary contacts between adoptive and birth parents, ensures a future in which it will be hard to keep almost any unclassified data from anyone who wants it. So what's the rationale for withholding adoptees' documents anymore? There appears to be none. Not to maintain people's anonymity, because they'll usually be found if someone wants to find them—with or without the help of birth certificates. And certainly not to fool children into thinking they weren't adopted, because almost no one believes that's a sane thing to do.

Sealed birth certificates and adoption records are a destructive anachronism. They didn't exist before the middle of the last century (Pennsylvania didn't join the closure trend until 1984) and one day they'll be viewed as a misguided historical aberration. But they still prevent some people from searching, particularly older Americans who entered their families during the period when secrecy and deception were defining characteristics of adoption. Like many of the children who are abandoned or who spend their early lives in orphanages abroad today, the adoptees born in America in the past still need all the help they can get if they want to find out about their backgrounds, because their personal information was usually poorly maintained, frequently falsified, and sometimes destroyed.

Bill Troxler has not been stymied in his search for Marianne only because he couldn't get his birth certificate. Even without it, he learned his birth mother's first name by shining a light through the ink blotting it out on the court order finalizing his adoption. He even located the doctor who arranged his adoption, but too late. The man had died, and his widow had discarded his files. Troxler has since hired a searcher, pored through the records of every courthouse in several counties in North Carolina (which his adoptive mother recalls as Marianne's home state), and become a political activist.

Several years ago, he helped to organize a campaign that ended with all but one member of Maryland's House of Representatives voting to give the state's adult adoptees access to their original birth certificates. The measure didn't become law because a couple of politicians bottled it up in a state Senate committee, but they only achieved a temporary and partial victory since a weaker version of the legislation was enacted last year.[3] Even without a complete success, the initial House action and the recent statutory change proved a central point in this seemingly obscure debate: The more people learn about the issues, the surer they are to come down on the side of openness.

That proved true in Tennessee, where politicians were extremely skeptical when an adoptee named Caprice East began lobbying them to unseal records. But on March 18, 1995, the state Senate approved the legislation, thirty to two. The House followed suit, ninety-nine to zero, after which the lawmakers gave Caprice a standing ovation. Oregon's referendum in 1998 sent an equally unambiguous message. After a public campaign in which the pros and cons were extensively aired, nearly sixty percent of the voters said all adult adoptees should be allowed to get their files. A handful of other states—Alabama, Delaware, Montana, Ohio, Colorado, and Vermont—also amended their laws in the 1990s to make it easier for most adoptees to do likewise.[4]

The Truth Can Hurt

The key to understanding the adoptee-rights movement is knowing that the people driving it believe so deeply in their cause, much in the way that anti-abortion activists and gun-control advocates do in theirs, that there's little anyone can do to diminish their determination. They are characters in a riveting, ready-for-prime-time melodrama whose characters include not only zealous adoptees, but also distressed birth mothers who insist their lives will be ruined if the children they relinquished decide to find them, and elated birth mothers who insist their anguish has been soothed by the children who found them.

The unapologetic idea behind sealed records was to keep secrets. Now they are relics that have somehow managed to survive the bad old days of deceit and denial; whatever they might or might not accomplish, they serve as an icon of discredited practices that most adoption professionals and triad members are trying mightily to overhaul. Still, the fight over their continuation offers a prism through which we can gain valuable insights about our nation's judges and lawmakers. And about ourselves.

Dr. Troxler is among many adoptees of his generation who grew up believing he was the genetic creation of the only mother and father he ever knew. He always sensed something was amiss, though, because visiting relatives would whisper to his parents while glancing over at him, and because he never saw one person in his extended family who looked anything like him. Once, when he was nine, he asked if he was adopted. His mother scolded him for even suggesting such a thing and sent him to his room as punishment. He wasn't suspicious by nature so he carried on, making friends, heading off to college, getting married, accumulating several graduate degrees, raising his son.

The paranoia didn't kick in until he was forty-six. In July 1993, while he was teaching at a small college in North Carolina, a student asked what relationship Dr. Troxler's father had with the institution. "None, I'm sure, since I'm the first person in my family to get past high school," he replied. "That's strange," said the young man, "because a portrait that looks just like you is hanging in our classroom." Dr. Troxler finished his lunch and walked over to the building the student had mentioned. "I'd never seen anyone who looked like me, so I was curious," he recalls. As he stared at the painting of a former president of the college, Alfred O. Cannon, his knees grew weak. He shivered. "It sounds crazy now, but it scared the hell out of me. There was this guy staring at me from out of this gilded frame and he looked exactly like me. . . . It was a very strange experience."

On the way back to Maryland a few days later, Dr. Troxler decided to visit an elderly aunt, uncle, and their children in his father's hometown of Gibsonville, North Carolina. The portrait fueled his desire to see his relatives, but he didn't intend to ask them anything about it; he figured the resemblance was "just an eerie coincidence." Still, it weighed on his mind, especially after his Uncle Walt—whom he hadn't seen in twenty years—inexplicably launched into a monologue about how Bill didn't look like any Troxler he'd ever seen. He went on and on, as though he was trying to tell his nephew something.

When he got home, Dr. Troxler dug out an album of his childhood photos, at the front of which was a copy of his birth certificate. It was much shorter and contained far fewer details than he'd expected, so he decided to get a look at the original. "I wasn't searching for anything," he says. "It really was just curiosity at that point." So, a few weeks later, he went to the Office of Vital Records in Washington, D.C., paid a few dollars and asked to see his file. He immediately knew something was wrong. The "original" birth certificate contained no doctors' signatures, no scribbled notes. All the information on it was perfectly typed, clearly at the same time. It didn't look like his son's birth certificate, or his wife's, or any other he'd ever happened to see.

"Don't worry about it," the clerk told him when he said something seemed odd. "It's valid, it's just not true." The words were in English, but Dr. Troxler had no idea what she was talking about. He asked for a translation. "It means you're either part of the federal witness protection program or you were adopted," she answered, smiling. "Which would you rather be?" Dr. Troxler discovered the document he was holding was a legal fiction, one of millions routinely created to reflect that adoptive parents had given birth to their adopted children. He reflexively asked for the original. The clerk said she was sorry, but she couldn't comply. "That would be illegal," she said. "It's under seal of the court."

Dr. Troxler left the office addled and angry. He didn't know what to think or do. He'd never given adoption a second thought, and now, suddenly, it felt like the epicenter of his existence. One effect took hold immediately: His father had died years earlier, but this newfound knowledge crumbled his image of his frail, elderly mother. She had lied to him all his life, deprived him of the ability to learn basic facts about himself. Now, as he was entering what should be the fulfilling years of his middle age, he felt empty.

The gravity and intensity of such sentiments can be very hard for most people to understand. The adoptee has had a good life and a successful career, so what's the big deal if his well-meaning parents omitted a little information? The people who ask the question, of course, have never had the most rudimentary facts about them hidden away by their mothers or fathers and locked up by the government.

Most adoptees start coping with identity issues by the time they're seven or eight. Developmentally, that's when children begin the transition from concrete to abstract thinking; for adoptees, it's the time when the word "adoption" becomes a multifaceted concept rather than just a description of a procedure. Most pointedly, they start to internalize a fact they might have known but never really understood: that, in order for their parents to have gotten them, someone had to give them up. And, as these children acquire a rudimentary grasp of reproduction, they add another volatile variable to their emotional mix: that the someones who gave them up were their mothers and fathers, too.

It can be a confusing, painful revelation. It causes some children to begin grieving, others to become angry or feel guilty, yet others to withdraw. Whatever its effects, it's one of a series of distinct stages in most adoptees' lives that can powerfully influence their maturation—perhaps making it difficult for a child to make attachments or, alternately, to become clingy—and presenting particular challenges for their parents.

The ensuing stages, typically during the teen years, are marked by progressively greater ranges of emotion, desires to assert independence or control, and, sometimes, resentment and depression.[5] Adoptees aren't necessarily tougher to raise because of their own concerns—certainly no more so than, say, the children of divorce or those with other familial issues—but it is important that adults, whether they're parents or teachers or psychiatrists, understand these phases so they can anticipate and respond to them.

How they do so obviously depends on the particular individuals and circumstances. An insecure ten-year-old boy who seems reluctant to ask questions of any kind, for instance, might need gentle reminders that he didn't cause his birth parents to relinquish him, while an assertive fifteen-year-old girl might need support for her genealogical research. At any age, adoptees benefit from reassurances that their anger, guilt, and grief are normal, that they are unconditionally loved, and that their current families are theirs forever, whatever they may do in their lives or whatever other relationships they choose to establish.

The more information adoptive parents have during these critical junctures, the better they can explain and demonstrate their points. Relationships with birth parents can also play an important role, when they're possible, because they allow children to obtain a firsthand grasp of the complex reasons someone might have had for relinquishing them. It can take years for adoptees to internalize the notion that an adoption placement itself is an act of love, a selfless decision intended to do what's best for the child.

The research on adoptees shows they generally grow up to be pretty much like everybody else, but some studies seem to conflict with others. Now that adoption is coming out of the closet, better and broader work is being done, but some points of consensus already have emerged from the clinical investigations, surveys, and personal experiences that adoption professionals have examined. Among them:

- Adoptees receive psychological treatment at higher rates than the population at large, particularly during adolescence. This disparity presumably stems largely from the tumult of having to deal with complex emotions and tough identity questions. Sensitivity to loss and fear of rejection, in particular, appear to become pronounced issues in a disproportionate percentage of adoptees as they get older.[6]

But the increased incidence of counseling is also attributable to the heightened consciousness of triad members to developmental and behavioral issues, as well as to the fact that most Americans who adopt privately are affluent enough to afford professional help. As a result, adoptive parents often seek assistance for their children more readily, and adoptees themselves request it more frequently than do other people who may assume (rightly or wrongly) that a specific problem occurs naturally in anyone's life.

- Adoptees, particularly those who get new families as infants, have comparable grades and self-esteem as their nonadopted friends by the time they are teenagers. Those conclusions are drawn from several studies, including the largest ever conducted of U.S. families with adolescent adoptees—a four-year survey of two thousand people released by the Minnesota-based Search Institute in 1994. It found no difference in outcomes between same-race and transracial adoptions, including on the question of whether adoptees wanted to meet their birth parents. Sixty-five percent said "yes."

  While heartening for adoptive families, these findings weren't one-sided and have to be viewed with a huge grain of salt. The adoptions in this study were arranged by agencies that carefully screened prospective parents; consequently, as a group, they were better educated, more affluent, more demonstrative with affection, and typically faced fewer complications like divorce. The children, meanwhile, were generally adopted in good health and at young ages—and, since they filled out their questionnaires while in their parents' homes, they could have felt pressure to give positive answers.

- Even children from institutionalized settings, in which they were deprived or abused, make sustained progress once they're adopted. Studies indicate about 20 percent initially have severe adjustment difficulties, but the number drops by half after five years. Children from well-run, well-established orphanages in countries like China and Korea (the overwhelming majority of whom are adopted by white parents) show no discernible behavioral or developmental differences from their nonadopted peers.[7]

  Most parents of internationally adopted children, wherever they were born and whatever their backgrounds, say that all but the most severe problems eventually become manageable or are overcome with the help of counseling, medical intervention, and persistent attention. And more than 90 percent of all these parents report that they are happy with their adoptions; one out of ten dissatisfied parents is far too many, but the numbers can't be much different among people who are raising their biological children.

Eliminating the Ignorance Excuse

Some indeterminable minority of adoptees say they're impervious to identity issues. Maybe it's the way their parents raise them, or maybe it's something ingrained in their personalities, but they insist they have no desire to learn about their genetic backgrounds. Most people who fit into this category are male, so the explanation seemingly has to do with chromosomes and/or culture. Those factors clearly play some role, since female adoptees frequently tend to express interest in learning about their ancestries while starting their own families. Whatever the reasons, adoption professionals agree one unmistakable indication of this gender difference is that at least 80 percent of the hundreds of thousands of adoptees searching for their birth mothers (and, less frequently, their birth fathers) are women.

Whether or not they're curious about their pasts, or want their birth certificates or try to find their birth relatives, all adoptees at various times have to deal with the consequences of being adopted. The worst-case scenario, for those who don't know they're adopted or who have no genealogical information, is that they can't take precautions to avert predictable health problems. Or can't get organs for life-saving transplants because they don't know who or where their biological matches may be.

An almost-laughable, corollary phenomenon has been taking place routinely for generations, and still does: People of all ages unwittingly use data derived from their adoptive parents' medical histories to fill out their own medical forms, to assess their own drug allergies, to decide which medications or preventative procedures they might need, and even as the basis for serving as subjects in medical research.

Mary Insulman, the Oregon woman who became a political activist as a septuagenarian after being denied her birth certificate, spent her life being tested for diabetes and limiting her diet to prevent its onset. It seemed the only reasonable thing to do, since her mother suffered and died from the disease. Mary's three children, and their children, took the same precautions. That is until Mary, in 1992, discovered she was adopted. "Can you believe that?" she asks. "It's just plain silly, isn't it?"

Other examples of the impact of everyday life on adoptees are equally subtle and may seem just as innocuous, if changing what you eat and spending your insurance company's money on unnecessary tests can be called innocuous. The most constant factor, yet the hardest for which to gauge the repercussions, is language. Nearly everyone at times has discussed adoption in ways that make adoptees cringe, that chip away at their self-esteem, that nurture the notion that "different" translates into "inferior."

Well-intentioned people casually ask, in front of an eight-year-old who is trying to figure out what adoption means, "Why did her real mother give her away?" The child might pretend she didn't hear, or she might ask that night why her parents aren't "real" or what she did that was so horrible that someone wanted to give her away. However she reacts or doesn't, whatever her real adoptive parents tell her, some damage has been done—or, at the least, another jagged piece has been added to her personal developmental puzzle.

Friends, coworkers, and complete strangers—people who wouldn't dream of asking, "Hey, did you have any miscarriages before you gave birth?"—think nothing of probing for the details of a child's adoption. They're only curious, but their ill-informed prejudices and preconceptions are always apparent.

"Did his mother drop out of high school?" "Was his father one of those guys who just disappear?" An acquaintance asked me those kinds of questions one day as Zack pulled at my shirt in a grocery store, trying to get my attention. He was five. Later, when I asked if he knew what the woman had meant, he said he wasn't sure. I haven't a clue whether the tone or content of her questions resides somewhere in my son's brain, waiting to click in. Maybe it never will. Or maybe one day, when I tell him what kind and smart people his birth parents are—because it's true and because he will always partly judge himself by how he perceives them— maybe then he'll remember that other grownups implied demeaning things about them. It can't ever do him any good.

Ironically, adoptees face the greatest risk from verbal ignorance in an institution designed for enlightenment: school. They're particularly vulnerable at the elementary level, when all children are molding their self-perceptions and typically want nothing more fiercely than to fit in. That's why some parents choose to keep their children's adoptions private (though not necessarily secret with family and friends) during this period, and why a growing number of others advocate educating teachers and administrators about positive language use and general sensitivity about adoption.

Teachers who deal forthrightly with the topic of adoption and with the adopted students in their classrooms will surely make mistakes, but no more than they already do by keeping secrets and operating with potentially detrimental misconceptions. Besides, dealing openly with adoption helps to cast it as a normal occurrence, as opposed to one that must be whispered about or avoided for some mysterious reason. As Joyce Maguire Pavao, a longtime therapist and adoption expert in Massachusetts, wisely observes: "People who have secrets about them think there's something wrong with them."

Our collective definition of "normal" is evolving every day and yet, in many ways, we cling to the concept of the biologically formed nuclear family. Our perceptions will catch up to reality only when everyone faces up to the fact that a huge percentage of our children are adopted and/or have divorced or single or gay or foster parents, or are a different color than other members of their families.

Regardless of what we think of all these arrangements, we have to remember that they were created by adults. Children all deserve to be treated with respect, and they all are "normal." So they need to draw family orchards instead of family trees. Otherwise, children embarrassed about not knowing the identities of their fathers will sometimes make them up, and adoptees striving to be just like their friends may lie about having been abandoned in China or Romania—even as the assignment itself triggers painful memories or associations. Or they may just learn to lie, denying that they're adopted altogether.

The lesson plan has to evolve to reflect real life, and to benefit the children. A teacher who kindly suggests that a nine-year-old adoptee should "choose" one of his families to use in a traditional tree, just to show how the process works, hasn't a clue about how much damage she has just inflicted. Likewise for the proponent of an environmentally marvelous, semester-long "adopt a tree" program in a middle school, who hasn't a glimmer of understanding that he's stirring an emotional cauldron within some teenagers struggling with separation anxiety; they need reassurance and stability, not induced doubts about whether adoption is really a form of marketing that can apply to trees or highways or children, and can be started and stopped at will.

Language will always be as imperfect as the people who use it, and we all learn to live with inadvertent slights and willful insults. But no society should tolerate systemic, identifiable practices that harm large segments of its population. When adoption was a secret, no one would tell friends or strangers that a question they asked, or a comment they made, was out of line. No one would tell teachers that they were unintentionally injuring our children. Well, it's not a secret anymore, and we're telling you to stop.

Success Comes in All Colors

The children who look nothing like their parents are most deeply steeped in reminders that they are adopted. That's true even in cases like mine, where a fair-skinned boy and a blond-haired girl are being raised by two olive-toned, Jewish-looking parents. But it's most stark, and the ramifications are most profound, when the participants are clearly of different races. Adoption has contributed hundreds of thousands of American families that fit this description, and it is adding tens of thousands more every year.

Mainly, they're white couples and white single women with black, Hispanic, or mixed-race children who were born domestically, or with Asian and Latin children from abroad. These most conspicuous of adoptees don't all react in the same way, of course. Some stare back with defiance or pride, others grow angry or embarrassed, and yet others—because they're either so self-confident or so indifferent—just shrug and move on.

Adoptees, like any other group of people, occupy the full spectrum of personality types and individual circumstances. Few transracial and transcultural adoptees are unaffected by their distinctions, however, because self-exploration is an integral part of human nature and because it's tough for anyone (adopted or not) to achieve color-blindness in a society that's both infused with bigotry and fixated on race.

Those are basic facts of life even for mixed-race adoptees like Mesha Goldberg, who are members of secure families and say they encounter little overt prejudice. Mesha, like many children who lived in foster care, has little incentive to examine or connect to her roots. "There's nothing I really want to remember or hold on to because it wasn't anything good. I kind of try to fix my eyes on the future," says Mesha, who changed her name from Tina Louise when she was adopted, to symbolize her new beginning.

Until she was five, Mesha and her brother, who is two years older, lived in Ohio with their biological mother, a prostitute. Authorities believe her father was a client, one of many men who physically and sexually abused Mesha, apparently with her mother's knowledge. While mom was conducting business, she locked her son and daughter in the basement, where they sometimes stayed for days on end. Their nourishment consisted of one meal a day, usually macaroni and cheese, plus water. Their ordeal ended one day when a man enraged Mesha's brother by holding her down to do something she doesn't want to think about anymore. Jimmy bit his sister's attacker on the thumb and ran to the telephone. The police rescued the two children a short while later.

Mesha, whose mother is white and whose father is black, moved into and out of a half dozen foster homes during the next seven years. Foster parents are paid a monthly stipend to cover the expenses of each child they take in, but few do it for the money. They are generally unselfish people trying to help children. Their biggest challenges are boys and girls who come from abusive circumstances like Mesha's. These children, like their counterparts from the worst institutions abroad, often deeply distrust adults, aren't equipped to bond emotionally with anyone, suffer from abysmal self-esteem, and can act out their anger and inner turmoil with self-destructive or persistently belligerent behavior.

Mesha could check off every symptom on that list. She struck her foster parents, screamed curses at them, broke things in their homes, ran away, and tried to kill herself a few times. She was too much for most people to handle, so she didn't stay anywhere for long. "I was like a terror," she says. "I treated everybody the way I was treated before, and I was real angry. I guess I still am some of the time. I don't know if you can ever completely get over what I went through. I sure hope so."

In 1993, a white psychotherapist and former nurse named Carol Goldsmith went to Adopt America, one of many fine organizations that help boys and girls with special needs, to look at pictures of children under state supervision in Ohio. Carol had always wanted to be a mother and, as she approached forty, she decided she'd better do something soon. She didn't want to raise a toddler and didn't have the money to consider adopting from another country, so she turned to the public system.

When Carol looked at Mesha's photo, the eleven-year-old girl stared back. There was no decision left to make. Within a year, the adoption was complete. The girl no one had wanted to keep suddenly found herself in a loving, permanent home; she still has problems, but she also has matured and thrived, one of tens of thousands of children whose special needs have been met—and exceeded—by determined adoptive parents.

Today, completing high school in a town called Delta, part of an extended family with adoring grandparents, uncles, aunts, cousins, and an adopted younger sister, Mesha says she never wants to look back because she now has everything. For certain, she wants nothing to do with her birth mother again. Or with her father, except she wouldn't mind at least knowing who he is or getting his picture. And she'd sure like to see more of her brother, who is in a group-care facility. And if she can, she'd love to find her maternal grandmother, who was wonderful to her whenever they met in a previous life.

Similarly, Mesha says race and identity questions rarely even occur to her. Unless you want to count the time, a few Sundays earlier, that the teenagers at church stayed away from her like she was a leper. Oh, and it would be cool if her mom would find a black guy to marry. And it's really great that Carol has friends with other adopted kids, especially the couple who has two black daughters. And Mesha does try to listen to black singers to "get in touch" with parts of herself that her white mom doesn't quite get. . . .

Color, ethnicity, and advanced age, meaning past perhaps five in the adoption world, add layers of complexity to a process that's complicated to begin with. One reason so many Americans turn to the orphanages of the former Soviet bloc, in addition to wanting children who share some of their characteristics, is that they believe they'll be able to avoid the frustrations of raising children with "special needs." That's the euphemism applied to a range of concerns—most notably race, age, behavioral problems, and physical disabilities—that can diminish children's prospects for adoption.

A significant minority of people who adopt from Eastern Europe for this reason, particularly those who bring home older boys and girls, discover that many of these children were abused by their birth parents and/or their institutional caretakers, suffer from the effects of fetal-alcohol syndrome, have problems caused by severe pollution or other environmental factors, and display an array of developmental difficulties. In other words, they often are in no better shape than their counterparts living in foster care.

This isn't meant as an argument against adopting from abroad. Those children need homes, too, many of them desperately. But it is to say that more prospective parents could look to America's foster-care system, and then use the tens of thousands of dollars they would have spent on an intercountry adoption for any necessary therapy, counseling, or maybe even a college fund. It is also to suggest that people should press for as much information as possible, whatever avenue they choose, and not allow their craving to become parents to blind them to potential problems or to lead them in directions they'd find morally or ethically offensive if they heard about them on the evening news.

Even if it lengthens or complicates the adoption process, there's an even better reason for insisting on accurate medical records, getting whatever data can be obtained about birth families, and participating in procedures that don't exploit biological parents or promote baby-selling. As ever, it's for the long-term benefit of the children. While love plays a glorious role in furthering any relationship, we all know it can't really conquer everything in its path. One way or the other, most adoptees today will eventually learn the circumstances that led them into new homes. And when they do, even decades later, what they discover can have a major effect (positive and negative) on their feelings about the people who created them, about the people who raised them, and about themselves.

The overwhelming majority of adoptive parents today wouldn't think of hiding their children's origins from them. They understand the need for information, even if they are intimidated by the idea of contact with birth families. Many, especially after a few years of bonding and building self-confidence, surprise themselves by becoming the most gung-ho members of their triads about opening up their adoptions.

That's today, in revolutionary times. It wasn't the norm during previous decades, however, so there are millions of birth parents—some who have decided to search and others who feel too embarrassed, afraid, or powerless to do so—living with guilt, pain, and a festering desire to know what became of their babies. And there are hundreds of thousands of adoptees, at least, who feel like they're living without a vital internal organ.

Yet nearly every state erects legal skyscrapers between blood relatives separated by adoption. There is no proof, much less any evidence, that the people involved want to harm anyone or don't want to be found. In fact, the vast majority of adoptee–birth parent contacts are made cautiously, discreetly, and without a hint of desire to jeopardize anyone or to pursue a relationship if one party isn't interested. The data show that overwhelming majorities on both sides want to at least meet.[8] But just in case, for the sake of the small minority who might not want communication, for the good of the minority within that minority who might not even want to be offered a choice, nearly every state just says no to all birth parents, all adoptees, and all adoptive parents acting on their children's behalf.

"I didn't sign any papers promising anything. I'm alive, I'm here and I have a right to know about myself. That's all there is to it," says Robert, a thirty-eight-year-old Louisiana businessman who asked that his last name not be used because he was unsure how his parents would feel about his publicly discussing his adoption. "What I think is that I, and any adoptees, should have the right to a first phone call. If the person at the other end isn't interested, I should hang up and that should be it. . . . If I push harder than the other person wants, there are laws against harassment or she can sue me or whatever. But the government can't tell me I can't pick up my own phone to call another person."

The woman Robert called in 1995 didn't ask him to hang up. He is the biological son of Sheila Hansen, the woman whose story I recounted at the beginning of this book. He is not a radical by any definition of the word and, in most respects, is no fan of the brave new world of adoption. "How can your parents feel like your parents if your biological mother or father is around?" he asks. And, even though he says he had a good up-bringing "just like any kid who wasn't adopted," he admits to having harbored some damning stereotypes: "Until I met Sheila, I had no respect at all for birth mothers."

Despite holding such views, Robert decided in 1993 that he wanted to find his first parents. "I got married, I had kids. I wanted to know if there was anything medical I should know and I wanted to be able to tell them something about themselves," he says. "I guess I wanted to know, too." So Robert asked his adoptive parents for whatever documents they had, which included adoption papers that contained clues but no names for his birth mother or father. Next he turned to an adoptee support group, "true believers," as he calls them, who told him how to dig more details out of state records.

After more than a year of searching, Robert found out that his biological father had died of a brain tumor years earlier. He talked to the man's widow and son, who willingly answered his questions. Then, in 1995, Robert made contact with Sheila, who quickly altered his image of birth mothers. They now enjoy each other's company, chat on the phone occasionally, and see each other a few times a year. "She's a great person and I'm glad she's around," he says, "but I wasn't looking for new parents."

The bias against adoptees is instituted immediately after they begin their new lives. Wherever they are born and whatever their ages when their adoptions are finalized, they become the only Americans to have their birth certificates sealed and replaced with official substitutes containing intentionally false information. All but a few states then forbid the adoptees from obtaining their original documents, except in exceptional circumstances.[9] That's because they might reveal the birth parents' identities (though many older records contain aliases and/or list no fathers at all), which could be used to locate them.

The states say that can't be allowed to happen because women were promised confidentiality. Violating that vow would be wrong and maybe illegal as a matter of principle, the argument goes, while in practice it could lead to distress for birth mothers who just want to forget, and humiliation or worse for those who haven't told their husbands and children about what they went through so many years earlier.

That's not all. Some critics of giving adoptees access to their records also caution that, if women don't believe they will remain anonymous, many will terminate their pregnancies rather than carry their babies to term and then give them new homes. "The whole point is, if you want anyone to choose adoption, it has to be as confidential as abortion," says William Pierce, who recently retired as president of the Washington-based National Council for Adoption, a large lobbying and trade association for mainly religious private agencies. "How many women do you know who want to wear an 'A for adoption' across their chests for the rest of their lives?"

For two decades, Dr. Pierce was arguably the most powerful force in shaping U.S. adoption laws in Congress, state legislatures, and the courts. His bottom line has always been, and still is, that openness damages adoption, particularly when it applies to obtaining original birth certificates or in any other way that makes it easier for triad members to contact each other. Usually, when an adoption-related measure has come before lawmakers or judges, Dr. Pierce and his supporters have been the best-organized and best-financed players in the game, and they've generally rolled over their opponents.

In most instances, they also have prevailed because their reasoning can sound so right to people who know little about adoption other than what they are being told at the moment. The Council was instrumental in securing court orders blocking implementation of the two highest-profile efforts in history to unseal adoptees' records, resoundingly approved by Tennessee's legislature and Oregon's voters. In both cases, opponents asserted that the new statutes would violate birth mothers' rights to remain anonymous; in Tennessee, a more conservative state, they also argued that the new law would increase the incidence of abortions while cutting the number of adoptions.

These assertions are often offered by the dwindling minority of practitioners who don't want to tamper with the status quo out of fear that their profitable businesses could suffer, and by a small number of religious fundamentalists who apparently believe that women who have children out of wedlock are sinners unworthy of becoming mothers. Some adoptive parents also accept such reasoning for closure because they are intimidated by the possible effects of openness to begin with, so they are susceptible to arguments that admittedly resonate on both an emotional and intellectual level.

Like so much else in adoption, however, the realities are more complex and frequently counterintuitive. The abortion-versus-adoption argument is a stark example. Pregnancy counselors, mental-health specialists, and social workers agree that the circumstances and mindsets of women who undergo abortions typically are very different from those who give birth. So, for instance, a woman whose convictions don't permit her to terminate her pregnancy ultimately has to decide whether to become a parent or place her child for adoption; conversely, a woman who views abortion as a viable option, and doesn't want to become a mother for whatever reason, is unlikely to want to deal with the social, medical, and personal ramifications of carrying a baby to term.

Most people approaching these two paths seriously consider only one or the other. Moreover, counselors at clinics that perform abortions often don't provide much advice about adoption, while lawyers and adoption agencies seldom discuss the possibility of terminating a pregnancy. So women typically head in the direction to which they're predisposed, and their inclinations are reinforced even if more information might have led them elsewhere. At the same time, an unintended consequence of the lingering stigma on birth mothers, as well as on pregnancy outside of marriage, is that some women who might otherwise have chosen adoptions for their children get abortions instead.

Studies, statistics, and real-life experiences support just one side of this debate, and it's not the one offered by the National Council for Adoption. The resident adoption rates in Kansas and Alaska, the only states in which adoptees' documents have always been open, hovered around fifty per thousand births in the 1990s, compared to 31.2 for the United States overall. Their abortion rates, meanwhile, averaged about fifteen per thousand female residents, compared to twenty-five for the entire nation. Most states with closed records report higher abortion rates and lower adoption rates than either Kansas or Alaska; furthermore, historically, the incidence of abortion in a given state has not dropped after it sealed birth certificates and other identifying information.[10]

The answers are equally one-sided to the question of whether adoptees and birth parents want to search or be found. Data from "confidential intermediary" records in eight states indicate at least 90 percent of all biological mothers and fathers desire or are amenable to contact, with 99 percent saying "yes" to date in Tennessee. Comparable studies of adoptees show that 65 to 80 percent want reunions, and experts agree that the ratio rises as they age.

The true numbers are probably even higher. Some birth parents are reluctant to admit even to themselves that they'd like to see their children—

but are pleased once they get the chance. Many adoptees haven't yet seriously considered the question or don't want to answer it honestly because they think it might hurt their adoptive parents. As they become independent adults, a large number of them covertly search for and even establish relationships with their birth parents without telling anyone in their adoptive families. The overriding point is that, wherever the totals stand today, they are sure to rise as everyone in and out of the triad grows accustomed to adoption's new realities.

Search and Obsession

While the media do considerable harm by accentuating adoption horror stories, they also get major credit for promoting progress by paying more and more attention to the positive changes taking place. By devoting additional space to the reforms in foster care, for instance, they are implicitly sending the message that it's okay to adopt from the public system. And by putting more adoptee–birth parent reunions on daytime talk shows (which, unfortunately, exploit the phenomenon), The Learning Channel (which airs a daily program called *Reunion*), television movies, and the nightly news, they demonstrate that search itself isn't strange and that relationships between consenting relatives don't generally pose grave risks to themselves, their respective families, or our society at large.

The very fact that press coverage is soaring contributes to the normalization of adoption within our culture by removing it from the realm of secrecy and making it something that people feel it's all right to discuss, debate, and learn about—even if the stories that provoke the dialogue aren't all comforting or comfortable. Here's an illustration of how a little knowledge can go a long way toward providing crucial context.

"Gail Gilpatrick" is a physician in Pittsburgh, a thoughtful and articulate woman in her late forties who loves her parents and, by her own description, doesn't tend to do "crazy stuff." While she has known since childhood that she was adopted soon after birth, she was well trained not to spend time dwelling on the subject; her mother and father preferred not to discuss it in any detail, and her schoolmates always "made it clear they didn't think it was something for me to be proud of."

Still, she thought about what it meant sometimes and used to daydream about her birth mother. Sometimes she appeared as an ogre who was mean to her daughter and didn't deserve to keep her; that made Gail glad to have been adopted, but afraid she might grow up to be like her mom. Occasionally, the faceless woman seemed to be afraid, as though her little girl had done something terrible to her; then, Gail thought she must have deserved to be given away. Most often, she was a kind, enchanting princess who gave her child toys and understanding; this is the mother who materialized when Gail was angry or upset or felt her parents weren't giving her enough attention.

Most adoptees have similar visions, especially when they're young and trying to figure out what it means to have had other parents—but also during their teenage years, as they rebel against authority figures and wonder what alternatives there might be. That doesn't mean they want their first mothers or fathers back. By this time, they harbor no doubts about who their "real" parents are. Besides, teenagers want to jettison the adults who tell them what to do, not acquire new ones. But the fantasies, which many children never share with anyone, brightly illuminate some of the most critical issues in adoption.

First, they demonstrate yet again the innate nature and strength of adoptees' desire to know about their origins. They also underscore the importance of providing accurate information in a positive manner, so the children don't think they did something wrong. Most dramatically, the daydreams show that birth parents—in some form, real or imagined—invariably appear in adoptees' lives. So adoptive parents have a choice: to acquire information and/or establish relationships that give their kids a true picture of the people who created them, and deal with the consequences; or to allow unpredictable, uncontrollable phantasms to become their partners in child-rearing.

Gail remembers the moment she decided to take matters into her own hands. She was twenty-two, during the year between college and medical school, and she was watching a made-for-TV movie about a woman who reunited with her birth mother. "Suddenly, I just started crying," she says. "All these identity and self-esteem questions I grew up with just surged—not knowing about your heredity when everyone else is talking about theirs; things like not knowing if I can get a relative's kidney if I need a transplant; wondering what you did wrong, even though logically you know you couldn't have done anything. . . . I realized that the only answer is knowledge."

So Gail found the telephone number for Dr. Pavao, whom she had recently seen on a news program. They talked for a while, and the Massachusetts therapist gave Gail the name of a volunteer searcher, one of hundreds of Americans—probably thousands, including detectives and others who charge fees—who help adoptees and birth parents look for each other. Gail didn't want to ask her parents for help because she knew they would feel hurt by her desire to find her birth mother, so she could provide the searcher with only a few sketchy facts her parents had told her over the years: the name of the home for unwed mothers in which the woman had stayed, the approximate dates she'd been there, some physical descriptions, and the hospital where Gail was born.

Nothing happened for years, but Gail continued to gather bits of information and provide them to a series of searchers, some of whom she paid and some who were volunteers. Then, in July 1985, a voice on the telephone told her, "Don't ask me who I am, just take down this number." Gail's hands shook; she still has the scrap of paper on which she scribbled her birth mother's telephone number in Washington State.

Gail stared at the paper for several minutes and then, "excited but scared to death," she dialed. The brief conversation that ensued is a haze in her mind. She recalls only that she gave her name, address, and phone number to Mary, who was attentive and polite as she denied ever having placed a child for adoption.

A few weeks later, Gail received a letter from the woman calling their chat "strange." It continued: "Needless to say, this accusation would threaten me, my husband would be furious, and my children appalled. If you ever call again, I will have to turn this whole business over to my attorney. . . . You sounded disturbed, and I wonder if you could not be satisfied with the gift of life. Someone cared enough to give you that."

Gail was confused. Information she'd received from her searcher left no doubt that this woman was her birth mother. But she hadn't meant to upset anyone, so she decided to back off. Yet the desire for contact continued to gnaw at her. Several years later, she decided to call again, but the woman had moved. Gail hired another searcher, who, now with much more information, quickly found Mary's new address and phone number.

This time, Gail didn't use the telephone. She decided to accompany a friend who was going to Seattle on vacation. In August 1989, Gail and her friend sat in a car outside her mother's house, waiting for her to emerge and then taking pictures with a telephoto lens once she did. Then they followed the woman to a supermarket and wheeled their own shopping carts around the cavernous store. Gail felt anxious, guilty, and excited. "It was wild. . . . I just wanted to get as many glimpses of her as I could," she says.

The next day, Gail positioned herself down the street from her mother's house and, when she took a walk, stopped her for a brief chat. They made a lunch date for the next day and, to Gail's surprise, Mary showed up. She only stayed a few minutes, though, and she used that time to fire a barrage of accusations at her daughter before fleeing: "Are you crazy?" "Is this a setup to blackmail me?"

The following August, by coincidence, Gail returned to Seattle for a conference. She decided to give her reunion one last try. She waited outside the house again until she was sure no one else was home, then rang the bell. The two women talked for about ten minutes, during which Mary denied her maternity less adamantly. At the end of their conversation, she promised she would amend her will to specify that Gail be notified of her death. "That was the end of that," says Mary's daughter. "My intent had never been to disturb her, but I thought at least I might get her to acknowledge my existence."

Adoptees rarely become as obsessed as Gail or tread so close to becoming stalkers. The adoption world is filled with far more accounts of happy reunions, and even the problematic ones are rarely as one-sided or unnerving as this one. But I chose to tell this story because it unmistakably shows that, even in the extreme cases, adoptees don't seek to embarrass or expose anyone. They only want to fill the void in their own souls. Gail would have stopped the second her mother said, "Yes, I did this and here's why."

For some, the very acquisition of an original birth certificate is enough to accomplish that awesome task, as though all they really need is proof that they emerged from a real human being. Others find the search itself to be sufficient without making contact, both because they obtain a good deal of information and because they finally attain some control in a process that others have always shaped for them.

Tens of thousands more adoptees each year, however, are deciding they want it all—from the documents to the people—regardless of whether they like what they discover or whether they decide to maintain communications afterward. "Sometimes things work out and sometimes they don't. There are no guarantees and no one should expect any," says Dr. Pavao, whose 1998 book *The Family of Adoption* is an invaluable resource for triad members (and anyone else) who want to understand the developmental stages and clinical issues in adoption. "But this whole movement of getting in touch with one's self, one's identity, is a very good example of how radically things are changing. . . . "

Through the tears of recounting her own journey, Gail offers the same bottom line. "Make sure everyone understands that it was very, very important for me to do this . . . whatever anyone might think of how I did it," she says. She's devastated, and yet she says she'd do it again without hesitation. Which, in a nutshell, is why the search phenomenon—mostly consisting of adoptees seeking their first mothers, but with an escalating number of birth parents looking for their children and siblings trying to find their brothers or sisters—is a bullet train that's gaining speed and can't be stopped.

It's an ever exciting, sometimes unsettling, increasingly integral part of the cultural reformation that's altering the way people in and out of the triad perceive adoption and its place in our society. And, just as the high incidence of divorce in this country has forever revised everyone's understanding of relationships between siblings, half-siblings, stepchildren, and multiple parents, the adoption revolution is adding a novel, decidedly American definition to the term "extended family."

5

Birth Parents:
A Painful Dilemma

Linda Scrivens is the terror in every adoptive parent's heart. Eighteen months after she gave birth to a boy, after she signed a raft of documents relinquishing her rights to him, after he had spent most of his young life with his new mother and father, Linda went to court and won him back. "I will never believe that adoption is full of happy endings," she says now, nearly twenty years after regaining custody of her son. "It's full of sad endings. . . . I was one of the casualties, and his adoptive parents were two more."

Linda's story is chilling, but not for the reasons you might assume. The actions she took were audacious and unnerving, to be sure. Viewed in the context of the times in which she was living, however, they also were understandable and even brave. Besides, whatever anyone might think of what she did, the anguish Linda indisputably caused wasn't ultimately her fault; it was the responsibility of a system that stripped her of her dignity, methodically tormented her, and finally manipulated her into a trap from which there could be no painless escape.

Ironically, seen from this perspective, Linda's experience provides lessons that are heartening rather than dispiriting. Because it not only illustrates the grinding pressure that used to be applied on single women to give up their babies but also highlights how massively things have changed. Because it not only summons the inner demon that adoptive parents seldom entirely exorcise—the fear of losing their children—but also demonstrates how rarely that happens. And because it shows that, when it does happen, it takes an unlikely combination of extraordinary will (by the birth parent), human mistreatment (of the birth parent), bureaucratic malfeasance, and legal errors.

Linda was twenty-six, a college graduate headed for the Peace Corps, when she became pregnant in 1978. The father didn't want the child, and she didn't want to become the subject of small-town gossip in her southern Vermont community. So she moved into a home for unmarried pregnant women in the northern part of the state, one of hundreds of similar, isolated lodgings around the country at the time. The residents of these facilities were allowed to use only their first names, or sometimes they were assigned phony ones; they were typically given wedding bands to wear when they went outside.

"I was in distress, I was in turmoil, and it was a secret. I didn't know if I wanted to be a mother or consider adoption. I was in no emotional state to know what I wanted, so I went to a place where I believed professionals would help me through a tough period and help me make a reasoned decision," Linda recalls. Instead, she was meticulously brainwashed and placed on an "adoption track." Her account of life in the home, which she did not want to identify but which still operates as an adoption agency, was corroborated by other women who spent time there and in other shelters of its type.

From the start, even before Linda indicated what she wanted, her case worker told her the "right thing" to do was to form an adoption plan. Linda kept repeating that she might want to raise her baby, but this woman firmly encouraged her to choose adoptive parents from several letters of application. After a few months, says Linda, "my baby didn't feel like mine anymore." In retrospect, she bristles at having succumbed to the pressure, but her isolation and desperation left her vulnerable to the kind of indoctrination that she and hundreds of thousands of other women used to receive.

So, although her ambivalence persisted, Linda chose an adoptive couple. On May 25, 1979, after canceling three meetings at which she was scheduled to sign the paperwork that would complete the process, she remained so anguished and uncertain about what to do that she despondently decided to flip a coin. It landed silently on the carpeted floor of her bedroom, with the adoption side facing up.

Four days later, she signed all the documents placed before her at a local courthouse. She says that, all during the lengthy bus ride home, she knew she had done the wrong thing; within hours, she was back in court asking that her paperwork be ripped up. But the clerk told her that only her case worker could ask for the files back, and had to do so by the end of that day. Linda called her case worker again and again, but the woman didn't answer the phone and didn't return the increasingly frantic messages left for her. Not on that day, and not ever.

Linda felt guilty, regretful, crushed, alone. How, she wondered, could any decent person want to give new parents to a baby whose mother wanted to keep him and had the resources to raise him? Her lone sin, if it was one, had been to bear this child outside of marriage, and the punishment seemed far too extreme. Along with her depression came dysfunction. To the extent that Linda could think cogently at all about what she'd done, and what had been done to her, she assumed she had no recourse.

While watching an episode of *Donohue* two months later, she realized all was not lost. A guest on the talk show was a member of Concerned United Birthparents, a national organization begun in Massachusetts by women who felt they'd been coerced into giving up their children. CUB played a key role in supporting the biological parents in one of the most famous instances of adoptive parents losing a legal battle for their child. In the Baby Jessica case, as with Linda's, the result was based on technicalities, mistakes adoption agencies and lawyers have learned from and now scrupulously avoid.

It's important to remember that women like Linda, who actively seek their children's return, have always been the exception and remain so today. "I'm not saying that it can't ever happen, but it's just not how things work," says Jeffrey Kaye, the cofounder of a Boston-based adoption agency and an official of the American Academy of Adoption Attorneys, a national organization with more than 300 members. "We're always on the lookout for red flags that they might want to change their minds, and always err on the side of advocating that they keep their children."

Linda Scrivens was able to gain custody of her son because, after a year-long legal battle that she initially lost, an appeals court in September 1980 found that a judge, rather than a clerk, should have overseen the signing of her documents. The adoptive parents were devastated, but went on to adopt again. Linda, now a mental-health counselor, says she regrets the suffering she caused, but has no misgivings about the course she took. "I know that what I did scares the hell out of adoptive parents, but I got my son back only because of a legal fluke, a mistake that was lucky for me and unlucky for them," she says. "I also know I lived through a period that I call the meat grinder of adoption. . . . I want to believe things have changed, and I understand they really might have. I sure hope so."

Homes for expectant mothers still exist, usually provided by adoption agencies as housing for unmarried women trying to decide whether or not to parent their babies. For the most part, they treat their charges with respect and counsel them to forgo adoption if they have misgivings; it's the diametric opposite of the direction in which such women used to be pushed. But there are still some walk-in counseling centers and residential facilities—mostly operated by conservative religious groups, but also by supposedly neutral agencies staffed by professional social workers—that continue to try to tip the scales by promoting adoption as the "right" thing to do in almost all circumstances.

Some fundamentalist Christian sects focus on pregnant teenagers, attracting them to special homes with the promise that they'll receive room, board, and nonjudgmental support. If they decide to parent, they are told, they will also get training and other help to ease their transitions into motherhood. As the young women's dependence on their benefactors grows, however, the drumbeat begins. They are advised that they are sinners, or are too young or too incapable to be good parents. As their delivery dates approach, the message becomes more and more explicit: Placing your baby in the care of a God-fearing, married couple is the only way to repent and ensure a decent life for the child.

Mainstream adoption authorities decry this kind of behavior, which effectively coerces or misleads people into taking actions that irrevocably alter the course of their lives and those of the human beings they carried. No one can predict their sentiments years down the road, but the best professionals believe birth parents should make adoption plans only if they feel certain about what they're getting into and why, because that knowledge will be their most formidable shield and compassionate ally when the pain and the second-guessing set in, as they almost inevitably will.

Some people, especially those scarred by experiences like Linda's, find it hard to believe that serious advances have been made in recent years. But they have, and the headway is continuing on many fronts. Unmarried, pregnant women have more choices and are subject to fewer social stigmas. Those who choose adoption usually play pivotal parts in selecting their babies' new parents and have considerable latitude to change their minds. And, again, a growing number are playing ongoing roles in their children's lives. Furthermore, as the revolution crosses boundary after boundary, birth fathers for the first time are fighting for and assuming greater responsibility at every step of the process.

All of which is to say that, for the most part, we're headed in the right direction. But we're not there yet by a long shot, as evidenced by the unchecked spread through the adoption system of the profit virus. Indeed, even the progress that has been made remains uneven. For instance, single pregnant women—without whom adoption would become as rare as the passing of Halley's comet—are still viewed disparagingly by many Americans, including some whose opinions of adoption are soaring in all other ways.

That's a major reason there are news stories about teenagers, afraid that their parents or teachers will find out why they've gained so much weight, who dump their newborns in toilets and trash receptacles. On the day I write these words, there's an article in the morning paper about a twenty-nine-year-old man in Arkansas who allegedly hired three brothers to kick his girlfriend in the abdomen until her fetus died because, according to a police affidavit, "he was afraid. He didn't want his parents to know" she was pregnant.

It is this same cultural climate that still can't come to grips with the idea of unmarried women deciding to give birth. Those willing to say that they plan to relinquish their children are seen as callous: "What kind of person would let someone else have her baby?" Those who intend to become parents are thoughtless: "She's so young; she's just going to ruin her life." And those who complete adoptions become demons, either because they were so heartless that they could part with their own flesh and blood, so unstable that they couldn't just swallow their decisions and move on, or so obsessed that they're willing to risk destabilizing their children's lives by trying to reconnect with them. The underlying notion is that these women, and men when they're involved or if anyone thinks of them, should be baby donors who do their jobs and then quietly go away.

"Most things about adoption are improving," says "Charlene Kelly," a twenty-four-year-old travel agent in Connecticut who chose her son's new parents six years ago. "But birth mothers are still seen as these terrible witches who give away their children." The fact that Charlene doesn't want her real name used underscores the truth of her observation; even so, she repeatedly says her experience illustrates that a seismic shift is occurring. "It's a far cry from the days when women couldn't even think about getting an abortion and couldn't consider keeping their children unless they were willing to live in disgrace and have their babies called bastards," she says. "I feel terrible for the women who suffered through all that . . . but I'm grateful to be living in a time when we have opportunities and choices that they didn't."

Charlene, a devout Irish Catholic, believed from the moment she discovered she was pregnant that she wasn't ready to raise a child alone. She didn't even consider telling her unemployed ex-boyfriend about her condition because she considered him too lazy and immature to participate in such a life-altering decision. "I want to start a family," she explains, "only when it can be traditional, with a mom and a dad . . . and I want to be sure it's a dad that I love and respect, so our child will as well." Kelly doubts she could have pushed herself to get an abortion, but it wasn't even an option by the time she concluded her procrastination, self-delusion, and denial about what was happening. "When I finally looked up and dealt with it," she says, "I was well into my fifth month."

So Charlene started looking for new parents in a place where she felt comfortable about the prospects: the classifieds section of the *Irish Voice* newspaper. Such ads appear regularly in publications throughout most of the country, and they're spawning like guppies on the Internet. Advertising to find birth mothers is illegal in some states,[1] but the World Wide Web has effectively rendered those statutes null and void, giving anyone with access to a computer the ability to read and respond to the entreaties of a growing array of adoption agencies, attorneys, facilitators, and prospective parents themselves.

The people who seek to adopt in this way run the gamut of modern families, from infertile couples to gay individuals to older Americans who have already raised birth children and are on their second marriages. The vast majority, however, fit a select profile: They are white couples who earn at least $50,000 a year, are in their late 30s or older, have failed to produce children in the old-fashioned way, have exhausted their insurance coverage and/or spent tens of thousands of dollars of their own for infertility treatments. And badly want a white infant.

Charlene picked a married couple in Manhattan, but she was too nervous to phone them herself, so she wrote out some questions and listened in as her roommate did the talking. She recalls James Ettore's reaction as he realized what the call was about: "The poor man nearly had a heart attack." Charlene considered other possible parents but, after a few more phone conversations that she conducted herself and a few meetings arranged by the couple's adoption agency, she stuck with her initial choice. She can't say exactly why, but she liked that James, a video documentary editor, made her laugh, and she was taken with the intelligence and warmth of his wife, Joan Humphreys, an architect.

Though Charlene could legally have turned over custody of her son within two days of giving birth, an agency social worker who had been working with her advised that she temporarily place the baby in foster care, giving Kelly time to sort out her feelings, consider her options, and achieve a reasonable level of certainty about what she wanted to do. The counselor explained to Kelly the emotional difficulties she faced, and encouraged her to consider the long-term implications of her decision.

One of the most productive functions adoption professionals can serve is to catch the warning signs of a change of mind as early as possible. Doing so benefits everyone concerned—the pregnant women who endure less angst by making their determinations sooner rather than later, and the adoptive parents who are spared the heartbreak of anticipating children who will never arrive. It can also lower costs, since many women receive assistance for medical and living expenses as long as they remain in the process.

Most women in these situations vacillate about whether to become parents, sometimes changing their minds several times before they give birth. Of those who believe they've settled on adoption, experts estimate at least half ultimately discover that they can't go through with it once they actually see their babies as living, breathing realities. And the delivery process itself, along with its emotional aftermath, produces an overwhelming feeling in nearly all women to keep their children. Charlene experienced it.

"It was so strange to see him come out, this beautiful, healthy boy. I didn't want to let him go," she says. "All my clarity about what I wanted to do, it just evaporated at that moment." The memory generates her only tears in an hours-long interview, and it reminds her to open the silver ball she always wears around her neck—a present from the adoptive parents—so she can show off the three tiny photos of her son inside.

The more she thought about it, though, the more certain Charlene grew that her instincts about adoption had been correct, a sense that was forcefully affirmed when she finally handed her child to his new parents. "What made me happiest was to see them and see how they reacted to the baby," she says. "They were so happy, and I knew they would be able to complete their lives and could give him the moon and the stars, which is what I wanted him to have but what I know I couldn't give him at this stage of my life."

The Trauma of Loss

There are birth mothers who believe with all their hearts that people like Charlene are blinding themselves, or are being blinded, from seeing a bottom-line truth: that any woman who parts with her child is emotionally and psychically damaged beyond repair. Once women realize that to be the case, these birth mothers argue, they will prefer to deal with any social, economic, or personal consequences necessary to raise their own offspring rather than endure the brutal, lifelong trauma inevitably caused by separation.

A few years ago, while attending a conference of the American Adoption Congress, I seated myself at a table with a group of women to listen to one of the most passionate lecturers and authors in the adoption community, Betty Jean Lifton. (Many adoptees revere her book *Journey of the Adopted Self*.) As we listened to her explain adoptees' needs to reconnect with their birth mothers, I whispered to the middle-aged woman next to me that I intended to do everything I could to help my two children establish relationships with their biological parents. I'd chatted with this woman off-and-on for about ten minutes earlier, and found her bright and engaging. That was before I poured verbal acid on her unhealed wound. She glared at me with a mix of agony and fury. "What are you saying? You love your kids and I gave mine up because I didn't? You people don't understand at all," she snapped, then abruptly walked away.

There could be no doubt about who she meant by "you people." To a small minority of birth parents, mainly women, those of us who pay large sums of money to adopt babies are the driving forces of a system that brutally severs primal bonds. The only acceptable adoptions in these critics' eyes are of those foster-care children whose biological parents have died, have abused them, or are patently incapable of caring for them. A small, indeterminable number of adoptees agree.

The common denominators among people who hold this view are profound pain and unhappiness. Some are teens and adults whose adopted parents treated them so badly that they rightly wish someone else had raised them. (Many people who grow up in dysfunctional biological families feel the same way, but they don't have readily available alternatives to fantasize about.) Most, though, are older women whose visions have been forever clouded by the drugs, deceptions, and disrespect that were used to induce them to give up their babies, without knowing their fates and without hope of seeing them again.

A majority of birth mothers, until recent years, got worse than nothing. Even if they had plainly wanted to become parents, they were supposed to accept their children's departure without a word of complaint, a session of counseling, or a second of consolation. As their punishment for committing the social sin of unwed pregnancy, they were forced to internalize their despair and literally instructed to move on as though nothing had ever happened. Cynicism about adoption has been soldered onto their souls.

It's a testament to the human spirit that the vast majority, however injured inside, have rebuilt their lives and developed a reasoned perspective on the institution that gave their babies new homes. The stereotype of birth mothers as stalkers trying to reconnect at any cost is as misguided and shallow as the one of them as victims who want only to remain anonymous. The conflict between these two frequently portrayed images is a tip-off that something's going on other than an effort to accurately describe human behavior.

Other similarly negative, and often contradictory, stereotypes provide more clues. Adult adoptees, for instance, are sometimes depicted as innocents who must be protected from being found because, presumably, they don't want contact with their birth parents; on the other hand, when they decide to look for those same people, they are transformed into ingrates willing to torment their adoptive mothers and fathers. Adoptive parents suffer from the fewest stigmas, but sometimes we are painted as selfish people who capitalize on the misery of others (that is, birth parents) and whose ability to raise their children (that is, the adopted ones) is diminished by our lack of genetic connection to them and our grief over not having produced our own offspring.

Given its history of stigmas and self-contempt, it's no surprise that adoption has generated so many erroneous, unappealing perceptions. People who harbor secrets all their lives must have something scandalous to hide, right? It's hard to straighten out misunderstandings, answer criticisms, or provide education about subjects that aren't supposed to be discussed. Those are among the major reasons many warped views about adoption came about, but they don't explain why the stereotypes haven't dissipated more quickly as the process has grown increasingly open. Part of the answer is that most Americans still don't have enough information with which to form a complete, accurate picture, but there are two additional factors as well: insecurity and politics.

Adoptive parents, at least at the start of our journeys and sometimes throughout our lives, harbor a gnawing fear that our bonds with our children might not be firm or permanent. It's a wrong-headed impression, but it's an understandable one. Nearly all of us have endured the pain of being "different" ourselves, cast by chance into the minority of our friends and relatives who are infertile. So we live with an insidious suspicion that biologically unrelated people can't ever feel completely connected; it's a doubt that has been nurtured in all nations throughout history in ways ranging from their legal practices (allowing inheritance only through "bloodlines," for instance) to their use of language (listen to the pride in a father's voice as he discusses "my own flesh and blood").

As a society and as individuals, for generations we deluded ourselves into thinking that the simplest way to make the uncertainty go away, and to ensure that we would never even have to consider competing for our children's love, was to make their birth parents disappear. Or, if that couldn't be accomplished, at least to turn them into lesser beings who couldn't possibly be the objects of anyone's desire.

The glorious, reassuring realization that eventually dawns on most adoptive parents is that our children love us deeply, even if they feel strongly about other people as well. But the hard accompanying truth is also that the best adoptions—or any other relationships, for that matter—entail accepting and dealing with their intricacies. Demonizing biological mothers and fathers in an effort to simplify our own complicated lives ultimately diminishes us as much as it does them, even as it undermines our children's views of all their parents and, as a result, of themselves.

Adoptees' insecurities generally don't stem from questions about what they do have, which are close ties with and powerful feelings about the parents who raise them, but from what they don't: an understanding of their backgrounds and the circumstances that thrust them into new families. Some seem to adjust well without much knowledge of their personal histories, but most build defense mechanisms to cope with the enigmatic, unknowable wonder of what might have been.

Those defenses can include resentment toward the people who relinquished them, and that can lead adoptees to embrace ugly stereotypes about birth parents. Alternately, or sometimes in addition, they may accept the negative depictions of adoptive parents, particularly if the adoptees are unfortunate enough to wind up with mothers or fathers who mistreat them. No matter what their circumstances, those without knowledge about their pasts often feed their neuroses by fantasizing about how good or how bad things might have been or, most destructively, what was wrong with them or what they might have done that was so heinous that a parent wanted to give them away.

The insecurities of biological parents, most pointedly of birth mothers, often run deepest of all—especially when their sense of loss isn't alleviated by contact with, or even information about, the children they carried. When they feel they had no choice, they can become bitter and self-deprecating, nearly as hard on themselves for having failed to exert more power as on the forces that divested them of it. Even those women who participate fully in their decisions, and feel confident about them, at least initially second-guess their judgment and question their self-worth. And the prolonged grief and guilt, irrespective of any other factors, can eat away at any woman who doesn't know if the child that once lived inside her is happy or troubled, healthy or needy, or even alive.

Charlene Kelly says she silently thanks her son's adoptive parents nearly every day for the letters and photos they regularly send. What gives her even more assurance and comfort, though, are the spontaneous, unscheduled arrivals: scribbles the child has produced at home, drawings he's made in school, notes about his accomplishments.

One day in March of 1997, when Sam was one and a half, his parents called to ask Charlene if she'd like to see the boy again. She considered the pluses and minuses of the idea for about a microsecond. They met in New York a few days later. "It was just creepy-incredible. He reminded me so much of myself," she says. "I absolutely loved it." During their hours together, Joan and James told Charlene that they'd begun explaining to Sam that she was his birth mother and asked if she wanted to play a recurring role in the boy's life. She declined, saying she thought "it would be too confusing for the child." (On a subsequent visit, in late 1999, Kelly began warming to the idea.)

Adoptive parents who fear that birth mothers or fathers will invade their turf don't understand this about the vast majority: Like parents of any sort, first and foremost they want what's good for their children. The fact that there are exceptions, the ones we see sensationalized in news stories, only proves the rule. Birth parents who aren't in open adoptions typically try to find their children only after they become adults, and when they search sooner, they contact the adoptive parents first and invariably respect any boundaries they work out. They want to be invited to the party, not to crash it.

Charlene remembers watching a television program about adoption when she was much younger, and thinking she could never give up a baby because she would forever wonder what had happened to him. "I think about my boy every day," she says now, her voice trembling. "But I have no regrets. It's all about options and choices, and I know I made the choices about his life as well as my own. I can change my mind about seeing him anytime, and that helps a lot. . . . And I never have to wonder. I know where he is."

Adoption is a television soap opera minus the cameras. An adoptive father sobs in his daughter's arms as she tries to reassure him that she kept her two-year relationship with her birth father secret not because she was ungrateful to the parents who raised her, but because she loved them so much that she didn't want to hurt them. Or a birth mother discovers that her search for the son she relinquished twenty years ago is causing serious tension with her husband, who is afraid of the disruption within their family if she succeeds in her quest. Make up a scenario, and it happens.

The current phase of adoption's volcanic transformation is its most active, therefore its most volatile and unpredictable. But personal experiences do more than just add complexity to individual lives. The intense emotions and tangled interactions in this drama also provide ammunition for what I call the politics of adoption, a big subject with two recurring components: internecine feuding among groups representing adoptees and their various parents; and fierce battles in legislatures and courts, generally involving adoption professionals as well as triad members, over the reform of laws and practices.

Neither of those occurrences is unusual. Every effort to implement change of any consequence, and certainly every major social movement, generates internal debates and external resistance. Conflict can serve a useful purpose, helping to define issues and forcing people to take stands, but it inevitably causes negative fallout as well. In the case of adoption, the internal and external friction has served—sometimes deliberately, often unwittingly—to perpetuate negative stereotypes, to prevent people who believe in the same goals from working together and, ultimately, to slow the pace of progress.

The most explicit examples involve the National Council for Adoption, a Washington-based organization whose ostensible mission is to promote adoption. For most of its two decades of operation, it received wide support from politicians, adoption agencies, and religious groups that were attracted to its name (who could oppose a council FOR adoption?), liked the sound of its arguments (adoption, not abortion!), and didn't pay much attention to what it was really doing. The Council began functioning at a time when adoption wasn't discussed much publicly, so it was the only player on the field during most of its existence, and it remained the biggest, best-known lobbying/advocacy organization until recent years. Its credibility was enhanced by journalists who, knowing little and with few other places to turn, regularly went to NCFA for information.

That's what I did when I began researching a series on adoption for the *Boston Globe* in 1997, but I was fortunate enough to be working during a period of greater openness, when reform groups like the American Adoption Congress and research organizations like the Evan B. Donaldson Adoption Institute were gaining greater prominence, and when it was relatively easy to interview triad members for firsthand accounts of their experiences. With more sources of information, I was able to gain a balanced picture of what was happening and what roles various actors were playing.

What I learned was that the NCFA's agenda has been to keep adoption closed. Its principal backers have been the adoption agencies of the Mormon Church—ironically, an institution that avidly promotes genealogy—along with a dwindling number of other adoption agencies, some philosophically averse to change and others concerned about the impact that reforms might have on their businesses; conservative Christian groups that consider unmarried pregnant women to be sinners who don't deserve to keep their children and/or believe openness will lead to more abortions; and adoptive parents who fear the consequences of communication between children and their birth parents.

William Pierce, the organization's president until he retired in late 1999, and his allies have been instrumental in blocking state efforts to allow adoptees access to their birth certificates and to implement laws simplifying searches. They have done that partly by efficiently providing politicians and judges with skewed or incorrect information, such as the contention that past birth mothers were guaranteed anonymity and that future ones will get abortions unless they receive similar assurances.[2] To a large extent, though, they've triumphed because they've been adept at preying on and promoting the negative images of triad members, and pitting them against each other.

At times, such as when he has argued for keeping records sealed, Dr. Pierce has depicted birth mothers as wonderful people who need to be defended against being "hounded" or "hunted down" by the children they relinquished. Alternately, when he has opposed the creation of registries that might actively be used by biological fathers and mothers, they became the heartless hunters while their birth children were transformed into potential victims in need of protection. Invariably, he has cast himself as the champion of adoptive parents and portrayed them as the heroes who will suffer most from any tampering with the status quo. Dr. Pierce unflinchingly labels those who disagree with his views as "anti-adoption." Once, while interviewing him in his office, I asked what he thought generally about the trend toward more openness. I expected a cautious, equivocal response; instead, he bluntly answered: "Pernicious, wrong, evil."

One way in which NCFA has been able to further its agenda is by recruiting triad members to speak out against pro-openness measures. These people undoubtedly are sincere about their views, and some presumably have legitimate anxieties about the effects a specific reform might have on their particular situations. What they are not, however, is representative of the populations for whom they purportedly speak.

Study after study shows that at least three quarters of adoptive and birth parents favor giving adult adoptees access to their own documents, and just as many think it's a good idea to expedite the search process for triad members who want to find each other.[3]

Too many judges and lawmakers are uneducated in these emerging realities, and therefore are susceptible to persuasion through the use of aberrational horror stories and faulty stereotypes. On the other hand, greater openness brings better information, so a growing number of jurisdictions are making improvements; sometimes they're slow or partial, but they're moving in a single direction—and it's not the one in which NCFA and its backers have been pushing. A few unmistakable indicators of where things are headed: Many adoption agencies and other longtime Council supporters have dropped their affiliations in the last few years, and Dr. Pierce has been declared persona non grata by some Capitol Hill politicians who used to welcome him as their adoption guru.

"He's a bad guy and he's done a lot of harm," says Senator Carl Levin of Michigan, who has promoted legislation since the mid–1980s to set up a voluntary national registry for birth parents and adoptees who want to make contact. It's a relatively small step that's cautiously worded to prevent intrusion on anyone's privacy by mandating that both parties sign up before either one could search. It may not have a huge numerical impact since the Internet, virtually overnight, has become reunion central. But implementation of Levin's initiative would help some searchers who are stymied because they and their relatives are registered in different states. Perhaps most important, a national registry would serve as a symbol of what's acceptable in the new world of adoption, and that's presumably why Dr. Pierce has lobbied—successfully—to kill the bill every year.

Levin is a Democrat and some of NCFA's strongest supporters are not, so it's tempting to conclude that partisanship is partly responsible for the dispute, but that's patently not the case. Conservative members of the GOP, such as Senator John McCain of Arizona, have been among the most vocal advocates of Levin's measure. "This important legislation will help thousands of Americans who want to learn about themselves and their birth relatives," McCain, an adoptive father and former presidential candidate, once said in a statement announcing his sponsorship of the bill.

Further evidence of NCFA's overarching mission, to keep adoptions closed, lies in the fact that it supports the so-called voluntary, mutual-consent registries that exist in half the states and operate exactly like the one Levin envisions for the country. Opponents of openness know usage rates for the state registries are abysmally low, however, because so few people know about them. The risk of a national equivalent is that, regardless of how widely used it might be, it probably would hasten reforms overall by raising public awareness and by essentially acting as a government stamp of approval for reunions.

Unfortunately, as rapidly as adoption is metamorphosing, some of the most ardent proponents of reform have inadvertently prevented even faster progress. They've done that in a time-honored fashion among true believers in causes of virtually any kind: by diluting their strength with internal squabbles over how to use their resources (a particularly tough issue since the three sides of the triad can have varying priorities); what strategies to employ; and whether they should accept short-term compromises in order to achieve their final goals. The feuding players' disunity hasn't only deprived their movement of its maximum potential impact; their passions sometimes have become so thick as to obscure their vision, leading them to distrust each other and to resort to the kinds of tactics and stereotyping that they're supposedly trying to eliminate.

It's easy to find members of Concerned United Birthparents, for instance, disparaging adoptive parents at meetings of the American Adoption Congress, to which many adoptive parents belong and the current president of which is an adoptive mother named Jane Nast—who helped her two children develop relationships with their birth mothers and works fourteen-hour days promoting reforms in adoption laws and attitudes.

Officials of the twenty-two-year-old AAC and other longtime adoption revolutionaries also receive criticism for having grown accustomed to fighting for partial victories rather than striving for knockouts. In fact, there might be circumstances in which they could learn something from the audacious maneuver Bastard Nation members executed in Oregon, where they revised the law on sealed adoption records by putting it to an unprecedented public vote. But, in general, activists who accept incremental progress and partial victories aren't selling out or setting their sights too low.

Far too few Americans know enough yet about the benefits of openness—or even realize how prevalent searches, reunions, and relationships between birth and adoptive families already have become—to turn their lifelong perceptions inside out overnight. After a few years in which they learn that adoptees will flock to see their unsealed records, but won't turn into vultures swooping down on their unsuspecting biological parents, more legislators and judges will become willing to lift the remaining restrictions. The same will be true when they discover only a tiny number of birth mothers will refuse contact if allowed by law to do so, because they overwhelmingly want to be found.

Unnoticed Birth Fathers

Whatever distance birth mothers still must travel to reach a comfortable and respectable place in society, they've indisputably come a long way. No one can argue that the men who were their indispensable accomplices in the formation of life have made nearly as much progress or even received nearly as much attention. When we think about an adoption, the only man most of us include in the picture is the one doing the adopting. Two of the only reasons Americans have noticed biological fathers at all over the years are the Baby Jessica case in Idaho and the Baby Richard case in Illinois.

"There are two stereotypes about birth fathers, and neither one is very appealing," says Fred Greenman, the lead attorney in the landmark Tennessee case and an important player in comparable efforts to expand the rights of adoptees and birth parents around the country. "They're these terrible men who are either going out the door or are in some way interfering with an adoption." Fred possesses a great deal of knowledge about birth fathers, not all of it accumulated in the course of his work.

In the spring of 1991, he received a call at his New York office from a man who said in an apologetic tone: "I have a rather embarrassing question to ask. Did you have a daughter in Boston thirty years ago?" Fred was about to respond when he realized he didn't have a clue about the identity, much less the motives, of the person at the other end of the line. "You're a lawyer, act like one," he thought, then asked the mystery man why he wanted to know. "If you did have a daughter," he replied, "I married her." Fred was flabbergasted. He never hid the fact that he and his then-fiancée had placed a child for adoption while he was attending law school, not from his family or his friends, but neither had he expected to ever see her again. "The answer," he told his caller, "is yes."

Adoption has changed enormously, but men's roles haven't. In part for biological reasons, they have never been or sought to be primary participants in the decisions about their children's fate. The sad truth, though, is that most birth fathers don't bow to the wishes of birth mothers just because they're nice guys who understand that women develop powerful ties to their babies. Rather, they're young or married to other women or chicken. They don't show the evidence of their actions and so they defer—or deny or flee—because they can. And society has insidiously reinforced their inclination to do so.

When Fred and his fiancée discussed what to do about their baby in early 1960, Margaritta wanted to get married but Fred was unsure. They decided to temporarily place the newborn in foster care, so they could discuss their options without the pressures of parenthood. After several months, they agreed they would wed and raise their daughter, so they went to the agency caring for her to sign the paperwork necessary to resume custody. But when the social worker asked what they wanted to do, Margaritta tore Fred's heart into pieces. "I can't do it," she announced. Fred winces as he remembers the words cutting through him. "It was one of the worst moments of my life," he says.

Fred was twenty-six, in his second year at Harvard Law School, living in an era when single mothers were debased and the only imaginable single fathers were those who were divorced or whose wives had died. Fred had never had insomnia before, but from that point on he suffered from disturbing bouts of sleeplessness. They never seemed related to anything specific in his life; they just sort of came and went. And they lasted for about thirty years, until they suddenly disappeared after his daughter's husband, using identifying information Jody had gotten from her adoptive parents, found Fred at work.

Just as society robbed generations of unmarried women of the right to raise their children, it placed that option out of the reach of men like Fred. In both ways, without malicious intent, it denied millions of children the chance to be raised by at least one of their birth parents. It's something of a cosmic payback that one way adoption is changing America for the better today is by creating more opportunities for single men to become fathers, thereby helping to make that a respectable choice for those who share genetic codes with their sons and daughters, as well as for those who don't.

Our culture, along with most others, long ago declared parenthood to be a dishonorable calling for all unmarried people. But, as with so many aspects of life, that moral judgment hasn't been applied equally to both genders. Men might not have felt empowered to become single parents, but they weren't mocked and denigrated if they engaged in sex before they walked down the aisle; in fact, they were often considered macho and cool. Nor were they humiliated or ostracized for creating a fetus. They generally went on with their schooling, their dating, and their work. Some small proportion presumably remained concerned about what had happened to the children they sired, but many more were relieved or even pleased that they didn't have to know.

There's no denying that parenting often reveals a gender gap in emotional connections and personal responsibility. It's on display when politicians announce programs to force affluent "deadbeat dads" to pay child support, and it's evident in the fact that more than two thirds of families on welfare are headed by single mothers. No one's insisting that the men absent from these situations should have a right to anonymity, that they need to be protected from their biological children, or that it would be wrong to disrupt their current families by exposing them as birth fathers.

Even in revolutions, some things change more slowly than others. Too few professionals seem very interested in disclosing or reforming adoption's nasty little secret: that birth fathers are often considered a nuisance, or even just sperm donors. The process usually doesn't concentrate on determining whether these men want to become parents if the mothers do not; instead, it focuses on persuading them to accede to an adoption or circumvents them altogether so they don't get the chance to make a choice.

In most states, the names or descriptions of birth fathers who must step forward if they want to contest an adoption (which they probably don't know is pending, if they suspect they contributed to a pregnancy at all) are printed in tiny type in the legal notices section of local newspapers. "None of these guys ever finds the citations, much less reads them," says Herbert Friedman, a well-regarded adoption attorney in Boston who has placed such ads for more than twenty years. "I've never had a birth father respond to one."

Meanwhile, a growing number of states—eighteen as of this writing— have established "putative father registries" that men must sign if they think they may have impregnated a woman to whom they're not married; if they don't, they lose their right to seek custody later. Other states mandate that men somehow indicate their interest, for example by signing the birth certificate or obtaining a court order establishing paternity, if they want to earn the right to parent a child or participate in an adoption decision.

Such devices are intended to avert repeats of cases like those of Baby Richard and Baby Jessica, both of which hinged on men's assertions that they didn't know they had sired children and therefore had been improperly denied the right to claim them. It's in everyone's interest to prevent recurrences of such painful incidents, however rare they may be, but legal gimmicks don't ensure that men will play a vital role in affecting their children's fates. They all but guarantee that they won't.

The only upside to this state of affairs is that, for the most part, it doesn't harm too many people. Because the somber reality is that birth fathers, as a group, have earned their reputations. Of those still on the scene when an adoption decision is being made, few express interest in participating and fewer still express a desire to parent the child.[4] And by all accounts the men who have to be sought out, as they increasingly are by private detectives hired by appropriately cautious adoption agencies and attorneys, usually sign on the dotted line without much hesitation or many questions.

But what about the growing number of men who don't fit the molds constructed by and for them? The men who want to help determine their children's future, who want to stay in touch wherever they may wind up, or who want to become their parents—they all tend to be thrown in and out with their prototypical brethren. "It's ironic that on the one hand, as a society, we want fathers to take more responsibility and get more involved with their kids," says Madelyn Freundlich, who is now the policy director for an advocacy group called Children's Rights, Inc. "But in adoption, we want to get rid of them."

Often that happens because birth mothers want to sever connections with the men who impregnated them. Some of these women, angry or afraid or just anxious, lie about the identity of the fathers or refuse to sign final documents until after the men do, to preclude the possibility of their ever gaining custody of the children. They don't like to admit it, but many agencies, facilitators, and attorneys advise women to do such things, usually because they genuinely believe birth mothers should have the near-exclusive right to decide, but sometimes because they're trying to expedite a profitable transaction. It can be hard to untangle people's motives when so much money is involved.

Empowering birth fathers is a controversial concept, in no small part because the last thing prospective adoptive parents want is another legal or emotional hurdle to jump. But it's hypocritical for an institution that is attempting to proudly throw open its other doors, proclaiming that hidden flaws can't be repaired, to continue blockading this one. Some of the issues will be easy to handle: Should rapists be allowed to help make any choices? Not on this planet. Others will be exasperatingly tough: What happens if two parents, perhaps who despise or barely know each other, differ on whether their baby should be relinquished or on which applicants should get to adopt?

Reasonable people will disagree on many of the nettlesome questions that will arise, but that's a terrible reason for avoiding them. There's a big principle that has to be addressed, and not only for the sake of the men who earn a place at the discussion table—or deserve to be fathers—by virtue of their character and conduct, and not just because they engaged in sexual intercourse. Adoptees can feel spiritually and emotionally wounded when they learn their biological parents were shabbily treated or were manipulated into giving them up. That applies to their fathers as well as their mothers.

It's in the interest of everyone striving to improve adoption to candidly admit and seize the high ground on the process's problems, so they can promote their own solutions to adoption practitioners and state legislatures. Otherwise, the people whose primary concern is profits will be left to lobby for their own answers to satisfy their own needs. Reformers also need to weigh in because their voices have to be heard by judges who have too often steered adoption in erratic directions because they've received too little information about the underlying issues or the impact of their pronouncements.

Nevertheless, the nation's judiciary has been sending some downright revolutionary messages regarding birth fathers. While courts still overwhelmingly favor women in family-related issues, important decisions have been handed down recently that impose a high price for ignoring birth fathers' rights. These rulings are noteworthy not only because they side with the men involved, but also because they received so little attention—whereas the Baby Richard and Baby Jessica cases provoked national uproars—and because they could fundamentally alter the course of adoption practices.

In September 1999, the Oklahoma Supreme Court unanimously upheld a district judge's ruling that a two-year-old boy be removed from his adoptive home and placed in the custody of his birth father, Joseph Ferguson. Both courts' reasoning was simple: The mother had concealed her pregnancy and the adoption agency hadn't promptly informed Mr. Ferguson that he had a child. He learned of Brandon's existence four months after the birth, and immediately initiated legal proceedings to become the boy's parent.

The decision was a warning shot aimed in the right direction, but it was neither the only one nor the loudest one signaling that the adoption revolution will have to include biological fathers. State and federal courts in recent years have clearly stated that, while women have the innate right to make determinations for and about their children, the wishes of men who provide physical, emotional, and/or economic support also must be taken into account. Those were general opinions, however. A U.S. Supreme Court action in early 1999 was more pointed and should have a more persuasive impact.

The court rejected a final appeal by a Beverly Hills attorney, David Keene Leavitt, who had been ordered by a jury to pay $7 million for deliberately circumventing the biological father while helping an unmarried

West Virginia woman place her baby for adoption. The case went nearly unreported, in yet another reminder of how little attention is generally paid to adoption, even though it ended with a devastating decision.

The fact that this was the highest court in the land speaking should count for a lot, but lower courts have varied wildly in their edicts on adoption matters, and lawyers on all sides know that future outcomes will hinge on the circumstances of specific cases and the predilections of individual judges. Legal opinions aren't always followed in daily practice anyway, because so few adoptions are disputed that there's no reason for anyone other than the direct participants to learn the details of what procedures were used.

The principal power of the Leavitt ruling wasn't in the legal lines it drew; it was in the mammoth penalty it extracted. It's one thing for people to take risks when they know adoptions seldom wind up in litigation, but it's another level of gambling altogether when the financial stakes soar into the heavens. So for the majority of practitioners trying to act honorably, this should serve as a solid reminder that openness and fair treatment can't be selective standards. For those whose main interest is cold cash, it should provide an awesome incentive to behave more ethically.

Search and Seizure

In many ways, the reforms now being advanced fall into two separable categories: cleaning up the mistakes of the past and creating a better process for the future. A small but growing number of states, for instance, won't open birth certificates and other records that already are sealed, but give new adoptees access to identifying information once they reach legal age.[5] Whether adoption practitioners believe in openness or not, the minority who continue to assure birth mothers that their identities will indefinitely remain confidential are being more than audacious. Given the shifting views of adoptive parents and the expanding capabilities of today's information technologies, they are lying.

The anecdotal evidence concerning triad members' sentiments about search—that they usually favor it or at least don't object—has been bolstered by research and surveys over the last decade.[6] But there are other concrete indicators as well. For example, only a trickle of birth parents have seized the opportunity to attach no-contact notices to birth certificates in Delaware, Tennessee, and other states where some or all adoption records have been opened. And there have been only a couple of legal cases initiated by birth mothers claiming their discovery caused grievous harm, though there are many instances of adoptees, adoptive and birth parents, and even biological siblings being upset by the idea of contact itself or by the behavior of those who found them.

A few women have sued lawyers and agencies for allegedly handing over confidential information to adoptive parents or biological children. In addition, in an unprecedented action, in 1998 a Florida resident named Patricia Austin filed a lawsuit against the investigator who found her. She claimed the private eye hired by her birth daughter, Lisa Franklin, had invaded her privacy and tormented her emotionally. Ms. Austin's attorney, William Graessle of Jacksonville, says the investigator apparently located Patricia by using records sealed under state law, and then badgered her into seeing Lisa. The lawyer adds that Lisa stalked her biological mother after the older woman had repeatedly made it clear that she wanted no communication whatsoever.

"She was a prosperous, independent businessperson until this happened," says Graessle. "Within three weeks of being found out, she was an emotional wreck and went into hiding." He maintains his client was shattered when she placed her daughter for adoption in 1963, and cried every day for five years afterward. The coping mechanism on which she had relied since then was to lock her skeleton in a faraway closet of her mind and never go near it; when she was forced to do so, Graessle adds, she fell apart again.

Lisa and the investigator, Virginia Snyder, tell a very different story. They say the birth parents' names were on documents the adoptive parents gave their daughter, so searching was a relatively simple task. Pointing out that the suit was filed four years after contact had been made and severed, they also raise questions about the birth mother's motives. It will be up to a jury, if the case goes that far, to determine whom to believe.

Opponents of search argue that aggrieved parties don't sue more often because, once any communication begins, the found person has irretrievably lost the treasure she was trying to safeguard. Maybe so. Some of the revolution's casualties will be birth parents whose lives will be disrupted. It's inconceivable that a colossus like adoption could make the breakneck leap from darkness into light without incurring or inflicting some injuries. Most will be temporary and transitional, I hope, but some surely will be the price for existing in the real world of people who pursue relationships, thrive or get hurt by them, and sometimes wind up in court. The reality is that women like Patricia Austin are a distinct exception, and it doesn't make sense to strip all adoptees of the right to meet their parents for the sake of the very few who might not want the encounter.

Erratic growing conditions yield imperfect crops, so there are adoptive parents who are paranoid or suffocating because they've been led to believe a birth mother's phone call could destroy their families; adoptees whose overblown fantasies about reunion have turned into unhealthy obsessions because they've been denied the perspective that comes with accurate information; and birth mothers who are so overcome by loss, so convinced their objective is just, that they break the laws regarding sealed records. One even wound up in prison, and she's a hero to many adoption activists.

This will undoubtedly be the first time most readers will have heard of Sandy Musser, who was fifteen when she gave birth in 1954. Because of her age and the era in which she was living, there wasn't much choice about what would happen next. She never stopped being heartbroken, though, and she never stopped envisioning the day she would again see the child who emerged from her. Still, it never occurred to her to do anything about her dream until she read a magazine story, while sitting in a doctor's waiting room, about a reunion. From there, she got very lucky.

Pennsylvania, where she had relinquished, had a loophole in its laws (which it has since closed): Adoption records were sealed, but birth certificates weren't. So when Sandy filed a written request for any available documents, claiming she was an adoptee born to a woman named Musser on July 18, 1954, she got back a copy of an amended birth certificate with the full names of her daughter and her adoptive parents. It turned out that Wendy, by then twenty-two, had been raised just forty miles from Sandy's home. The two women reunited in April 1977, and they have had a seamless relationship ever since.

That experience transformed Sandy. She started the first chapter of Concerned United Birthparents in Pennsylvania, counseled other birth mothers, and marched in protests. When she moved to Florida in the early '80s, she remained a secretary by day and an activist on weekends, but by 1988 she decided to do more. In a small office in Cape Coral, she started the Musser Foundation to find biological relatives separated by adoption. Over the following five years, sometimes for fees and sometimes for free, Sandy facilitated more than 500 reunions—nearly all for adoptees and birth mothers, but for a smattering of birth fathers, siblings, and grandparents as well. Many of the people who hired her had first looked on their own, but hit an impenetrable roadblock when they needed legally unattainable records. "We got around that little problem," says Sandy.

She did that by using dozens of unpaid and well-paid searchers around the country like Barbara Moskowitz, a birth mother in Ohio with an uncommon talent for persuasion. Though law enforcement officials suspect Sandy's agents got some of their information from documents spirited out of state and federal files, most of it apparently came from government employees who believed they were just doing their jobs. Barbara would phone a given state's Office of Vital Records, for instance, tell the clerk that she worked for the Social Security Administration or for a judge whose name she made up, and the clerk would straightforwardly provide her with names, addresses, and other identifying information that purportedly had been shut away forever.

In March 1993—after a sting operation in which a New York State investigator called the Musser Foundation, pretending he was a birth father seeking to reunite with his daughter—Sandy and Barbara, then fifty-four and fifty-three, respectively, were charged in a thirty-nine-count indictment with conspiracy, wire fraud, and theft of government property. Barbara, in return for her cooperation, was allowed to plead guilty to a single felony and served two months in a halfway house. Sandy refused to concede she'd done anything wrong; she was convicted of thirty-five offenses and sentenced to four months in a penitentiary, followed by two months' house arrest wearing an electronic monitoring device and then three years' probation. It was a tougher punishment than some first-time offenders get for dealing drugs or pointing guns at people while stealing their money.

Evidently because of a bureaucratic snafu, Sandy also received an unplanned extra penalty. She arrived at Marianna State Prison late on a Friday afternoon, as instructed, but that turned out to be after the processing office for new inmates had closed for the weekend. There was only one place to store her, she was told, a small room in the maximum-security wing. Sandy, who had suffered from claustrophobia all her life, was placed in solitary confinement. When the guards opened the steel door on Monday morning, they found her curled up like a fetus in a corner of the cell.

Two other birth mothers, Rita Stapf and Barbara Lewis, were arrested at about the same time as Moscowitz and Musser, also after a sting. They ran a covert search-assistance operation out of Albany that helped hundreds of birth relatives in New York State find each other over four years. Their job was relatively easy, since Barbara was a computer operator in the government agency that stored birth certificates and adoption records. The two women received fines and five years' probation each for their crimes.

The felony sentences described above may be the only ones ever imposed on searchers, and Sandy evidently is the only one ever to have been imprisoned for such activities. But that's not because there are so few people out there doing what these birth mothers did. Today, thanks to the explosion in computer technology, the number of professionals and amateurs who help triad members in their quests has skyrocketed into the thousands. Some are private detectives with licenses and the savvy to know where to look legally, while others are Internet entrepreneurs who understand little about adoption or traditional investigation, but use their technical skills to tap into a growing market.

And many, if not most, don't fit into either of those categories. An unknowable percentage of searchers operate within a loosely knit, virtually unreported underground network that has existed nationwide for two decades. They are adoptees, birth parents, some adoptive parents, and other true believers who use pseudonyms, intermediaries, and mysterious codes to protect their identities and methods, which include surreptitiously copying sealed documents obtained from sympathetic or bribed government workers, hacking into computer records, and making phone calls for judges who don't exist.

Whatever anyone may conclude about the morality or legality of their actions, a couple of manifest lessons can be drawn from the fact that a spiraling number of people are trying to locate their biological relatives, irrespective of whether they're doing their own legwork, listing themselves in scores of registries on the World Wide Web, handsomely paying professional investigators, or turning to the search underground.

First, it's clear that probing one's history is such an essential need that it can fester for a lifetime if unfulfilled and can drive a person to commit (or commission) illegal acts. With the de facto permission that accompanies adoption's nascent normalization, birth relatives are already seeking each other out in droves, and the phenomenon will spread as openness becomes the standard practice. The extensiveness and success of the search movement also makes it apparent that the institutional construct of secrecy, whether relating to documents or identities, has all but crumbled. All that's left is a façade, a thin statutory wall that prevents a random selection of Americans, because they were born in certain years or live in certain places or don't know about the search underground, from obtaining basic details about themselves that most people take for granted.

Critics are quick to point out that, whatever their problems, Americans aren't entitled to pick which laws we obey and which we don't. Even the people with the most poignant stories—who were brutalized into giving up their babies, who have been denied by the courts at times of medical need, who are elderly and don't believe they'll be around long enough for registries or agencies or even historical currents to produce results for them—have to understand that they must stay within the boundaries of acceptable behavior that every society draws for its citizens. That's what good, moral people have always done. Except when they haven't. "It wasn't a criminal act when Rosa Parks sat at the front of the bus," Musser points out. "It was an act of courage and conscience."

6

Adoptive Parents: Infertility Begets a Family

As Judy and I understood the rules, which were strictly adhered to by all other members of our immediate families, the process after marriage was supposed to work something like this: Through an act of love and passion, we would ignite a new spark of humanity imbued with our finest traits. We would cherish every day of the following nine months, the proud father-to-be monitoring the expanding belly of the expectant mother, who would be reveling in the fulfillment of her enduring dream to feel a baby grow inside of her. Then we would become doting parents who would give our nearly perfect child all the warmth and wisdom that we could muster and that he or she could tolerate.

This is what happened instead: We discovered that we are among the ten percent of American couples who can't produce a viable fetus.[1] Both genders suffer equally from infertility, but women account for a steadily escalating proportion of the problems as they get older because their eggs and uteruses age with them, while most men continue producing new sperm. Only about ten percent can't get pregnant when they're in their twenties, but the number skyrockets to nearly ninety percent by the time they reach their late thirties. That's the vital statistic that explains why career-minded, late-marrying baby boomers began herding into fertility clinics in the 1980s and 1990s, and why many who left empty-handed—

success rates are rising, but they still only hover around twenty-five percent[2]—kept going right into the offices of adoption agencies and lawyers.

My wife and I were right there with the pack. We tried valiantly to provide nature with as much assistance as our inner fortitude and our insurance plan would allow. Fertility drugs, in-vitro fertilization, donor eggs, the whole shebang. The only penetration in our baby-making ritual ultimately entailed my inserting a needle into my wife.

No one who hasn't confronted infertility can fully grasp the raw brutality of being deprived of something so fundamental as the ability to reproduce. Any biologist will tell you we were built to do it. Every culture glorifies it. Whatever power put us here secured its commanding role in life by making it a compelling instinct and an ecstatic experience. So sometimes, though I agree with the principle, it's hard for me to hear another earnest social worker or aggrieved birth parent or disaffected adoptee chant the reformist mantra that "adoption should be all about finding parents for children, not children for parents."

Some of the brightest, most responsible adoption activists, people who try to speak and act with sensitivity toward other triad members, don't add any conciliatory caveats when they express their idealistic goals to groups that include adoptive parents. They don't flinch when they explain that infertile people have to "get over" the notion that they're "entitled" to become the mothers or fathers of babies. They admonish us to remember, if we're intent on becoming parents, that there are lots of special-needs infants and older children in need of homes. And they remind us that there have always been adults who simply had to accept that they would remain childless.

It is as though we are being asked to pay the price for violating a social norm, as though our feelings of shame, embarrassment, or inadequacy aren't penalty enough. We're supposed to swallow our loss, internalize our pain and move on. It all sounds hauntingly, disconcertingly familiar. Some people undoubtedly aren't cut out to be parents and shouldn't reflexively turn to adoption just because they assume adults are meant to have babies, but isn't that the same reason some of our fertile friends try so hard to get pregnant? Unquestionably, more of us should also adopt challenging children—a phase of the revolution that has, in fact, begun—but shouldn't that be an equally responsible option for couples with perfect plumbing who are thinking about enlarging their families?

Disparaging infertile people for following their elemental impulses, while implicitly suggesting denial as a coping mechanism, is neither a compassionate nor effective way to accomplish anything. Until we arrive at the point where everybody's wishes are granted, the most productive course we can take is to try to understand and address the core realities of all of adoption's major players. This imperfect arrangement of ours will improve more quickly, and will normalize its place in society more readily, if people in and out of the triad temper their stereotypes and expectations with empathy.

That may seem self-evident, but so many changes are taking place that they're dizzying even for active participants, and it's hard to think through all the implications of the tumult. Despite the resulting uncertainty, the confluence of all these events has created a heady, hopeful time for birth parents and adoptees. And a hopeful, confusing one for adoptive parents and Americans considering adoption. The old directions might have ignored other people's needs and caused them distress, but at least they were easy to follow: Adopt an unmarried woman's baby, pretend the birth parents cease to exist, and then, blinders firmly in place, plow straight ahead as though the child was born to you.

The trip today is characterized by seemingly ceaseless choices rather than simple instructions, often starting with whether to undergo fertility treatments, which ones and for how long. Then come more bewildering questions: domestic or intercountry adoption, through a lawyer or agency or facilitator or on your own, an infant or older child, a boy of your own race or a girl from another culture, and where's the money going to come from? Before and after resolving those issues, parents-to-be have to reveal personal details in multitudinous forms; interview and be interviewed by birth parents; take classes to adopt from foster care or make provisions to travel abroad; and, finally, agonize over whether they've got the strength or the money to try again after the pregnant woman who selected them realizes, after her baby is born, that she can't part with him.

And those are just the preliminaries. Once your child is firmly ensconced in your home, living in this selfless, inclusive new world of adoption means letters and/or phone calls and/or visits with birth parents, learning about and keeping your daughter in touch with her racial or cultural roots, becoming vigilant about the sensitivity of schools and relatives and friends toward adoption, and wondering every time a behavioral issue comes up for your son whether it's the result of adoption or something innate or something you did, of too much information too soon or too little openness too late.

Yet I've never met adoptive parents who would magically make their most aggravating moments disappear, or would travel back in time to start over with healthy eggs and robust sperm, if it meant not getting the children they have. "In the end, it gives you so much that you forget what you went through," says Georgia Salaverri, a marketing executive in

Massachusetts who with her husband adopted an infant several years ago. "I do believe somebody up there has a plan, and this was all part of it. One thing I want to tell Daniel is that we couldn't have a baby because God wanted us to have Daniel."

Nearly all adoptive parents express some variation on that theme, or at least think it, because we inevitably come to believe we were destined to have the children we do. That adoptive parents bond with their children as securely as any others is itself a reality many Americans, including those first considering adoption, can't quite accept because it's so outside their own experiences. At the same time, because of the don't-ask/don't-tell nature of past practices, most people's firsthand observations of adoptive family life are relatively new and superficial. All of which helps explain some unsettling findings published in 1997 by the Evan B. Donaldson Adoption Institute, drawn from the most comprehensive national survey ever conducted on adoption-related issues.[3]

The poll succinctly showed that birth parents aren't the only triad members who still suffer from negative perceptions, even as opinions about adoption itself are soaring. On the plus side, ninety percent of all respondents viewed the process positively and ninety-five percent agreed it serves a useful purpose. Fully half, however, said adoption "is not quite as good as having one's own child." In addition, about a quarter said it's sometimes harder to love a child who is "not your own flesh and blood," while nearly one third doubted children could love adoptive parents as much as birth parents. What the people who hold those opinions are saying comes down to this: Adoptive families are disadvantaged, not quite whole, unlucky compared to the rest of us.

They couldn't be more wrong, but people with such views have a broad negative impact. If they only express their sentiments through words, they perpetuate harmful stereotypes and bruise the emotions of adopted children, as well as other triad members. But if they formulate or implement policies—the easiest example is within schools, but there are many others—they can foster discriminatory attitudes and practices.

In 1998, Milwaukee Judge Daniel Konkol ruled that a federal employee named Scott Albrecht could not adopt his one-year-old orphaned niece. The girl's mother, Susan, was Scott's sister. On her deathbed, she asked him to become the baby's legal father if both parents died. Scott and Susie had been inseparable throughout their lives; he said yes, of course. As fate would have it, just weeks after Susie succumbed to cancer, a car accident killed her husband, Steve. True to his word, Scott quickly applied to adopt his sister's child under a state law expediting the process for immediate relatives.

The night before the court hearing, however, the toddler's godparents filed a petition contending Scott was not legally a "blood" relative because he and Susie had been adopted from different families (which they'd always known). The judge agreed and awarded custody to the godparents, one of whom was Steve's cousin. The decision was reversed on appeal, and it induced state lawmakers to enact a statute formally giving adoptive and biological families equal rights. But it's extremely unlikely this was the only time this judge ever based a ruling on his view of adoption, and any lawyer who has ever handled adoption cases will testify that our courts are riddled with judges just like him.

Wills are sometimes contested on grounds that adoptive siblings and mothers and uncles aren't true relatives. Golf clubs and other facilities that routinely admit members' children still debate whether their rules apply to adoptees. Some executives of a national philanthropic foundation recently tried, unsuccessfully, to prevent the adult adopted son of a founder from serving on its board, as birth children automatically do.

Fortunately, one major way in which the adoption revolution is remaking America is to undo people's ill-conceived and sometimes bigoted predispositions, while revising some of the nation's laws in the bargain. The changes are aimed at triad members, but their potential impact is far more sweeping because prejudices that hold whole groups to be subordinate inevitably take a toll beyond their intended targets and contribute to a corrosive, generalized sense of social inequality and resentment.

Most distressing to me in the Donaldson survey was a statistic that sounds pretty good at first glance—that seventy percent of Americans consider adoptees to be "first rate," a term that's not explained but presumably refers to their quality as human beings. Twenty percent answered "second rate" and ten percent said they weren't sure, which means at least one in five people who learn that my kids are adopted start out thinking they're somehow inferior, without knowing a single thing about them.

Learning from and for Children

One of the most gratifying, enriching, and frustrating things adoptive parents learn about their children is that we have to treat each one as unique. We have no other choice. We can't look at our sons or daughters and think they're talented or stunning or smart because they inherited some characteristic of ours. So they teach us to be less vain and more appreciative. We can't necessarily anticipate their interests or predispositions or allergies based on hereditary clues. So they teach us to be more attentive and responsive.

To be sure, there are adoptive parents who wish they had progeny who mirrored a part of themselves or who regret they won't get to pass on some family trait to future generations, but those sorts of ruminations needn't reflect on their sentiments about their adopted children. Neither a man who loses his daughter to a childhood disease nor a woman who wonders all her life about the son she once relinquished feels any less love for or devotion to the children they subsequently raise. Anyway, biological offspring don't come with guarantees about what they'll look or be like either, and all parents get the chance to shape the final products with the nurture they give to the nature they got.

Ellen Goodman, a *Boston Globe* columnist whose work is nationally syndicated, provided a sharp perspective on what everyone can learn from adoptive parenting in an eloquent commentary she wrote nearly a decade ago. In it, she told the story of a couple of her friends who had adopted a boy from another country (she didn't say which). She described how this man and woman watched their son, took cues from him, gave him latitude to figure out his own way of doing things, adapted their conduct to accommodate him. Here are a few paragraphs of the conclusions Ellen then drew:

> I have been a parent for over two decades. A biological mother, a child-raising mother, an adult child's mother . . . the works. And it seems to me that my friends started out in the parenting business one step ahead of the rest of us.
>
> Those of us who give our genes as well as our love to our children set out to reproduce ourselves. We deliver unconscious expectations in the birthing room. We think we know them. Because they are "ours." . . .
>
> Only later, sometimes much later, are we forced to get to know our children as they are, to stop assuming and start listening or watching. In adolescence they begin to insist, noisily, sometimes angrily, on their own identities. In their 20s we stop, finally, raising them, and start, finally, listening to them. Or we lose them.
>
> What I have learned from my friends and from their son is that our children may be our own but we can't claim ownership. What I have learned is that sooner—in their case—or later in mine, we must learn

to share children. We share them with the world. But most particularly, we learn to share them with themselves.

When they are adopted, even when it's not part of the game plan, we also share them with their birth parents. That happens because adoptees fantasize, some only occasionally and others frequently, about the mothers and fathers they don't know; consequently, the biological parents influence their children in intangible ways that neither they nor we might ever understand or suspect. But it also happens because adoptive parents bring the spirits of our counterparts into our homes, too.

If we have met them, we think about and discuss who our children look like, whether our children might one day want to meet their first parents, and how to factor those sorts of considerations into the way we raise them. If we've never as much as glimpsed a photograph of their biological parents, we think about and discuss the same things. The birth parents affect our lives and our decisions whether we write them sporadically, see them regularly, or move to another state to hide from them.

"It is incredible, the things our parents do to keep us from finding out. It hurts them and it hurts adoptees, because most of the time you discover the truth anyway, and then you just become resentful and distrustful," says Ron Morgan, a building contractor in San Francisco who was thirty-six when he discovered his mother and father had deceived him all his life. It was early 1991, and both of them had died within three months of each other. Ron, heartbroken, was leafing through his parents' old stationery box when he found a document that electrified his nerve endings: a medical release form from his birth mother. "I know it's a cliché," he says, "but I really felt like the floor opened up and I was falling down an abyss. This lie was so fundamental. It was about my history, my ethnicity. All that I'd internalized was thrown out the window."

Bill Troxler discovered his truth even more obliquely, as the result of teaching one summer at a college in North Carolina. There, during an episode described in Chapter Four, his curiosity about his past was piqued by the portrait of a former president of the college who looked eerily like him. As it turned out, Alfred O. Cannon was no relation, only a ghost who briefly surfaced to shatter a middle-aged man's falsified image of himself.

As hurt and betrayed as he felt after learning he'd been adopted, it took several months for Dr. Troxler to broach the subject with his mother, Lurline. (His father had died years earlier.) She was getting old, and he didn't see any point in causing her unnecessary pain. But once he hit a dead end in his search for Marianne, after the widow of the doctor who arranged his adoption said she had destroyed all her husband's records, he saw no other alternative. So he waited until December 28, 1993, his son's sixteenth birthday and coincidentally his parents' wedding anniversary, summoned his courage, and nervously drove through a snowstorm to his mother's suburban Maryland home.

"I want you to give your grandson a present," Bill told his mother. "It may break your heart, but I want you to give him his history, because I can't." Lurline didn't flinch. Or cry. She only looked resigned and relieved as she talked for three hours straight. She told her son that she and his birth mother had discussed his adoption over lunch six days before taking him from the hospital, that Marianne had said she didn't want to give up her child and was trying to figure out a way to make ends meet so she could keep him.

The next thing Lurline knew, after she took her baby home, she saw Marianne periodically driving or walking down the street in front of the Troxlers' house. Sometimes she stopped and sat and stared, but usually she just kept going. She never knocked, never imposed herself, never said a word. After a few sightings, Lurline called her doctor to ask what she should do, and Marianne never made another appearance. But it's clear from the vividness and intensity with which Lurline described her that Marianne never went away. She will forever remain a part of Lurline's life, and of Bill's, whether he finds her or not.

The knowledge that adoptees have an innate need for connections, or at least for information, can be daunting throughout adoptive parents' lives—but especially at the beginning, when most of us are anxious about bonding with our children and already feel jealous of the affection they might one day feel for their birth parents. My wife and I certainly experienced that. In fact, we chose the nonprofit agency for our first adoption specifically because its policy was to introduce the two sets of parents only after a child's relinquishment was complete. The idea was to protect us from any disappointment in case the biological mother or father changed their minds; after suffering the pain of infertility, and with the failed treatments for it, we wanted any protection we could get.

Today, Judy and I use a single word to describe our thinking about Zack's adoption: Wrong. Our gratitude to the agency we used stretches beyond the stars, because it joined us with a boy whom we love as much, and appreciate even more, than any child we could ever have conceived ourselves. But not a week goes by without our wishing we could have spent considerably more time with his parents, as we did with our daughter's.

Intuitively, it may seem that anyone who gets to know birth parents will forge a mental link between them and their child, thereby undermining any feeling of entitlement to become the new parent. For better and worse, however, there's a lot about adoption that's counterintuitive. Birth mothers aren't generally young teens trying to "get rid" of a problem; adoptees who search for their roots almost never do so out of dissatisfaction with their adoptive families; and adoptive parents who meet the people who blessed them with their children seldom wish afterward that they hadn't had the opportunity.

Our extended experience with Emmy's parents had a powerful effect that many adoptive parents share and appreciate: It solidified our own recognition as her parents far more quickly than otherwise could have occurred. That's because, in both a real and visceral sense, our time together amounted to explicit permission to make this extraordinary little girl our daughter from the only two people who had the right to make that decision. "You're going to make a great mom and dad; she'll have a wonderful life," Emmy's mother told us again and again. It was reassurance she undoubtedly needed as much as we did, and I hope it continues to give her as much strength as it does us.

There's another potent incentive for people to meet and stay in touch with the men and women who allow them to become parents, and it's a principal reason this is becoming the common practice today: It's good for the children. Whatever level of contact the various participants settle upon, it's simply true that the more information adoptive parents receive, the more we can share. That's the case whether we're telling our kids their adoption stories (which they love to hear), describing her birth mother to a daughter who asks why she has blue eyes, or explaining to a teenage son that he has to watch his cholesterol because there's heart disease in his birth father's family.

Judy and I are fortunate to like both our children's parents enormously; they are bright and engaging people who we feel enthusiastic about seeing again. At this writing, our communications are still limited to regularly sending them pictures and letters, but we know much more now about the value of sustained contact than we did when we agreed to that arrangement. So we're trying to establish more-personal connections for ourselves and, we hope, for our children once everyone's ready. At a bare minimum, although we hope regular interaction becomes the norm far sooner, we'll eventually give Emmy and Zack their documents and, if they want, help them locate their birth families.

Our pattern is typical. The more secure adoptive parents grow, the more concretely they internalize the understanding that their children aren't confused about who their "real" parents are: the people who hug them, help them with their homework, tuck them into bed. And the more confident adoptive parents become, the less intimidated they are by the notion that their kids might also be able to love other people, like grandfathers or aunts or birth parents, without it posing a threat to their own relationships.

A quick analogy to highlight the point: Ten years ago, I went on a trip with my older brother to Poland, where we both were born. We visited the town where my parents grew up. We went to the city in which I spent my first three years and found an elderly woman in our old apartment building who regaled us with her recollections about our family. We traveled around for weeks, taking in the culture and the history, the good and the bad. It was a wondrous, emotional pilgrimage into a past I barely remembered, and it gave me a fuller understanding of who I am today. I want to go back again, to stay in touch with that part of myself, to fill in more of my personal blanks. But I don't want to return to Poland to live. The United States, my adoptive country, is my real home.

Normal, but Different

Families that include children with special needs have concerns that involve definable problems and highlight important issues about adoption. In contrast, the amorphous worries of adoptive parents reveal more about the fragility of human nature than about the process itself. Most people with apprehensions about the love and loyalty of their children, for example, either aren't paying enough attention to recognize how powerful the chemistry between them has become or are so insecure that they can't see the potency no matter how hard they look. Or they aren't doing a very good job as parents, in which case they should feel uneasy if they have biological children, too.

Even more dissonant are the attitudes and feelings many adoptive mothers and fathers exhibit toward the people who brought their children to life. In microcosm, people afraid that a birth parent will show up on their doorsteps generally base their paranoia on a made-for-television movie they once avoided or a newspaper story they partially read, at most, and probably on no evidence at all. The ultimate incongruity, of course, is that all this trepidation and stereotyping is aimed squarely at people to whom adoptive parents typically express undying gratitude, for whom they thank God in their prayers, and about whom they talk glowingly to their friends and children. And mean every word of it.

Joyce Maguire Pavao, the psychologist, calls this internal conflict "the paradox of hopes and fears" and attributes it largely to reasonable inse-curities among people who travel an emotionally turbulent road to get their children. But Dr. Pavao identifies another factor as well, one that not only contributes to the onset of anxieties but also is primarily responsible for their persistence even when it seems clear that they are unwarranted.

> Though lots about adoption is changing on the ground, in practice, there are still broad beliefs and attitudes that haven't changed much since the 1950s . . . and they're perpetuated by outdated laws and bad policies. Back then, many of the people who were adopting were told that the birth parents died in car accidents, things like that. And it's so easy to beatify people who aren't there, whether they die or just go away, never to be seen again. Everyone does it all the time with relatives they don't like; once they're gone, we only remember the good stuff and romanticize much of the rest.
>
> Adoptive parents, like all parents, look at their children and think, "This child is perfect. This child is the best thing that ever hap-pened." They want those special qualities to apply to the birth par-ent, too, and it's easy to do if you simply create a reality to validate your scene, rather than dealing with the good and the bad of how things really are. The fear is of the unknown. People can be perfect in our fantasies but not in real life, and the way things used to work al-lowed adoptive parents to indulge in fantasies. Some of them unfor-tunately still do that, and it's not good for anybody.

The people who appear least conflicted about contact are those with a mix of open and closed adoptions. Parents with only open adoptions may wonder during the rough patches whether the benefits are worth the ef-fort, while parents with no communications with birth families see only uncertainties because they're looking primarily through the prism of their own insecurities and stereotypes. Adoptive parents who have experi-enced both ways, even if their relations with the birth parents sometimes are stormy, generally agree that they'd much prefer to open their closed adoptions than close their open ones.

"There's just no doubt about it," says Carol Wierzba, an accountant in Tennessee who reintroduced her daughter Kelly to her birth mother at the age of two. Carol and her husband, Michael, have tried for several years to establish a relationship with the birth mother of their son, Andy, who is ten, but she hasn't been interested. The couple also have a nine-year-old biological daughter, LeeAnn. "To tell the truth, Andy's a bit jealous

and sometimes so is LeeAnn. Kelly has all these people giving her attention . . . like Donna's mother and father. Both Michael's and my parents
died, so Kelly's the only one with grandparents. It's understandable that
the other two wish they had that, too.

"The main thing, though, is that Andy wants to know more and more
about himself and what happened with him, the normal things he'd want
to know, and there's really just one way to give him the information he's
going to want as he gets older," says Carol. "I'm not saying our relationship on Andy's side would turn out as good as it has with Donna, because I think our relationship's unusually good, but it doesn't matter. If
we all get along well or don't, it's just so much easier when you have
something to look at versus facing the unknown, having all those questions you can't answer, you know?"

None of this is to imply that things always work out for the best.
Sometimes, communications between birth and adoptive families can be
undesirable or become untenable. An adoptee may not initially want any
direct links or may develop problems later on, one of the adults may have
a troublesome personality, or an extraneous issue in a participant's life
may undermine the arrangement. The dynamic simply turns out to be
more frustrating than fruitful, and counseling doesn't seem to help.
Circumstances can and do change, however, so even people confronting
these sorts of situations usually find it valuable to at least keep track of
where all the parties are, through an intermediary if necessary, so they
don't jeopardize their ability to reconnect if they ever choose to.

And then there are situations in which the adoptive parents have little
choice about their connections. At one end of the spectrum, the identities
of biological mothers (and occasionally fathers) are almost always known
in the foster-care system, and the judges who approve public adoptions
generally decide whether and how often the birth parents will see their
children, under what conditions, and whether the visits will be super-
vised. Conversely, it can be exceedingly difficult to determine, much less
communicate with, the biological kin of children adopted from orphanages abroad.

The gulfs between adoptive and birth parents can be vast and vastly
unfair, from their economic disparities—biological mothers, at least in the
stage of life at which they make adoption plans, typically are much less financially and socially secure than the people seeking children—to their
positions at opposite ends of the relinquishment-acquisition process.
That's a stark reality that can make interactions awkward, strained, or
even contentious, at least at the beginning. But there are also some paral-

lels between them that are striking, and recognizing them can be an effective way to build bridges.

The most profound is that distress usually is the reason their paths intersect and deprivation becomes their lifelong companion. This isn't an upbeat sort of similarity that adoptive and birth parents can idly chat about, but it is a shared sensibility that can provide a basis for empathy and understanding. It's also not to say that birth parents, particularly those who were coerced or mistreated, shouldn't feel bereaved or angry. But why at the adoptive parents, whose only crime is to want children? Likewise, it's common for adoptive parents to feel uncertain about attachment, at least at first—but nothing's accomplished by translating that anxiety into fear or mistrust of birth parents.

Sadly, many Americans assume that birth mothers (most people don't factor the fathers into their thinking) simply forget the babies they nurtured inside their bodies, and that adoptive parents can't conceivably feel as much for children who don't share their genetic configurations. That triad members are among those who believe such nonsense is extraordinary. It's an unmistakable measure of how pervasive and entrenched social dogmas become when they're accepted even by people who should know better. And that prevalence, in turn, explains why the normalization of adoption can't be achieved solely though institutional changes; the nation as a whole must participate in the transformation.

Laws preventing adoptees from seeing their own records have to be repealed, laws regulating the role of money have to be written, and laws forcing people to do emotional calisthenics to accomplish an adoption, or live with one, have to be revamped. Governments have always helped to shape public attitudes and behaviors by defining what's legally and socially permissible. Just as they've shown little reluctance to address the overarching problems in foster care, legislators should correct the major flaws impeding quicker progress for adoption and its participants.

Society's central mistake in the past, which led to nearly all the faulty statutes and misguided behaviors we still live with, was to try to force adoption into the same mold as "normal" (defined as biological, same-race, heterosexual) family formation. That required one secret to be stacked onto another, until the truth was nearly buried. No one should regret its reemergence. Today, it's becoming increasingly unnecessary to hide nontraditional family relationships. It's also getting very hard to pretend that there's just one way to be normal, though parents of virtually all types do share at least one common denominator: All of them are responsible for, consumed with, and frequently controlled by their children's needs and desires, their educations, their health, and their safety.

When we got home with Zack, my mother off-handedly offered one of her typically sharp aphorisms: "Okay, now you can worry for the rest of your life." Bull's-eye for all parents. And for those of us with adopted children, onto the normal anxieties of life we add an overlay of specialized concerns, just as people who are divorced or hold two jobs or share their homes with frail relatives have to deal with their distinct issues. They're not better or worse, just more complicated sometimes, and different. It would be easy to exaggerate the differences since families of every construction spend most of their waking hours proceeding through similar, unremarkable routines. Still, there's no escaping that adoptive parents' lives encompass activities that other people would not consider normal for themselves, including some that other Americans wouldn't abide unless they had no other choice or found themselves under criminal investigation.

First, the very decision to have children is an intensely personal one for most adults, and anybody who suggested a screening process to determine who should be permitted to become parents would be vilified for treading on sacred ground. The earth on which triad members walk has never been so hallowed. Outsiders regularly make decisions that shape our lives, and another of the many ironies of adoption is that doctors, social workers, and file clerks know details about us—such as the names on an adoptee's original birth certificate—that we are regularly forbidden to learn about each other. People considering adopting, in particular, discover that they have to all but abandon their privacy if they want to have children to tuck in at night.

If we're having trouble conceiving, the most explicit aspects of our sexual functions and relationships are revealed to medical personnel and their secretaries. People who adopt through an agency or the public-care system provide all that data, along with a few years' worth of income tax returns and a long list of other personal information, on a slew of application documents and during discussions with social workers. Prospective parents who adopt from abroad or publicly give the government copious accountings of their lives, along with their fingerprints, to comply with federal regulations.

Whatever process is utilized, even if all the arrangements are made directly with the birth parents, all fifty states mandate that would-be adoptive parents undergo home studies before, and sometimes after, a child is placed.[4] Essentially, a social worker attempts to determine whether we'll provide a loving and safe atmosphere by asking questions about such subjects as how often we engage in sexual intercourse, whether we ever argue, and how we plan to raise our children; the cost of these examinations, usually paid directly by the applicants, ranges from several hundred to several thousand dollars depending on the agency and the locality. In all states, the parental wannabes also pay for state and federal law enforcement agencies to conduct criminal background checks.

No wonder many adoptive parents feel stressed out, protective, and paranoid by the time they get their children. Devote that much energy to anything, not to mention all the money usually involved, and you're going to cling to it like a prized possession. There aren't many better indicators of how powerful the parental drive can be than the fact that millions of Americans each year subject themselves to infertility treatments and hundreds of thousands trudge through the adoptive process, despite the discomforts, emotional strains, expenses, and legal and bureaucratic mazes they typically have to go through.

The headaches and hardships are thrust into unmistakable perspective literally within seconds of glimpsing your child, however, and they fade like a morning fog as soon as you hold him. To the extent that we remember the turbulent moments at all, they become the morning sickness, pregnancy backaches, and labor pains of adoption. We transform into parents, plain and simple, with all the soaring joys and crashing disappointments the word entails, trying to do right for our kids and making lots of mistakes along the way.

Fueling Stereotypes

On May 24, 1998, Connie Chung presented a report on the ABC News program *20/20* that drove adoption reformers wild. It was about sealed records, searches, and reunions, and it was "balanced" in the way journalistic presentations often are, especially on television; that is, the host showed the issue's two sides by questioning participants on-camera about their conflicting points of view. Ms. Chung began by saying that a growing number of adoptees believe it's their right to meet their birth mothers, but that some of the women "desperately want to maintain their privacy." A group of adoptees is then shown chanting, "No more secrets," followed by Ms. Chung's description of the controversy:

These adoptees are demanding that their adoption records, which remain sealed by law, be opened so they can learn the identities of their birth parents. For them, it is a right worth fighting for. Pulling at the other end of this emotional tug of war are birth mothers who desperately want those records to stay sealed. When birth children want to find their birth parents, is it a matter of civil rights?

The first voice to answer is that of a birth mother identified only as Cindy. She says: "Not any more than yelling 'fire' in a theater is a matter of free speech." The television program found Cindy's daughter, whom she hadn't seen since shortly after her birth twenty years earlier, and put her on the air next. The young woman, named Riki, said she'd long felt a "burning desire" to find her biological mother, primarily so she could learn her origins and understand why she'd been placed for adoption.

The reason was that Cindy had been raped, couldn't go through with an abortion, but couldn't bring herself to keep the baby either. "She looked like my rapist," Cindy explained. Still, she never stopped thinking that one day she'd like to see her child again and, once her psychic wounds had healed, even establish a relationship with her. Soon after her child turned eighteen, Cindy notified the adoption agency she'd used that she was willing to be contacted; it turned out that Riki had registered, too. The two women took things slow, exchanging photographs and letters as a prelude to a reunion.

After an upbeat beginning, however, Riki mentioned an interest in meeting her biological father. Cindy became afraid that Riki would find the man and, innocently, give him information that could lead him to his onetime victim. She halted all contact with her daughter and retreated into anonymity—until Connie Chung asked her to tell her story. Riki, for her part, expressed regret that she'd ever said a word about her father, because it drove away a woman she still longs to meet. "I feel bad that I had the curiosity," she said.

On the show's next segment, Ms. Chung told the tale of Lisa Franklin, an adoptee who hired a professional searcher to find her birth mother, Patricia Austin, in Florida. Their eventual reunion led to an unprecedented lawsuit in late 1998 in which Patricia alleges that the investigator invaded her privacy and tormented her emotionally to induce her to contact Lisa. Details of this drama appear in Chapter Five. Ms. Chung concluded her own account of the case with this brief commentary:

Birth mothers are handicapped by an obvious paradox. How do you fight for your privacy if you have to go public to do it? What some have discovered is that hiding in the shadows isn't enough. By fighting back in court and speaking out in the media, their birth children are finally getting the message and letting go of their dreams of a happy reunion.

Though the *20/20* report dealt directly with only adoptees and birth parents, I'm injecting it into the discussion of adoptive parents because so many of them base their views of fellow triad members on skewed accounts like this. One of the women in these stories was raped and the other claims to have been harassed. They hold strong opinions as a result and raise the important issue of how to deal with birth mothers who covet their anonymity, but they are demonstrably unrepresentative of the vast majority of their peers.

When a highly respected, nationally televised news program insinuates that they are typical, it might make for a sexy feature, but it's also grossly misleading, it breeds fear within adoptive parents, and it promotes inaccurate stereotypes in the minds of millions of Americans. Not to mention that Ms. Chung didn't disclose that she is an adoptive parent, which some viewers might have factored into their understanding of her presentation.

Nearly all examinations of adoption, by the media or in research, have an impact on adoptive parents for another reason. While we may be prime beneficiaries of the process, we also deal most overtly and extensively with its day-to-day issues, at least until our children are grown. This isn't a contest. Everyone in the triad has weight to carry, but adoptive parents have to cope not only with their own tribulations but also with their daughters' identity crises and their sons' family-tree projects, with the hurtful comments that people unthinkingly make to their children, and, increasingly, with scheduling calls or meetings with their children's birth parents and siblings.

This isn't to suggest that the press should report only good news to make adoptive parents' jobs easier. On the contrary, adoption's controversies should be media magnets, because they're laden with emotion and provide insights into both broad social matters and into a segment of the U.S. population that was shrouded in secrecy for so long that journalists essentially ignored it. Extensive coverage of the issues in Oregon's open-records referendum, for instance, undoubtedly contributed to the historic initiative's passage by presenting the information that voters used to make up their minds.

Media coverage also helped to instigate an important change on the national level several years ago by pointing out a way in which adoptees and their parents had overtly been discriminated against: Until the mid–1990s, most children who suffered from psychological or physical problems at the time of their adoptions weren't automatically covered by their new parents' health insurance. If these firms had enforced a waiting period for people's biological offspring to screen for "pre-existing conditions," the outrage in our nation would have been so intense that no one could have ignored it. Yet it took federal legislation, sponsored by Senators Edward M. Kennedy of Massachusetts and Nancy Kassebaum of Kansas after the problem was reported in television and newspaper stories, to force insurers to systematically extend coverage to adoptees.[5]

Press accounts about a 25-year-old adoptee's plight may also help bring about a much-needed revision in U.S. citizenship regulations. John Gaul, who was adopted from Thailand when he was four, was convicted as a teenager of car theft and credit card fraud. A 1996 Immigration and Naturalization Act amendment required deportation for any non-citizen found guilty of a felony, so John was sent back "home" in early 1999, though he didn't speak the language and knew no one there. Congress had intended the law to apply to illegal immigrants, but its authors hadn't considered that it could also affect foreign-born adoptees—whose parents are supposed to apply for citizenship for them, something U.S. citizens with biological children born abroad aren't required to do.

As of this writing, a handful of additional adoptees had also been deported under circumstances similar to John's. He was living in a facility provided by Holt International and wanted to come home even if it meant being imprisoned. His parents, who can be faulted for having waited too long to apply for their son's citizenship (as can the INS, which lost his paperwork while he was on trial) were fighting vigorously for his return. And Senator Don Nickles of Oklahoma and Representative Lamar Smith of Oregon had submitted legislation that would confer U.S. citizenship automatically and retroactively, to birth, for all adoptees born in other countries.

This case certainly isn't typical of the types of travails adoptive parents experience. But disparities in such basic areas as citizenship, health insurance, and legal treatment clearly demonstrate how high the walls can get for families built through adoption—and, consequently, how different life can be for the millions of Americans who strive not to be confined by them.

A Cautionary Tale

There's no way to know what percentage of the people who adopt from overseas do so with the fantasy of starting out with a blank slate. There are no comprehensive studies on the subject, and practitioners don't always probe for the reasons their clients make the choices they do. But it's safe to say, based on my scores of conversations with adoptive families, social workers, researchers, and adoption professionals around the country, that a sizable majority of Americans who travel this route are motivated at least partly—and sometimes entirely—by the desire to lock out biological parents.

Much to their own surprise, it's these same people who frequently come to wish the most that they could make contact. That's chiefly because a universal truth of parenting eventually dawns on them: that the decisions we make "for ourselves" invariably turn out to be decisions we've made for our children. It's an axiom with special relevance to adoptive relationships and with particularly acute impact on families in which the adults and the children come from obviously different races or cultures.

When they're very young or perhaps not until they're teenagers, these adoptees are going to start firing off impertinent questions. They were always the children who could not be lied to about being born to their adoptive parents, but the generic response to them for generations was hardly responsive either: "You're my child and you're an American. That's all you need to know." Today, partly as a result of adoption's new openness and partly because of a steady relaxation in the parent-child dynamic in the United States since the late 1960s, few adoptees are likely to settle for such evasions.

Thankfully, the number of adoptive parents who fool their children, or try to shut them up, is shrinking for the same reasons. A looser social climate, abetted by behavioral research, has led to a generalized understanding that children grow up healthier if their intellectual and emotional needs are honestly addressed. At the same time, unrelenting scientific strides are imposing the realization that people without hereditary roadmaps will benefit from fewer advances and, in relative terms, will receive inferior medical care.

So sooner or later, because their minds snap into gear or because life would be easier if they knew whether their son's birth father also had hyperactive tendencies—and what treatments worked for him—adoptive parents without much information yearn for more. Many think or even say things out loud like this advice I recently overheard the adoptive father of two Latin American children giving to a woman who was considering an adoption from Guatemala: "If some sort of relationship with a birth parent is the price for keeping my daughter healthier and making my job easier, it would be cheap. I'm sorry nobody impressed that on me when I was adopting, but I want you to know it."

One of the most serious criticisms parents level against the people who arranged their adoptions, especially in retrospect, is that they didn't provide enough guidance about difficult issues beforehand or enough support afterward. They complain that any cautions their practitioners might have been offered were drowned out by pep talks about the positive aspects of adoption and by upbeat assurances that a child would soon be coming.

Prospective parents share the responsibility for the difficulties and surprises they encounter, however. Many people do more homework before they buy a car than before they adopt a child. By the time most of them decide to go this route, they have become so fixated on reaching their goal that they can't see or don't want to see the red flags their agencies or attorneys have posted along the way. Moreover, those people who turn over much of their savings in order to adopt too often delude themselves into believing they should be getting not only a flawless service, but a faultless product as well.

It's yet another example of the ubiquitously detrimental effect of money on adoption. Biological parents pray for perfect babies but love whatever they get; it's unhealthy for adoptive parents, nearly all of whom would have been thrilled to accept whatever children resulted from pregnancy, to conclude that they suddenly deserve perfection because they've plunked down their hard-earned dollars.

The level of competence among the practitioners they hire also will always be erratic, because that's the way it is in almost any industry and because of an unintended consequence of adoption coming out of the shadows: Entrepreneurs who don't necessarily know or care about families suddenly see the opportunity to cash in on a new business—especially on the Internet, where startup costs are low—in which people are anxious to hand over tens of thousands of dollars at a time, and results need never be assured.

This is an area begging for regulation, but it's also the place where prospective adopters can appropriately play their role as consumers, the purchasers of services and not goods. People blinded by their passion to become parents are too readily drawn by promises, even guarantees, of healthy babies within specified time limits. Whether the practitioners are fly-by-night profiteers or have been operating for decades, their clients shouldn't check their ethics and judgment at the door; they have to wonder about and demand answers to important questions. What's going on behind the scenes that makes a woman's placement of her child a sure thing? Or: How can anyone ensure that a baby won't develop mental or physical problems, even if she appears problem-free at birth?

The people who arrange adoptions strive for precisely the same goal as the medical personnel who try to cure infertility. They are our doctors, and we have every right to expect them to behave professionally, ethically, and compassionately. Too many lawyers, agencies, and facilitators have not an inkling that this is their true vocation, however, so they believe it's enough to offer sufficient information to get everyone through the process, provide efficient legal and logistical aid to keep things running smoothly, and consider their jobs done once the children arrive in their new homes.

Nearly every adoptive family would benefit from post-placement counseling and periodic advice, but that's something it takes most people years to grasp. For at least a while, it's consuming enough to revel in tiny smiles and reconfigure busy schedules, so new parents generally conclude it's just as well if their adoption providers stay away. For a variety of reasons—from persistent insecurity to a seemingly instinctive reluctance by adults to admit they need help raising their children—even as time rolls on, adoptive parents typically remain the least likely triad members to seek help for themselves.

The general exception to this overall scenario is adoption from public care, for which most states require would-be parents to take training courses and for which post-placement counseling, and usually money for treatment, are available for a specified period. Those are critical pieces of assistance because most of the children involved have varying degrees of special needs. But they're also essential because the people who utilize the system on average have lower incomes than those who adopt privately, whether domestically or abroad, which is one reason many of them travel the public route.[6]

Even in the public system, though, the aid usually stops within a predetermined number of months or years, depending on the state and the circumstances, while developmental and pathological problems can last indefinitely. And that translates into a potentially explosive downside to the exodus of children from foster care.

The politicians who instigated this segment of the adoption revolution got the first step right, placing children in permanent homes more quickly. But they didn't account for the long-term medical and psychological help that hundreds of thousands of new parents will now require to deal with the special needs of their sons and daughters. Unless and until governments take step two, offering sustained financial aid and counseling to the families they prodded into being, the adoptive parents will have to fend for themselves. Some will pull it off and some won't, but it's hardly a formula for optimal success.

America created its foster-care system, which is discussed in detail in Chapter Eight, during the early part of the nineteenth century in order to get children out of institutions. Now Americans are doing that again, by the tens of thousands every year. The vast majority of the adoptions that have taken place from overseas for half a century have been from orphanages and comparable group-care facilities, and there have always been difficulties as a result: Children given so little attention that they came to their new families with attachment disorders, children treated so poorly that they arrived with physical or emotional impairments, children whose medical needs were so routinely ignored that they suffered irreparable damage from treatable infirmities.

In the past, however, the principal "sending" countries—South Korea, Colombia, and a handful of others—seemed genuinely concerned about the conditions of and for their orphans. Moreover, the number of children involved was relatively low until the mid–1990s, so only a very small percentage of adoptive parents faced obstacles that were large or long-term. The experience with China has been similar, though it's not clear whether its orphaned girls are generally healthy because they receive good care or because those who are sickly aren't made available for adoption abroad.

Eastern Europe is another story altogether. Decades of poverty, alcohol abuse, pervasive smoking, pollution, and pathetic medical care converged to produce unhealthy residents of all ages. And, for some unfathomable combination of cultural, political, and economic reasons, the communist regimes there created institutions for homeless children that were (and some still are) abominations. Most were grossly understaffed, and some of the people they did employ were incompetent or sadistic. The orphanages run by caring professionals often received too little funding to do more than an adequate job, and those run by bureaucrats with no training or concern about their jobs oversaw shoddy and perverse practices.

It's no wonder that white Americans began adopting in droves from the former Soviet bloc. They could simultaneously rescue a young person from purgatory while adding rapture to their own lives. The perfect adoption, achieved at the intersection of giving and getting. For the majority of people who chose this path, things have indeed worked out very well, if sometimes imperfectly. Their children exhibit relatively few or only mild effects from institutionalization, and they're making solid progress in loving homes with good medical care. Others are working through tougher issues, but with minimal complaints since they were prepared for the task beforehand by their social workers and agency employees; they adore their children and are satisfied with their decisions.

But there are also thousands of parents whose lives have been turned inside out, many of whom maintain they not only weren't sufficiently informed, but were deceived and abandoned by their practitioners. "I haven't heard from my agency since I stepped off the plane and brought Juliana home," says Lois Hannon, a former real estate agent who became a full-time mother when she and her husband, Wallace, adopted their daughter from an orphanage in Romania in 1991.

The Hannons' agency had cautioned that their child could have "issues" ranging from stunted growth and developmental delays to an aversion to being touched. Still, they were assured that good nutrition, medicine, and lots of love would overcome most of the problems and would make the rest manageable. Lois explicitly told her agency that she was willing to tackle challenges like these but, after undergoing treatment for a cancer that rendered her infertile, she didn't feel emotionally ready to cope with severe disabilities. "Don't worry," she was told. "You'll get what you're looking for."

Thousands of would-be parents were descending on Romania at the time. The country's longtime dictator had been deposed, and bedlam reigned. People were bribing officials, paying birth parents directly, rescuing vagabonds from the streets. Some cut their own deals and others brought lawyers, but most contracted with adoption agencies because they had no desire to enter the fray themselves.

Lois and Wallace had considered adopting domestically, but they thought the process was too cumbersome, lengthy, and expensive. They also had been told that they probably would get an older child, and they had hoped for an infant. When they saw the madness in Romania, broadcast live on their living room television set, they decided this was the right opportunity for them to become parents—but only with the aid of the professionals they hired to guide them and help them feel confident about the outcome.

On July 2, the Hannons received a phone call from their agency advising them to go to Romania within days. Their daughter was waiting. They had wanted an infant, but asked for a three-year-old, figuring that most serious health questions would manifest themselves by that age and could be evaluated by the doctor their agency had promised would be on the scene. The Hannons' child-in-waiting was described as a dark-haired "baby doll" who suffered from developmental delays and lived with her indigent mother.

Wallace couldn't leave work on such short notice, so Lois went alone. In Bucharest, she met up with a group of other Americans for whom her agency was arranging adoptions, and they all drove to Fagaras, a town so poor and disheveled that it looked like it had been bombed. They arrived at their boarding house at 2 A.M. on July 8. Late that afternoon, a local lawyer hired by Lois's agency brought a tiny girl into her room. She was a dwarf with mental impairments, along with such blatant developmental disorders that it was clear she'd suffered prolonged deprivation of sensory stimuli. She'd lived in an institution, not her mother's home.

"I didn't feel I could handle this girl," says Lois, who was so dazed by what had just happened that it took several hours of soul-searching before she could mutter "no" to the lawyer. "I felt betrayed and confused. I wondered, 'Is this my one chance for a child? Am I just being selfish and heartless?'" The pressure was all the more intense because all of the other people who came with Lois seemed to have gotten children without a hitch.

She didn't find any consolation during the next stop on her journey. Rather, she encountered a scene that could have been lifted from a Federico Fellini movie or, perhaps more aptly, from a chilling tale set in some scary-sounding place like Transylvania. Which happens to be the region of Romania in which Fagaras is located.

The adoption agency didn't send any of its American employees on the trip, but its on-site facilitator told her distraught client not to worry. "There are other children," she said, and there were. That night, Lois was taken to an office shared by three attorneys. There, she watched a surreal horror show. Local people dressed in rags shuttled emaciated children in and out, some asking outright for payments and others pleading for someone to give their child a decent home. One adoptive father-to-be was grumbling that the daughter he'd gotten was too dark, apparently the child of a gypsy; he traded her for a lighter-skinned girl. The three lawyers paraded children in front of Lois, inviting her to choose the one she liked best. "The whole thing was too bizarre," she says. "I couldn't do it."

Neither did she want to go home alone. So the next day, one of the lawyers drove Lois to a nearby orphanage. There, sitting on a bench, her eyes met Iuliana's (whose name she later Americanized). The girl was three-and-a-half, weighed less than twenty pounds and couldn't speak. Faint reddish lines streaked her cheeks where she had clawed herself. She fondled blades of grass as though they were the first she'd ever touched. But her eyes blazed with a brilliance that captivated Lois. She was shown other children, but all she could see was this one girl's image. Neither the lawyer who escorted her nor the personnel at the orphanage spoke English, so Lois couldn't get any specific information, but she felt sure that nurture and medicine would bring the child around.

The next day, Lois returned to Bucharest and called her husband. They decided to proceed and, after three weeks of bureaucratic shuffling, Lois flew home to Atlanta with her daughter. The proud new father met them at the airport, video camera rolling. He couldn't stop smiling. Then both parents showed remarkable patience, probably abetted by a dose of denial. They knew it took time for an institutionalized child to catch up, so they gave her toys, took her to doctors, showered her with affection, waited and waited.

More than a year later, a psychologist in a special school program jostled the couple into facing reality. She called to report that Juliana wasn't getting any better. "I cried and cried. I just stared at the phone and wondered what to do," Lois says today, after eight years of caring for a daughter who still doesn't speak and has multiple other problems, a form of autism specialists attribute mainly to early sensory deprivation. "I didn't trust my agency. They were the ones who deceived us in the first place, and they'd never shown any interest in us since. I felt no one was there to give us any help."

So she decided to help herself. After crisscrossing the country in search of medical assistance, and conducting voluminous research, Lois discovered that few doctors learn to identify or treat problems linked to institutionalization. She also found many other parents like her who had no idea where to turn for guidance. In 1993, Lois and Thais Tepper, a mother in Pennsylvania who had a similarly nightmarish experience in Romania, formed the Parent Network for the Post-Institutionalized Child. The two thousand–member group presses for reforms, sponsors seminars, and provides forums for families with Eastern European adoptees to provide support and exchange information.

The relationship between the Parent Network and international adoption agencies is, to say the least, strained. It is yet another example of how people who should be on the same side—trying to better the process, nail the profiteers, and improve education and post-placement programs—instead are at loggerheads.

Ethical agencies are right to say that many adoptive parents are so resolute about getting children that they don't hear the advice they get, pay little attention to warning signs along the way, and don't avail themselves of the help they're offered. And they're right to point out that prospective adopters get far better preparation today than they did during the tumultuous period following the Iron Curtain's fall. Even well-intentioned professionals can be so self-assured or defensive, however, that they can't seem to get beyond the critical messengers to hear their vital message: that practitioners, especially of adoptions from problematic places, have to become more adamant about providing information beforehand and more forthcoming with resources afterward.

"In spite of it all, I am very pro-adoption. We've got a beautiful daughter, and I can't imagine life without her," says Lois, whose process wound up costing about $18,000 (not including tens of thousands of dollars in subsequent care for Juliana). "But the money's so blinding, there's almost no regulation to speak of, and too many people are getting into the business who shouldn't be there. . . . Adoptive parents pay so much, and the stakes for the children are so high. They have every right to expect the best services available, and that they won't be forgotten the second they take their children home."

PART THREE

Tough Challenges in a Promising Future

7

Special Needs,
Diverse Families

They are every society's disgrace, the scarlet letters that proclaim our leaders' inability to transcend their political differences even for the most noble cause, the flesh-and-blood evidence of people's capacity to be selfish and closed-minded. So many of the earth's children languish in "transitional" facilities that most countries don't or can't keep track of how many they have. We do know that more than a half million are citizens of the wealthiest nation in history during the most prosperous period it has ever experienced.

Most of the boys and girls living in America's foster-care system were removed from parents who severely mistreated them, neglected them, or abused alcohol and drugs so intensively themselves that they could barely function. The majority eventually will return to their mothers after rehabilitation, will be taken in by relatives, or will remain under state supervision until they turn eighteen and, with dubious prospects for success, venture out on their own. But more than 117,000 of them—teenagers who have bounced into and out of innumerable foster homes, infants with emotional or physical disabilities, babies born to prostitutes and people with HIV, and children of all ages who are black, Hispanic, of mixed race, or possess other "special needs"—are available for adoption.[1]

White, middle-class, married couples are not flocking to get them. Judy and I certainly didn't turn to the public system after we accepted the finality of our infertility. And we were so set on having a baby, an instinct

157

for which no prospective parent should ever have to apologize, that we'd probably head in the same direction again if we somehow found ourselves transported back in time, into the same circumstances and with the same information. But maybe not if we were starting over today, because two things have changed dramatically since we first decided on how to form our family.

The first is personal and evolutionary: We have come to understand how purely adults meld with whatever children they get, as evidenced by a black mother who devotes herself to her son with Down's syndrome or a white adoptive couple who embrace a new culture for the sake of their Asian daughter. The second change is institutional and revolutionary: States have begun to overhaul their regulations so that they are less onerous and exclusionary for would-be parents and, most important, so that children don't remain entrenched for nearly as long before they become eligible for adoption.[2]

Few people outside the foster-care world even consider the enormity of this shift in concept and practice, though its ripple effects are already being felt in additional political and cultural arenas. Not to mention that it is reshaping the lives of children in public custody, as well as their caretakers and all the academics, social workers, and other professionals who design and implement U.S. social-welfare programs.

Foster care's reformation means single people are adopting at an unprecedented rate, as are those with disabilities who couldn't have dreamed of becoming parents before. It also means escalating numbers of overtly gay and lesbian adults are adopting for the first time in history, increasingly as same-sex couples. No one keeps statistics on the personal traits of those who utilize the public system, but researchers and practitioners agree the surge in public adoptions is partly attributable to the participation of "nontraditional" parents.

"We no longer take a two-year-old and say, 'We're going to torture him for a few years while we figure out a way to get him back to his biological family or until we can find him parents who are somebody's stereotype of appropriate,'" explains Barbara Holton, director of adoption services for Tressler Lutheran Services in Baltimore. "Most of our adopters are still straight and married, and that's how I'm sure it will stay, but we know all kinds of people make good parents."

Racial and ethnic minorities account for more than sixty percent of the children in "out-of-home care" (encompassing foster homes and group facilities for those with the most challenging problems), and forty-six percent of these boys and girls are black. But African Americans make up only fifteen percent of the U.S. population. So the jump in public adoptions points to another significant social transformation: White men and women, married and single, are forming transracial families at an unparalleled pace.

As always, hard figures are scarce, but here's a glimpse of what's happening: Of the 31,000-plus public adoptions monitored by the Department of Health and Human Services in 1998, nearly one third crossed racial or cultural lines; that's five times the ratio of just a few years earlier, and there's no letup in sight. In fact, laws and financial incentives initiated in the mid–1990s to promote adoption from foster care—combined with private campaigns by organizations like the Dave Thomas Foundation for Adoption, Steven Spielberg's Children's Action Network, and the North American Council for Adoptable Children—virtually ensure that the numbers will continue to climb.

Superimpose the hundreds of thousands of intercountry adoptions, about sixty percent of which involve children whose skin isn't white, and a clear trend comes into focus. "We're fast approaching a time when unconventional families, whether because they're transracial or headed by a gay or single parent, not only aren't unusual but are a normal part of the landscape," says Peter Gibbs, executive director of the Center for Adoption Research and Policy at the University of Massachusetts Medical School. "Adoption obviously benefits from all this diversity but . . . in ways people haven't fully understood or even realized yet, it's also fueling the changes."

Just a decade ago, the odds against a woman like Carol Goldsmith becoming a mother would have been prohibitively high. She certainly couldn't have done it by giving birth; in 1984, when she was twenty-eight, an operation left her incapable of achieving a pregnancy. Adoption would have been nearly as impossible. Until recent years, most judges and adoption practitioners believed it was irresponsible to place children with unmarried people such as Carol, and not many would have imagined making a parent out of someone with limitations as pronounced as hers. She suffers from an acute case of Ehlers-Danlos syndrome, a genetic defect in her bones' connective tissue that makes it painful for her to perform even simple tasks like lifting a bag of groceries, or a child.

"It was a little scary at first, even thinking about doing this," she admits. "How could I not wonder sometimes how I would manage everything that raising children entails. But I knew that it would be easier because I'm not a baby person, and they're really the ones who need more chasing around and picking up and all that sort of thing. Once I decided I wanted an older child anyway, I knew for sure that I could do it, and fortunately the people at the agency believed that, too."

Thanks to a combination of loosely related factors—including legal and logistical assistance stemming from the Americans with Disabilities Act, increasingly positive public perceptions of people with physical impairments, and the major revisions being made to the nation's foster-care system—today Carol is bringing up two daughters, by all accounts very happily and very well. "They can come sit in my lap without my having to put them there," she says. But she's not the main beneficiary of all the legislative, procedural, and attitudinal improvements that brought them together. Her children are.

Mesha, a biracial eighteen-year-old whose story appears in Chapter Four, exhibited an array of behavioral problems during her seven years in six foster homes before Carol adopted her in 1995. Now she's a high school junior considering a law-enforcement career, inspired by the police who saved her from a life in which she and her brother were locked in a basement while their mother turned tricks. Belinda, a black girl who was eight when she entered Carol's family in 1998, passed through five temporary homes after she and her twin brother, at the age of three months, became the eighth and ninth children their mother voluntarily ceded to state custody. Though her aggression and anger still surface sometimes, Belinda's attention deficit and hyperactivity disorder is getting under control, and she's learning to show affection and to trust adults again.

There aren't nearly enough adults willing to do the hard work that children like these require. The bitter truth is that they are our equivalent of institutionalized children from overseas and, to varying degrees, most have incurred the same kind of harm anyone would if subjected to abuse while deprived of intimacy and stability. They are classified as having "special needs" not only because their complexions are dark or because they are no longer infants, but because they have truly special needs: About 60 percent cope with serious issues like asthma, HIV exposure, and developmental delays, while many others are at risk of eventual illness because of prenatal exposure to drugs or alcohol.

The picture looks bleak, but the children's prospects needn't be. Because, like their counterparts abroad, most aren't so far gone that they can't improve if given sufficient attention and care. Nearly every study of boys and girls who spent their early years in foreign orphanages shows the great majority rebound impressively after they're adopted,[3] and their conditions were generally far worse than those of children in foster care. Yet middle- and upper-income Americans eagerly spend large sums of money to adopt from other countries rather than seek sons or daughters from the United States for next to nothing.

Ignorance (not in a pejorative sense) and racism (a word without any neutral connotations) undoubtedly are among the reasons why. Another is the much-publicized research showing that children's early development is particularly important in shaping who they'll be forever. Some would-be adopters conclude it's too late to do any good for foster children. They're wrong, but until very recently, they had no way of knowing it because no one was educating them. Here, again, decades of secrecy inflicted the most harm on the youngest members, or potential members, of the adoption triad.

Only recently have state agencies and advocacy groups begun adequately using the media to tell their success stories or to explain the recuperative effects of stability and care. That's not to imply there aren't children so challenging that only the most saintly among us would think of tackling their behavioral and physical problems (though, thankfully, there are many such inspirational foster and adoptive parents). Moreover, no matter what we do as a society or individually, some children will stay in the system and others will return to it because they're so hard to handle. Even acknowledging those realities, it's still true that most of what Americans know about foster care, like most of what they know about adoption in general, is misguided or wrong because it derives solely from the sensational accounts that sporadically make their way into the headlines.

The professionals determining these children's fates inadvertently helped to create this status quo. For decades, within their own insular world, they tried earnestly and valiantly to achieve their vision of perfection in two principal ways: with relentless efforts to rehabilitate biological parents so they could get their offspring back someday and, failing that, by attempting to match children with same-race adoptive couples.

To say the very least, the picture is changing. In the most fundamental paradigm shift in modern child-care history, the federal and state governments during the 1990s began revising the nation's social-work and judicial objective from single-minded "family preservation" to "best interests of the child" through permanence. It's such an obvious goal that it almost sounds silly, but generations of Americans lost sight of it while addressing other pressing social concerns or pursuing more materialistic desires. Most specialists still believe children's interests are indeed best served by restoring their original families, which is what happens in most cases, but they're also becoming more amenable to quicker adoptions, and they're becoming less insistent on accepting only new parents who share a child's skin color.

The vast majority of the children in public care are adopted by their foster parents.[4] But some are still moved from one temporary setting to another, sometimes for years, by social workers and supervisors who think it's best to wait indefinitely for the biological mothers to get back on their feet or for another black couple to be recruited as adoptive parents. And there are still wide swaths of the country in which limits are placed on what kinds of adults may provide families for the children who need them most.

Florida is the only state to ban gays and lesbians from adopting in any form (New Hampshire revoked its prohibition last year), and Utah last year became the first state to legally mandate that only heterosexual, married couples can adopt children out of its custody, but five additional states—Arizona, Indiana, Michigan, Oklahoma, and Texas—are considering similar legislation. Arkansas, meanwhile, recently decreed that only straight, married couples can become foster parents, but magistrates and social workers all over the country take it upon themselves to apply that same standard every day.

For all the caveats and complaints, the water level in this glass has long since passed the halfway mark and it's continuing to rise. Americans excluded from parenthood in one jurisdiction can adopt with increasing ease in another and, especially since the advent of the Internet, they are doing so with mounting frequency. So the people hurt by all these prejudicial restrictions ultimately aren't the adults at whom they are aimed, but the children in the affected states who will continue to deteriorate in supposedly temporary situations because not enough of the "right" sorts of parents are available.

What's more, here's a news flash: There have always been homosexual parents, biological and adoptive. And their ranks have been growing steadily as our laws, popular culture, and common attitudes have gradually opened up to their coming out. Between 300,000 and 500,000 were thought to be mothers and fathers in 1976, the overwhelming majority probably married and hiding their sexual orientation. Twenty years later, guesstimates of the number of lesbian mothers varied from one million to five million, and of gay fathers from one million to three million.[5] In 1990, the only year for which I could find even vague statistics, it was believed that between six million and fourteen million children were growing up in households headed by homosexuals.[6]

Nearly everyone who works in the fields of reproduction, child care, and adoption agrees the rate of gay and lesbian parenting is climbing exponentially. Men inseminate female friends or paid surrogates, while women deliver babies produced with donations from male friends or withdrawals from sperm banks. Both genders, meanwhile, are adopting in record numbers, frequently by pretending they are heterosexuals getting children individually. Uncountable thousands of lesbians—gay men, too, but a far smaller number since single males as a rule are still widely viewed with caution when they try to adopt alone—employ such ploys every day to take in children from countries like Korea and China, which allow unmarried applicants but not homosexuals, as well as from Florida, Utah, and every other jurisdiction regardless of its legal restrictions.

Child-placement professionals everywhere are also taking matters into their own hands, both by knowingly ignoring factors that would preclude some applicants from adopting in their states and by discreetly suggesting ways to circumvent regulations. Some agencies, for example, imply to homosexuals that they should state only that they're unmarried and should put way their partners' belongings during home studies, while individual social workers in particularly restrictive locales might coach people with disabilities on how to word their answers to minimize concerns back at the home office.

The agency that helped "Jim Larson" adopt his son didn't suggest that the white, 35-year-old Pennsylvania psychologist should disguise his homosexuality, but it didn't insist on full disclosure in his paperwork either. Instead, a case worker told Jim that he should restrict his search to the few states with relatively liberal public-adoption policies; back in the summer of 1994, they were Idaho, Oregon, and Washington. Like most people who think about starting families, Jim had always wanted to compose a child from his own chromosomes, a baby. When he explored his options, though, he learned that surrogacy was laden with difficult ethical issues, offered no guarantees for success and could be very expensive—usually between $15,000 and $25,000—while the chances of adopting an infant at the time were infinitesimal for any single man, much less a gay one.

"So I looked inside myself and decided that, by training and disposition, I could probably handle an older kid with some level of difficulties, and I figured that's the kind of child it would be easiest for me to get. It was a practical judgment," Jim says. A growing number of Americans are adopting from foster care as their first choice, but most heterosexuals who turn to the public system do so for pragmatic reasons, too. The married men and women who still constitute a majority of adoptive parents, as well as the unwed couples and individuals who form a larger and larger percentage of the total, typically discover that infertility treatments and private adoptions cost more than they can afford; both straight and gay singles can usually adopt special-needs children, but they find out that the youngest and healthiest are still invariably reserved for married couples.

It's a tacit, mutual manipulation that serves everyone's ultimate interests: The nontraditional parental aspirants know the waiting lines for some children are extremely short, while the practitioners know these unmarried, gay, and disabled applicants are seldom in any position to negotiate. That intersection of decidedly unfair circumstances has contributed not so much to the overall rise in public adoptions as to a slower, but by all accounts consistent and appreciable, increase in placements of boys and girls for whom it has historically been the hardest to find permanent homes.

Older black children are benefiting most because, as a group, their defining characteristics have always been considered the least desirable by Americans looking to adopt. Every serious examination of the issue reaches the same conclusions: Parents' first priority usually is to get the youngest children they can find, so infants' race rarely counts against them, and it's barely a consideration through preschool age; the older they get after that, however, the more of a factor their surface color becomes.

The most extensive research ever conducted, by Richard Barth of the University of California, Berkeley, found that thirty-three percent of the black children but only eleven percent of the white ones were still in his state's public system six years after going into foster care. Among the four thousand cases he tracked, the white children were also five times as likely to be adopted, partly because there were disproportionately more white adults seeking to adopt and transracial placements were discouraged.[7]

A smaller but equally telling study, in New York State in 1998, showed that the children there who spent the longest time in the system waited nearly twelve years for homes, essentially their entire childhoods. These children were predominantly black and male, and they suffered from the greatest disabilities.[8] Other research, as well as social workers' experience, reinforces the role of gender and race: Black boys who stay in foster care until about eight, and black girls who stay past ten, are unlikely to ever be adopted.

From the time he was ten days old, when he was removed from his parents' apartment to protect him from further physical and sexual abuse, no one wanted to keep "Eddie." Some of his relatives tried periodically, but he was too loud and aggressive. The authorities in Oregon tried returning him to his mentally impaired mother in between foster homes, but those efforts stopped when police seized the four-year-old boy after he had watched his father beat and handcuff his mother while holding her hostage. Eddie was an emotional and behavioral tornado by the time he was nine, when he was told that both his parents had voluntarily relinquished all rights to him. Then he really freaked out.

He was living in a residential facility in Portland, his tenth home during a brief life in which the only constant had been rejection. Everyone assumed he'd be there until he turned eighteen. Then Jim Larson, while looking through three states' books of children's pictures in his agency's office in Pennsylvania, decided there was something about this boy's face that appealed to him. And the sketchy biography accompanying the photo, in addition to laying out Eddie's grim past, said he possessed at least average intelligence and displayed some limited social skills. In Jim's mind, that meant he was trainable.

After filing his request for custody with Oregon and completing three months of parenting classes taught by his own agency—nearly every state requires such training for people who want to adopt from foster care—Jim flew to Seattle on February 10, Eddie's tenth birthday. He planned to spend ten days with the boy to assess his needs, see whether they clicked, and "find out his reaction when I told him I dated men." Jim had never intended to hide his sexuality; he just didn't want a faceless bureaucrat or judge to disqualify him without acknowledging the real reason why. "I wanted to be evaluated for who I am and what I can do. Then when I said, 'I'm gay,' which I always told the individual people I was dealing with, at least I'd know exactly what the issue was."

When he walked into Eddie's room, the boy was pacing along a window sill, bristling like a reptile preparing to crawl out of his skin. Jim barely recognized him. The lanky, chiseled features that had been so striking in his photograph were gone, softened by water weight from the four drugs he took every day to control his anger and sedate him. After a little small talk to try to calm Eddie, who had been told only that his visitor wanted a tour of the group home, Jim decided to take a straightforward approach. "I'm considering adopting you and I'm here to figure out if it's a good match for both of us," he said. Eddie couldn't stop pacing, wouldn't make eye contact. He looked apprehensive, uncertain, confused. He shrugged his shoulders and mumbled, "Okay."

For the next few days, the two were inseparable. They ate burgers, talked about basketball, and took in the sights of the city. Then Jim knew it wouldn't be fair to wait any longer. If his homosexuality was going to doom this relationship, he didn't want to raise the boy's expectations and cause him more pain by letting their bond develop any further. So on day three, while they were chatting in his hotel room, Jim dropped the bomb: "I'm gay. Do you know what that means?" Eddie said he didn't. "I date men instead of women. I don't date children," Jim replied, emphasizing the last clause.

People who oppose gay parenting often believe homosexuals are deviants upon whom "normal" society should bestow none of its benefits—or that lesbian mothers, and gay fathers in particular, will steer their children in their own sexual direction and may even engage in carnal acts with them. Never mind the research and empirical evidence that gender preference isn't imposed or taught (nearly every homosexual in history was raised by heterosexual parents) or the fact that ninety percent of all incidents of sexual abuse reported in America, against boys and girls, are committed by straight men.[9]

Fortunately for countless thousands of foster children, homosexuals are shattering the nasty stereotypes about themselves. Consequently, Jim got the chance to make his case to Eddie, who didn't say a word or lift an eyebrow when the kindest man he'd ever met made a baffling statement about not being physically attracted to women.

Eddie had grown accustomed to not understanding everything people told him, and he'd long since learned not to believe anything adults said anyway, but his curiosity got the better of him as he and Jim were walking into the hotel's parking lot a few minutes later. "What do you mean you date boys?" he asked. Jim stopped in his tracks, looked at the boy in the eyes and repeated, "Not boys. Not ever. Men. Grown-up, adult men. Do you understand?" This time, Eddie was pretty sure he did. When Jim arrived to pick him up the next day, the boy was waiting with an announcement of his own. "I've made my decision," he told his father-to-be. "I want to come and live with you."

Indians + Mormons = Controversy

It's a revealing insight, as well as a damning social commentary, that the parents of children in public care were frequently raised in foster homes themselves. It's a destructive cycle that's linked inextricably to the core reason so many adults wind up unable to raise their offspring in the first place: poverty. Compared to the rest of the U.S. population, fewer of the people who emerge from the system continue with school, work at well-paying jobs, or receive enough medical attention to enhance their chances of becoming productive members of society. Simply put, they're less likely to be physically and mentally healthy, and more susceptible to the lure of drugs, alcohol, and crime.

In a perverse way, Eddie might have ultimately benefited from his mother's growing up in such a precarious environment. If she had received better mental-health care, or if the bureaucrats who arranged her placements hadn't lost track of her records, they might have been able to get information about her family's background. She knows she's Native American, and she looks like she's nearly full-blooded—as does Eddie, though his birth father is Caucasian—but they're both officially classified as unaffiliated because there's no way to determine their tribal roots. And that made it far easier for the boy to be adopted, because Indians operate under different rules than other U.S. residents.

As semi-autonomous nations, tribes exercise considerable sovereignty over their own affairs and those of their members; since 1978, when the Indian Child Welfare Act became law, their jurisdiction has included foster care and adoption. Essentially, in recognition of their historically communal decision-making, the legislation recognized that tribal courts share responsibility with parents for determining when children should be removed and who should get custody. Its unambiguous intent was to keep Indians in touch with their specific tribes, and with their heritage in general, throughout their lives.

The act has been controversial from day one. Its detractors note that Native Americans suffer from the highest rates of poverty, alcoholism, suicide, unemployment, and certain health problems of any ethnic group in this country,[10] so a disproportionate percentage of their children need new homes. They argue that the law complicates this task and drives away prospective parents by giving priority to Indian applicants. While critics want to revise the act, however, most oppose its repeal—an effort being led by the National Council for Adoption, which maintains that tribal courts use their power with the unconstitutional effect of discriminating against white parents.

Some Indian leaders agree their child-placement regulations need streamlining. Nevertheless, efforts to win congressional support for even minor changes have fallen short for two principal reasons: First, after a long history of trampling on Indians' rights, legislators are appropriately wary of doing anything that might continue that pattern. But the advocates of revamping the act have also failed because they've tried to present the elephant's tail as if it were a description of the whole animal; that is, they've tried to manipulate lawmakers on Capitol Hill by providing them with only partial information.

While non-Indians who want to adopt Native American infants do indeed have to jump through extra hoops, for instance, the fact is there's no dearth of applicants willing to do so. (There isn't a long line for older Indian children, any more than there is for any other older minorities.) Furthermore, showing disrespect for ancient traditions isn't a great way to win friends unless you can show seriously negative repercussions, and there's no evidence of tribal officials intentionally abusing their authority by keeping children in harmful conditions or preventing them from being moved to safer ones.

Most important, the critics gloss over the reason the Indian Child Welfare Act came into being: Before 1978, at least one quarter of all Native American children were being taken from their families, and nine out of ten were placed in non-Indian homes as well as boarding schools or institutions that immersed them in Christian religions.[11] Proponents of keeping black children with parents of their own race may worry about retaining their heritage, but the African-American population is growing and so is its influence on our nation's culture. The percentage of Indians who are full-blooded, on the other hand, fell from about sixty in 1980 to thirty-four in 1999 and is expected to drop to less than half of one percent by 2080.[12] And, while their prospects and image may be improving, only a verbal contortionist could argue that an ancient civilization should entrust its survival to thriving casinos and popular movies like *Dances With Wolves*. This isn't to suggest that Native American children should remain with their own people regardless of the circumstances. Any society that knowingly leaves its young in perilous situations, for any reason, is unconscionably derelict. This law may indeed need to be amended. But its central objective—to maintain connections to Indian heritage—is more than just a reasonable attempt to fight extinction or to offset the damaging negative depictions Indian children regularly encounter. It's also a basic tenet being embraced by a majority of researchers and practitioners, as well as an exponentially multiplying number of adoptive families whose members come from different races, cultures and countries.

If all this is so, then why is a vocal minority trying to scrap the Indian Child Welfare Act? It's a much weightier question than it may seem because the answer, in ways that range from obvious to Byzantine, affects the entire institution of adoption in America. To understand how, it's essential to know that the principal opponents of this law are the same people who have fought in courts and state legislatures for decades to keep adoptees from getting their birth certificates, make it harder for biological relatives to find each other, and prevent other major changes in traditional adoption practices. That's no secret. The National Council for Adoption (NCFA) and its supporters ardently disapprove of virtually every aspect of open adoption, and they're entitled to their views.

Their methods are another matter altogether. From their contention that open records lead to more abortions, which is statistically false but remains a powerful emotional ploy nevertheless; to their recruitment of anonymous birth mothers to imply that most such women oppose being found, even though every major study shows otherwise; to their dissemination of only pessimistic information about Indian adoptions, they have consistently fought (and frequently won) their battles by utilizing faulty data and distorted arguments.

Perhaps they are simply true believers who see their cause as so momentous that it justifies the use of dubious means; zealous triad groups have certainly played their own dirty tricks. But the gamesmanship on the pro-openness side, while unproductive, can be fairly described as internal bickering, maneuvering to gain priority for one faction's position over another's, and it hasn't been used to deceive judges, politicians, or the public.

It would be difficult to overstate the effects of the deception. Lawmakers in both parties agree that sleight-of-hand lobbying by Dr. Pierce and his allies has blocked approval for nearly a decade of a voluntary national reunion registry. By tying up the cases in court, they also stalled implementation of open-records laws in Oregon and Tennessee for years, and they have bottled up similar efforts in legislative committees all over the nation. Win or lose, their strategy works: It not only causes delays, but clouds the issues, stalls their adversaries' momentum, and deprives them of favorable publicity.

One effective way in which NCFA has promoted its agenda is by compiling a very official-looking *Adoption Factbook*, the third edition of which came out last year. Some professionals joke that it should be called the "fiction book" because it not only contains some questionable information, but most of it is devoted to essays by people whose views coincide with the Council's rather than to data of any kind. But journalists, students, and other Americans assume it's an unbiased presentation of reality, so its contents become "the truth" through wide dissemination.

"The plain fact is that as long as the Indian Child Welfare Act remains law, there will be those who wish to install racial and ethnic apartheid in America who will want their own versions. Black Child Welfare Acts, La Raza Child Welfare Acts and other versions will logically follow as America's child welfare system becomes increasingly balkanized," Dr. Pierce writes, hyperbolically, in a section listing "barriers" to adoption in the 21st century. Among the others are "the fact that more unmarried women are deciding to try and parent their babies" and "the fact . . . that the stigma of nonmarital childrearing and dependency on public assistance continues to be reduced."

It doesn't take a specialist in subliminal communication to understand the message underlying these observations, and it helps put NCFA's activities in perspective: The idea is to do everything possible to increase the number of adoptions. Not to help pregnant women make informed decisions about what's best for them. Not to induce practitioners to adhere to high ethical standards. Not to ensure that only those children who need new homes get them, while helping those parents who can and want to keep their offspring.

There's no way to determine whether this more-is-better philosophy stems from political, ideological, or financial considerations. But one clear effect has been to bolster the adoption business, the primary function of which is to service its clients, people who neither know nor care about any behind-the-scenes machinations. They just want to start families. And it will be easier to provide them with the infants they prefer if the laws governing Indian adoptions are relaxed and more single women relinquish their babies.

All these seemingly disconnected dots form a pattern, but its shape is hard to discern because it's obscured by secrecy. Not relating to adoption but to the Council itself, the membership and funding for which has come primarily from adoption agencies affiliated with the Church of Jesus Christ of Latter-Day Saints, the Mormons.[13] Their participation seems to explain a great deal, including why NCFA continues to promote practices that most of the adoption community is abandoning.

For example, Mormons consider it an integral part of their faith to expand their numbers, both by having large families and through conversion. In fact, their church has become one of the fastest-growing in the world through evangelism. What is virtually unknown outside their community is that Mormons also view adoption as a means of achieving growth. In Utah, where seventy percent of the population is Mormon, adoption rates are among the highest in the nation,[14] and researchers believe more Indian infants are adopted there than in any other state. That's attributable partly to the fact that most Native Americans live in the West, but it's also because the Latter-Day Saints are the only religious group with an adoption service devoted solely to placing Indian children.

A few more essential pieces of background: The Book of Mormon states that adoptees should consider their biological roots to be the same as those of their adoptive families. The Mormons have a special affinity toward Jews because they accept the biblical notion that they are God's chosen people. And the church teaches that Native Americans migrated from lands in which they mingled with Jews, so Jewish blood therefore courses through them; some believe Indians belong to a lost tribe of Israel.[15]

These elements come together into a cogent, if circuitous, explanation for the vehemence with which NCFA (the Oz everyone sees while the church stays behind a curtain) argues for easing the Indian Child Welfare Act's strict custody requirements: If adoption is a positive way to spread Mormonism, then who better to bring into the fold than some of the Lord's anointed favorites? The church's admonition about adoptees assuming their new families' ancestries follows a similarly logical path; that is, if a religion believes it offers its adherents the singular roadmap for spiritual fulfillment, what better way to assure that converts don't stray than to cut off the routes to their past?

The Latter-Day Saints' operations are worthy of examination in their own right. Law enforcement agencies and former members have accused the church and its members of all sorts of misbehavior, including child abuse and coercing pregnant women to give up their babies for adoption.[16] Moreover, it seems reasonable to understand why, for instance, Mormon leaders in Utah would want to devote their resources to opposing the release of adoptees' birth certificates in Tennessee, or why they would want to alter an ancient people's traditions and maybe even undermine their long-term survival.

Maybe the answer is identical to the one Dr. Pierce offers when explaining NCFA's pursuit of exactly the same causes: that it is guided only by a principled desire to topple the walls of prejudice and to maintain practices that protect everyone's privacy. Or maybe the answer is that the people exhorting the doctrines of secrecy and more-is-better want to keep the adoption business going strong. Or hope to further the agenda of a religious group with a vested interest in the outcome. Child-care officials, policy makers, and politicians should learn the motives of everyone who tries to shape their thinking.

A Panoply of Parents

Children like Eddie with fathers like Jim are part of an even faster-progressing sociological reconstruction than the advent of openly gay parents, the renovation of foster care, or the growth of transracial and transcultural families. During the three years that ended in 1998, the number of single fathers in America shot up by twenty-five percent.[17] In all, the percentage of families headed by married couples has declined in the last thirty years from eighty-five to under seventy. During that time, the number of single male parents rose from one in ten to one in six, and more than one third have never worn a wedding ring. Among current single mothers, a majority have never been married.

Each of those converging trends is taking place for an array of reasons, ranging from a soaring incidence of divorce to plummeting marriage rates,[18] from an escalating occurrence of racial intermarriage[19] to a steady decline in the percentage of the U.S. population that is white,[20] from specific legal protections for various categories of minorities to increased tolerance for, if not embrace of, many diverse lifestyles. The United States is metamorphosing into a very different place in the 21st century and we, as a society, revel in discussions of the complex causes and effects of the transformation.

But sociologists, historians, and politicians seldom mention adoption as a way in which America is changing, much less as a significant contributor to the changes. Yet there are schools from Virginia to California that are revising their teaching about family composition because there is one Asian boy in an otherwise white class, and he has two mothers. There are health-care providers around the nation who are screening all their patients more carefully because they finally figured out that adoptive parents' medical histories offer no insights into their children's genetic proclivities. And there's barely a community anywhere that hasn't confronted ethical, legal, or vocational issues stemming from adoptions by residents who are single, cohabitating but unmarried, gay, or disabled.

Many aspects of daily life obviously are affected by the revised processes and precedents resulting from adoption's emergence. It's too early to grasp some of the repercussions (children who learn that "there are all sorts of families" presumably won't grow up with the same views about divorce, single motherhood, and multiculturalism as their parents have), but others are already unmistakably clear. Adoption isn't the reason homosexuals are less covert about their identities, for example, but it is a primary method by which many are starting families and are working themselves into the social mainstream. Likewise for an array of disabled, infertile, single and middle-aged people.

Contributing to and accelerating the ability of nearly every type of adult to become a parent is no small or insignificant feat. Their empowerment will alter attitudes, reshape institutions, and cause controversies, all of which has already begun to occur. These outcomes are all the more striking because they're diametrically different than the ones the architects of our public system had in mind in 1909, when President Theodore Roosevelt invited two hundred experts to a White House Conference on the Care of Dependent Children. They agreed that orphanages and group homes harmed children and, as a result, decided national policy should be to keep families intact whenever possible. Within twenty years, forty states had enacted Mothers' Pensions to assist the most affected parents at the time, generally poor widows and women abandoned by their men.

Those programs evolved into the modern welfare program, Aid to Families with Dependent Children, in 1935. And as poverty and drug abuse proliferated, so did the number and types of beneficiaries, fundamentally changing both the system and the public's perception of it. What did not change was the categorical objective of keeping children with their parents, even as crack and alcohol abuse became facts of daily life.

This leads to a critical way in which the two types of adoption within this country differ. In the private process, children are typically relinquished voluntarily, while those in public custody were nearly all abandoned or removed from abusive and neglectful homes. So it is revealing that even some of the most badly treated children remain interested in their backgrounds, while many others want to see or know about their parents even if they shudder at the thought of moving back with them. And the mothers, almost regardless of their circumstances, want to see their children, too.

In this sense, at least, private adoptions are just catching up to their public counterparts: Because foster children have always been older, the intense connections between them and their parents may have been legally broken, but they haven't been denied. It's a lesson Americans who adopt from other countries are also increasingly taking to heart—not surprisingly since their lives most closely parallel those of parents who adopt from foster care, whose families also are often transracial and/or multicultural.

Nearly gone are the days when couples like Garnet and Michael Chappell brought children of color to white communities like Dimondale, Michigan, and essentially behaved as though they'd just come home from the maternity ward. "That's what we were instructed to do, and there seemed a certain logic to it at the time. After all, they were going to be Americans," says Michael, whose three-year-old son arrived from Korea in 1972 and whose next three children, two biological sisters and a brother aged two to seven, came together from the same nation in 1978. "But if we knew then what we know now, we'd be aggressive about keeping our kids in touch with all of the parts of who they are."

Today the people who adopt internationally attend cultural festivals with their children and send them to "culture camps" so they can immerse themselves in their heritage and befriend other children who share their backgrounds. Moreover, the adoptive parents who can get in touch with the biological mothers invariably do so or, when their children get old enough to express a desire for information or contact, help them search.

Many come to regret that they can't. But children who come from orphanages were usually left at the doorstep without any identifying documents, and many of the institutions do a terrible job of maintaining whatever records they do receive. Even when they have little to go on, however, a growing number of foreign-born adoptees—often supported by their American parents—are returning home to fill in their blanks, as well as to look for their relatives. By all accounts, more and more of them are succeeding.

In August 1996, after a lifetime of insisting she wasn't interested in any aspect of searching, Crystal Chappell flew with her two siblings to meet their birth mother. "Hyun Joo! Joo Mee! Jong Suk!" a voice yelled out as Crystal, Brooke, and C.J. walked off their flight in Seoul. Hyun Joo, whose story begins in Chapter Three, fell into her mother's arms and the two of them cried together. "Don't worry, it's okay," the younger woman whispered, summoning a few of the words she'd learned in her native tongue.

The days that followed brought introductions, to the three young people's grandmother, stepfather, uncles, and aunts. And they brought answers, most pointedly to why they had been relinquished for adoption: Their father was struck down by a train and their mother, grief-stricken after three years of struggling through poor-paying jobs during a national recession, decided her children would get their best chance of decent lives in America. Only after they were gone did the emotional locomotive hit her.

For years afterward, whenever she saw children, she wept. She would have committed suicide had friends not persuaded her to stay alive in case her son and daughters wanted to see her again one day. Now here they were, sobbing as she told her story. Their very presence, knowing they turned out as well as she dreamed they would, helped her finally come to peace with her decision. And making contact with their mother gave them a sense of resolution. "I understood I could have both my American family and my Korean family," says Hyun Joo. "I was able to complete the circle of my life."

Two years later, her birth mother came to visit Michigan for a week. The Chappells were nervous, but they'd gradually become accustomed to Crystal's ties to her Korean roots, and she was as loving and devoted as ever. The only time Garnet had felt a twinge was when her daughter first told her she'd located her mother. "That was a zinger; I wanted to say, 'I haven't been lost,'" Garnet recalls, laughing at the memory.

When her birth mother arrived at the Chappell home, two flags were flying outside: one of the United States and the other South Korean. The two mothers cooked together, laughed together, and traded stories as best as they could. "I liked seeing the similarities between her and our children, and I like her," says American Mother, as she was called for the week. "Crystal especially looks like her." Asked after the experience whether she had any regrets about it, Garnet sighed: "Only that it didn't happen sooner."

The genie has escaped its bottle without a reentry route. Like the internal reformation of adoption itself, the cultural and demographic reconfiguration of the American family has already achieved unstoppable momentum. It is an eventuality that our society will have to adjust for, conform to, and accommodate, for better or worse.

Lots of people clearly think it's the latter. In addition to the states that make it hard or impossible for homosexuals to adopt, individual courts in Colorado and Wisconsin have denied adoptions for straight couples because they weren't married—effectively penalized the offenders for their infertility rather than their matrimonial decisions—while judges in several states have refused to give custody of children to their parents, biological and adoptive, for no reason other than the adults' sexual orientations.

"While the evidence shows the mother loves the child and has provided her with good care, it also shows she has chosen to expose the child continuously to a lifestyle that is neither legal in this state, nor moral in the eyes of its citizens," Justice Champ Lyons wrote for the Alabama Supreme Court in 1998, explaining why it unanimously decided to remove an eight-year-old girl from her home and send her to live with a grandparent. The mother's transgression wasn't that she was a lesbian, but that she didn't hide it.

Several years earlier, a Florida circuit judge used a similar rationale to transfer custody of a twelve-year-old girl from her lesbian mother, who reportedly had been a good parent, to her remarried father, an alcoholic who had been imprisoned for killing his first wife. The message here is downright scary on lots of counts, from what it reveals about the twisted thinking that homophobia can spawn to what it might mean for the daughter's upbringing to what it indicates about our judicial system. One can only hope that the ruling would have been overturned by a higher court, but we'll never know since the mother died of a heart attack in early 1997, while her appeal was pending.

The targets of prejudice are never its only casualties. As the United States has learned from its civil rights travails, and as other nations from China to South Africa have discovered during their internal struggles, whole societies suffer the consequences of institutionalized fear and distrust. And there are always unintended victims. Innocent American boys and girls aren't dying during hate-driven violence, as they have in the Middle East and Northern Ireland, but the lives of thousands have been shattered because many people in authority in this country have chosen to relegate children to a corrosive system rather than allowing them to be raised by the "wrong" kind of parents.

The Multiethnic Placement Act of 1994, along with amendments passed in 1996, were supposed to help by making it illegal to prevent transracial adoptions. These laws were somewhat effective, but it wasn't until President Clinton launched two subsequent initiatives—Adoption 2002 in 1996, the goal of which was to double the number of adoptions for special-needs children, and the Adoption and Safe Families Act of 1997, which provided financial incentives for states to increase public adoptions—that the rocket took off. Even with all those measures in place and despite the improvements that have occurred, though, the foster system remains maddeningly bureaucratic, capricious, and discriminatory because of the intransigence of some states and individuals.

And so, while many Americans who look abroad for their children could find equally appealing prospects back home, it's also true that many people decide it's worth the trouble and expense of adopting overseas because the experience here can range from inconvenient to exasperating. At least one study even indicates a majority of adults who adopted transracially from other nations had initially wanted to do so from foster care, but found the process too vexing or were told they weren't suitable applicants.[21]

People now increasingly choose intercountry adoption for an array of reasons, from seeking children of a specific color (Asian girls and white European boys are particularly popular) to embracing a new culture and finessing issues of marital status or sexual orientation. Whatever the totals, it's clear that social-service personnel who worry about parents getting foreign-born children, when there are so many already living here who need permanent homes, have sometimes hurt their own cause.

"I absolutely wanted a waiting child, but I was rejected in both Virginia and Maryland because I was single," recalls Kathryn Creedy, who lives just outside Washington, D.C., near the border of the two states in which she tried to adopt. "I thought about D.C., too, but things were in so much disarray there that I couldn't get the same answer twice about what to do, so I decided not to hitch my star to that chaos."

At the time, in 1990, Kathryn also knew that unmarried women who signed up for private domestic adoptions could wait for years, with no certainty that they would ever get a child. So she did some homework, learned that Guatemala's civil war was creating large numbers of orphans who were available with relatively little red tape, and paid a local agency to handle the arrangements. Until, one day, she asked why some-one who applied after her had gotten a child first, a question the case worker clearly didn't like and refused to address. That kind of non-re-sponse, whether meant to calm an anxious client or to convey a more ominous message—like, you might lose your place in line if you don't keep quiet—induces most prospective parents to do as they're told.

Fortuitously, as Kathryn was pondering whether to switch agencies, another international crisis eclipsed Latin America in the news and beck-oned her to take a less conventional journey to motherhood. It was early 1991, Romania's dictatorship had just collapsed, and Kathryn joined the multitudes searching for children there. By the time she arrived on March 7, orphanages had closed their doors to individuals, so she hired a local adoption facilitator to drive her from village to village. "It was very strange," she says. At each stop, they asked an elder if he knew of a child who needed parents. Six weeks of maybes and heartaches later, Kathryn gave up and made plans to fly home alone.

The day before she was scheduled to go, however, she received a call from a Canadian woman who had flown to Romania with her. "I've got-ten a child, and my facilitator has another girl, in a place called Pitesti," she said. The facilitator arranged for Kathryn to go to the industrial city, northwest of the capital, a week later. The girl's mother was waiting in a tiny house that someone chose for their meeting. Through the facilitator, Maria explained that she and her three older children worked tortuously long days on a communal farm, and she wanted better for her baby. After two weeks, during which paperwork was processed and Kathryn met regularly with Maria, the American woman headed home with thirteen-month-old Alexis.

Kathryn's experience finding her second daughter, three years later, was far less adventurous. A friend who had adopted a child from Bolivia recommended the facilitator she'd used in the South American country. Through him, Kathryn adopted a five-month-old girl, whose mother she met during a twelve-day stay. The two women remain in touch, and Kathryn has made it clear to Brooks—who only recently began to express interest in her biological relatives or her Indian heritage, after years of be-ing exposed to family photographs, books, and cultural events—that she's welcome to develop her own relationship with her birth mother, or other relatives, if and when she wants to do so.

Kathryn has been equally diligent about keeping her older daughter connected to her roots, including with visits to a biological cousin who was adopted by a couple in British Columbia. Alexis has developed a solid sense of herself as a Romanian-American as a result, and she talks enthusiastically about visiting her native land one day. She's not yet sure if she wants to look for her family members, who haven't responded to Kathryn's periodic letters. But the photos Kathryn took of Alexis's birth mother occupy two central pages of their daughter's "life book."

Every November, during National Adoption Month, Kathryn's children are asked to bring their life books to school as part of a lesson on various kinds of families. Fellow students flock around to look at the pictures, listen to the stories, and, sometimes, express a little envy. "It used to be, especially in school, that kids hid their adoptions so they wouldn't get teased or be different. . . . And, not very long ago at all, when people saw me with my girls, who are dark-skinned and don't look like me, they assumed I was their nanny or something," says Kathryn. "Now they assume they're my kids, my adopted kids who never have to lie about who they are. Pretty good progress, don't you think?"

Before the 1990s, single mothers and fathers accounted for fewer than five percent of all adoptions. Today, the rate is at least fifteen percent nationwide and as high as twenty-five percent in some communities.[22] That's a breathtakingly rapid ascent that is obviously changing the face of adoption, particularly since the vast majority of the parents involved are unmarried women, but it also is contributing mightily to the national explosion in both the number of single-parent households and interracial families.

Color and Conscience

Though the Multiethnic Placement Act amendments of 1996 prohibit anyone from delaying or denying foster care or adoption based on either the child's or the prospective parent's race, color, or national origin, it's hard to fault people who take those factors into account if everything else is equal. In a nation still divided by race and battling racism, it's also hard to argue against the notion that minority children may be better prepared for real life if they're raised by parents who truly understand the challenges they'll face.

Both the federal statute and nearly half the states' laws bow to that reality, as well as to the bonds children develop with their relatives, by giving priority to "kinship care." In fact, nearly a quarter of the children in the system are placed with their grandparents, aunts, or uncles, and the ratio is even higher among African Americans, who have a long tradition of child rearing and informal adoption in extended families.

Moreover, the 1996 law that bans the consideration of race tacitly acknowledges its significance by mandating that any state receiving federal assistance for its child-welfare programs must make "diligent efforts" to recruit foster and adoptive parents who reflect the "ethnic and racial diversity" of the children in their communities. That means public outreach programs are being created, while organizations such as One Church, One Child and the Institute for Black Parenting (both of which are particularly effective) have initiated their own campaigns to find more black and Hispanic adoptive parents.

There aren't nearly enough of these efforts, however. Furthermore, all the states retain policies that undermine the positive actions they take. For instance, regardless of the income levels of those involved, kinship caregivers often get smaller payments than unrelated foster parents, while most foster parents receive higher subsidies than those who adopt special-needs children.[23] So the states press for permanency and genetic preferences with one hand, while with the other they provide incentives that attach a higher value to strangers than to relatives and to foster care over adoption.

Whatever the remaining problems, at least they're being frontally addressed, albeit not just because policy makers woke up one day and decided to improve children's lives. Instead, a variety of pragmatic factors sparked this portion of the revolution, including lawsuits alleging mistreatment of foster children and discrimination against adults who wanted to adopt them, tenacious lobbying by groups like the North American Council for Adoptable Children (one of the longtime greats in the field) and the Dave Thomas Foundation for Adoption, and the belated official realization that the system not only didn't accomplish its ostensible mission but also was sapping America's resources.

Until the passage of the Adoption and Safe Families Act, which awards millions of dollars annually to states that increase their special-needs adoptions, Washington offered no incentives to encourage permanency. It provided only money to care for children already in the system; consequently, as their numbers mushroomed, federal contributions to state treasuries skyrocketed.[24] So financial considerations undoubtedly contributed to the push for reform, and it's probably no coincidence that the states began doing the right thing during a time of economic prosperity— and once cash was attached.

Whatever the reasons, sentiment about public care is more upbeat than it has been in decades. The optimism is justifiably tempered, however, by a fear that there won't be enough post-placement services for everyone who will now need them. More money for this purpose will improve the odds of success for families with special-needs children, and it will encourage more adoptions by drawing adults who have stayed away because they don't have the wherewithal to remodel their homes for a wheelchair, pay for long-term counseling, or provide whatever other assistance a child might require.

At the same time, making it easier for otherwise qualified adults to adopt related children, and even encouraging them to do so, would help to ameliorate at least some of system's racial tensions. So would increasing the funding and priority for recruitment programs for minority parents. Few states are aggressively pursuing this part of the law, in some cases because of bureaucratic inertia and in others because officials contend it's discriminatory to seek parents of a specific color (raising the question of whether they would feel the same way if large numbers of black adults sought to adopt white children).

Launching high-profile campaigns to recruit black adoptive parents would be a particularly effective response because it would address several of foster care's problems at once. It would constitute a powerful official statement in support of minority inclusion, regardless of how many adults eventually signed up or children were adopted; in addition to promoting positive social policy, that would help to lower the volume in the debate over transracial adoption. Most important, the effort would inevitably find more homes for children, which is supposedly the bottom-line concern for everyone involved.

That said, if every state of the union started concerted recruitment efforts tomorrow, it seems implausible that they would bring out enough black parents quickly enough to meet even current needs. That's not because people of one race are any more or less concerned than another. But there are important economic, cultural and historical differences. Among them: To whatever extent economics influences the ability or desire to adopt, minority income levels are lower than those of whites; blacks have a long tradition of caring for and informally adopting family members' children; and some African Americans, especially older ones, bristle at the thought of participating in any activity that simultaneously involves money and the custody of an unrelated human being.

This lingering emotional vestige of slavery mainly affects sentiments about independent adoptions, which explicitly involve financial transactions, but it also tinges some people's feelings about the process in general. "That stigma was a visceral part of my parents' reaction, for sure," says Mike Burkette, a computer consultant in Atlanta who with his wife, Rita, adopted a girl privately and then a boy from foster care. "They said, 'You're going to give a child a home and somebody's profiting from it?' My mom asked, 'The people making money from getting you a baby, are they white?' Once we explained it to them, that it's a fee for services and not for the purchase of a child, they understood that pretty easily, but you can't blame them for how they felt in the beginning."

Mike acknowledges he had some reservations at first, too, when Rita suggested that they adopt rather than spend tens of thousands of dollars for infertility treatments that might or might not work. "My issue was that I was reluctant to give up the idea of my own biological child. I have to admit it was mostly about my own ego, maybe a male thing, like it was a personal blow that we couldn't do what most people take for granted," he says. With a little help from Rita, though, Mike realized he wanted a family more than he wanted to feel unsettled about himself, so the couple picked an adoption agency with a Christian-sounding name out of the Yellow Pages and dialed the phone.

Then those pesky dollar signs appeared again. When an agency employee started describing the costs involved, Mike and Rita couldn't quite believe the numbers they were hearing. It had nothing to do with slavery or ego or income level. Like adoption applicants of every type, they were taken aback by the concept itself. Then, like nearly all anxious parental wannabes, they forged ahead anyway without a question or a complaint.

Their initial irritation dissipated as they learned that their money would go for running the agency, paying salaries, and helping with birth mothers' expenses, but Rita and Mike also came to understand that adoption is one of the uncommon American social institutions in which being black could work to their advantage. In 1994, when they took two-week-old Sinclair home, their agency was charging couples who adopted white babies up to $15,000 each; the Burkettes were assessed just $3,000 in fees.

That was $3,000 more than they paid to adopt their son, Michael, four and a half years later. They were living in Chicago, where they had moved for Mike's job, and had been talking for months about expanding their family. This time, after hearing a radio report about foster care, they signed up for parenting classes, went through another home study, and got very lucky: Just a week after being approved as foster parents—the first step toward adopting from the state in Illinois—a social worker called to tell them about a boy born a month earlier to a drug-addicted mother. Once they saw him, Mike told his wife, "That's the son I've always wanted. Let's pack him up and go."

One of the fastest-progressing trends in public systems today is called "foster-adopt" or "fost-adopt," a concurrent-planning process that requires prospective adopters to first serve as a child's foster parents for a designated period, typically less than a year. The biological father could stake his claim during that time. Or the mother could complete her rehabilitation course and be deemed fit to resume custody. Or a grandparent could step forward. Traditional foster parents have signed up knowing that children will be placed with them only temporarily, even if they wind up developing strong bonds or adopting them. In these new programs, however, the foster parents care exclusively for children they hope to make their own. The emotional gamble can feel enormous.

"It's always in the back of your mind. All this love and nurturing and caring I'm giving this baby, and the mother might come to take him at any moment. It was scary," Rita recalls. Most of the time, the waiting period ends, the new parents adopt a child—or a sibling group, as is occurring more often—with whom they already share strong connections, and their son or daughter gets a permanent home more quickly and at a younger age than otherwise would have occurred. That's the idea, but some adoption advocates don't like it because it can send prospective parents on such a turbulent ride.

Maybe so, but nothing's going to change systemically or significantly without some tough going along the way. The Adoption and Safe Families Act certainly sets the majority of biological mothers and fathers on a jagged road, mandating that they lose their parental rights over children who have been in state custody for fifteen of the preceding twenty-two months. That means some good people who could have become responsible parents, if only they had a little more help, will lose their sons and daughters. But that's a sacrifice society has decided is worth imposing in an effort to unlock a cruel trap that has confined generations of children. Besides, as a result of the nation's new laws and standards, the scales are increasingly being tipped in favor of people who want to adopt, whether they decide to start out as foster parents or take any other route. "I can only tell you that, for us, it was absolutely worth any risk we took," says Rita.

For all of its positive aspects—the process was quick, Mike got the namesake he'd dreamed of, there were no costs involved—in the end, the Burkettes' story isn't a ringing endorsement of adoption through the foster-care system. They would pay a private agency if they decided to have a third child. Not so that they could avoid a waiting period or be assured of an infant, but to ensure that phone calls are returned, appointments are kept, and questions are answered the same way twice.

Sloppy procedures, lack of personal concern, and institutional ennui are persistent complaints about governmental entities of every type, but many public agencies have become more effective in recent years. Foster-care officials typically have lagged behind, however, partly because they've perceived their mission as so different—they're charged with determining the future of children, after all, not fuel-efficiency standards—

that they haven't felt as compelled to examine the mechanics of their own operations.

Setting time limits and establishing mandates might not be enough to help the maximum number of children. More and more lower-income, single, homosexual, and disabled people will certainly adopt special-needs children as the maze becomes easier to navigate. But middle-class and more affluent Americans expect a neatly drawn map and a competent guide as well. It seems like simple common sense that somebody should be trying to provide whatever assistance they deem necessary, since their participation would make the biggest difference, the most quickly, for the greatest number of children.

8

The Money's the Problem

In October 1999, the *Washington Post* ran a short article about a security guard in Virginia who placed an ad on the Internet seeking to adopt a "young boy who needs a dad." He explained that his own child had died in 1996, and he badly wanted to raise another "to be a Godly and a responsible young man." The FBI was investigating whether an Ohio couple had sold their fourteen-year-old son to the guard for about $400. The boy told authorities that his parents had previously swapped some of his siblings for a swing set and new clothing, among other items.

Several months earlier, a California woman in her last days of pregnancy was charged with fraud and grand theft after she allegedly told six different couples and one single woman that they could adopt her baby. The indictment said that Kimberly Ussery, 21, and her boyfriend had received a total of about $16,000 during the previous few months from the parental hopefuls, each of whom had thought they were the only ones providing assistance for housing, medical care, and other legally allowable expenses.

Not long before that, an Oklahoma judge sentenced a woman to ten years in prison and gave her husband a six-year suspended sentence for "trafficking in children" in five states via the Internet. Brenda and David Morgan, operating as Chosen Angel Adoption and Kaufman Adoption, had created phantom embryos and promised them to people who paid thousands of dollars in agency fees. Then the Morgans told their clients that their baby had died at birth or that the biological mother had changed her mind.

There have always been predators and profiteers eager to cash in on the misfortune of people who couldn't produce the children they wanted. Most of the abuses in the past weren't solely financially motivated, however. Rather, they grew out of misguided but prevalent cultural convictions—that unwed mothers shouldn't keep their children, for example, or that adoptive families are better served by fabrications than the truth. The baby boomers have been changing all that.

They were limit-testing teenagers in the 1970s, and one of the entrenched conventions they rejected was the bias against single parenthood; today, one of every four children in this country is being raised by a single parent, usually the mother but increasingly the father.[1] Then as 30- and 40-somethings, still more socially liberal and more flexible about their personal lives than previous generations, they ushered in a radical new era of adoption in which pride began to replace secrecy and relationships with birth parents started to burgeon. But other of the boomers' defining characteristics, in tandem with geopolitical factors over which they had no influence, have yielded less constructive results.

Because so many of them gave first priority to their careers, and because this was the period in which women entered the workforce in earnest, they became the oldest group of Americans ever to try to produce offspring. This society-altering phenomenon itself constituted only part of a breathtaking chapter in world history that also included Moscow cutting loose its satellite states and Beijing implementing a modernization program that included a one-child limit on Chinese families; both actions had momentous effects, one of which was to exponentially increase the number of children available for adoption. Medical science developed at the same stunning pace, creating hope in many areas, such as treatments for the infertility that became an unintended consequence of a generation's lifestyle choices. And, of course, the Internet reconfigured one reality after another.

All these events took place in the context of mounting affluence in America, the ascendance of global capitalism, and an increasingly prevalent, generalized sense that the marketplace works wonders if it's left alone. This laissez-faire philosophy indisputably bought material benefits, but at a considerable human cost. Applying the same economic theories to medical services as to toaster prices wreaked havoc on our nation's health-care system, created a monstrous gap between those who could and couldn't afford therapeutic marvels like in vitro fertilization, and allowed cash-fed infections to thrive in adoption, an institution that is supposed to help some of the earth's most-vulnerable inhabitants.

Money is a huge and growing problem in many areas of the field. Left mostly unsupervised and uncontrolled, as it is today, its influence could cause grievous damage and undermine much of the progress that has been made. It's long past time for everyone involved in adoption to say: "Enough." Enough secrets. Enough ethical gymnastics and moral compromises. Enough being left alone. Adoption cannot conceivably require less-attentive monitoring and regulation than cable television. Yet abuses and injustices are proliferating with barely a whisper of protest, much less demands for reform, from most lawmakers, triad members, or even practitioners, who know full well what's going on.

Charges of flagrant child-selling and fraud are unusual, but I offered them as initial illustrations for two reasons: First, they clearly show that no part of the adoption world is impervious to financial seduction or subversion. And, while the number of such incidents may be low, it is steadily increasing as people realize how desperate prospective parents can get, how easily the system can be manipulated for profit, how little supervision or regulation goes on, and how simple the Internet makes it to execute scams.

There is a bright side to this disheartening assessment: As a society, we are still appalled by efforts to capitalize on susceptible children and adults when we hear about them, and people who step over the line are prosecuted when they're found out. For now, though, the bad news outweighs the good. We don't hear about most abuses because the culprits don't get caught, the industry isn't trying to squeeze out its dubious activities, and it's getting harder to know who is stepping over the line because it's moving.

Last September, for instance, the on-line auction house eBay removed an offer from a birth mother to place her baby for adoption with the highest bidder. The price climbed to $109,100 before the site's managers expunged the listing. "It is illegal to sell a body, an unborn baby or a body part on eBay, just as it is in the land-based world," a spokeswoman explained. Nevertheless, there are sites on which prospective parents, after signing up with an adoption attorney or agency and receiving passwords for entry into special chat rooms, can receive instructions about how to use financial incentives to persuade ambivalent pregnant women to relinquish their children. I know of several adoptive parents who were advised on-line by adoption professionals, some of whom worked for large, well-known firms, precisely how much money they could channel into various categories of legally explainable expenses without raising anyone's suspicions.

In one case, an employee of a nonprofit agency based in the Midwest suggested to a couple in Illinois that they could send several hundred dollars in cash every month for medical care to the pregnant woman with whom they were in contact, even though they knew she was on Medicaid, and could send her a couple of thousand dollars in cash to cover anticipated rental payments for housing even though she lived with a relative. "We were led to understand, in so many words, that the more we gave her, the more obligated she'd feel to give up her child, which she ultimately did," the adoptive father told me.

Birth parents who feel pinched by difficult circumstances, or just want to cash in, also are finding friendly territory in cyberspace. While few practitioners explicitly offer economic inducements, many use their web sites to highlight the fact that everyone who signs up with them will be particularly well taken care of—the implication being that they'll receive far more than just good medical attention. "I'm not offering an opinion about whether this is good or bad," says Benjamin Rosen, a New York State attorney who been handling adoptions since 1975. "But it's just the fact that more and more birth mothers want to know all the rules and are asking to be matched with couples in places where the legal climate's most permissive or least attentive. . . . I'm not saying it's baby-selling, but the empowerment of birth mothers is making it more of a seller's market."

Ethically challenged adoption practitioners, child-hungry adoptive parents, and distraught pregnant women have always engaged in questionable activities, of course, but there have never been so many opportunities (and implicit invitations) for them to do so before. And it's never been possible before to scour the planet for co-conspirators with just a few clicks of a mouse. The World Wide Web is filled with so many faceless, unaccountable people willing to cut any deal that the proliferation of improper and immoral behavior seems inevitable in the absence of internal or external regulation.

The adoptive father who sent a California birth mother cash for medical and housing expenses was one example. He and his wife, both of whom described themselves as religious Christians, "wondered a lot about whether we were doing the principled thing." But, like the thousands of Americans who travel abroad each year with tens of thousands of dollars hidden on their bodies, the Illinois couple decided they wanted a child more than they wanted to deliberate the ethics of their actions or of their advisers.

"Anyway," said this father, "if our agency told us it was an acceptable thing to do, which they should know—and I must add that they were very warm, compassionate people—then we can live with it." By the time his daughter's adoption was finalized earlier this year, he and his wife had spent just over $28,000, including about $7,000 in "expenses" for the birth mother and nearly $18,000 in fees to their agency.

That's not an abnormally high sum nowadays. The numbers have been climbing for a decade, coinciding with the escalating interest in adoption by affluent baby boomers. The total spent by most people for adoptions outside the public system today seems to wind up between $20,000 and $35,000 regardless of whether they use a nonprofit agency or a highly paid attorney, whether they stay in this country or head abroad. Since Congress enacted a $5,000 tax credit for adoptions in 1997, a growing number of practitioners have been raising their charges about $5,000. Subjecting children to the pressures of the free market almost guarantees they'll be treated as commodities.

Is that assessment overblown? Lauren and Bill Schneider don't think so. A few years ago, they joined the throngs of Americans telling their stories on Internet sites, hoping pregnant women will select them as the new parents of their children. Their open letters, invariably accompanied by pictures, explain who they are, why they're seeking to adopt, and how they'll try to ensure wonderful lives for their sons or daughters.

Seven years ago, when Judy and I started the adoption process, would-be parents produced similar pleas, but most of us wrote them on paper and placed them alongside flattering photos in colorful binders that were shown privately to women considering who might make good mothers and fathers for their babies. Some practitioners still operate that way, but the Net has become the venue of choice because it reaches far more people, and far more rapidly, than any agency or lawyer possibly could in any other way.

Among the Web surfers who noticed the Schneiders' letter was a Hungarian émigré named Tamas Kovacs. On March 14, 1999, he e-mailed Lauren and Bill at their home in Minnesota, explaining that he was helping a divorced friend from his homeland find loving parents for her two-month-old daughter, Nikolette. A picture of the pretty little girl was attached to the computerized message, which described her as a "completely healthy, white Caucasian . . . available for adoption immediately."

The situation was almost too good to be true. The birth mother was in New York to sign the relinquishment papers and the birth father was an American, so the infant was automatically a U.S. citizen for whom the Schneiders wouldn't have to negotiate the bureaucratic labyrinth that international adoptions often involve. And the news got even better. Kovacs said the birth father would cover all expenses because he wanted his daughter placed with a family as soon as possible to avoid paying child support. So the adoption would cost Lauren and Bill next to nothing. Kovacs faxed them copies of every sort of legal document they might need, and told them to contact anyone they wanted to make sure the arrangement was legitimate. Lauren and Bill called their lawyer, a well-respected adoption attorney in Minneapolis, and she advised them to proceed.

"We were suspicious. How could we not be? But no one was asking for anything and Kovacs seemed willing to oblige any request," says Bill, an orthopedic surgeon who revealed his lucrative profession and displayed his impressive home in the letter he and his wife posted on the Net. "How could we just turn around and walk away?" The next morning, a Friday, the Schneiders flew to New York and took a cab to a destination Kovacs had suggested to further reassure the couple: a pediatrician's office.

The kind-sounding, gentle-looking Hungarian intermediary arrived with a child in a car seat, along with a diaper bag full of food, toys, and other necessities. After a doctor pronounced the girl in perfect health, Kovacs handed Nikolette to the excited mother-to-be so that the couple could take her to their hotel for the weekend. "It was magical," says Lauren. The fact that a total stranger was nonchalantly giving them custody of a baby seemed more than a bit odd, but it also helped persuade the Schneiders that everything was on the up-and-up, since no one had asked them for anything in return.

It turns out that the Internet provides clever capitalists with opportunities they previously couldn't have imagined. For example, there are now hundreds of Web sites on which adoptees and birth parents can list their names in order to find each other—which they are routinely doing without birth certificates or other legal documents. Nearly all these registries are operated for free by triad members, agencies, and lawyers who believe adults should be allowed to make contact if they want to. But at least a few practitioners, without permission or disclosure, sell the names on their lists to detectives and other search professionals, who then contact the registrants to offer their services for a fee.

The newly public exhibition of intimate "Dear Birth Mother" letters has not so much created a new category of entrepreneur as it has, for the first time, identified an inexhaustible pool of potential targets for a type of merchant who has plied his wretched trade throughout world history: the seller of human beings.

After a day of caring for Nikolette, of fantasizing about becoming her parents, the Schneiders went to a local diner at which they were to return their almost-daughter and find out what they needed to complete her adoption. Kovacs told them without flinching: $60,000 in cash. They were getting off cheap. Later, in court, it came out that the Hungarian had offered Nikolette to at least two other couples, one of whom he had asked for $120,000. The New York District Attorney's office also gathered evidence that he sold two infants to Americans in the past for undisclosed sums, but their adoptive parents didn't blow the whistle on him. They paid up instead, as an indeterminable number of other people undoubtedly have done and continue to do, because no one is watching.

Kovacs got caught only because he was unlucky enough to have targeted principled people. As much as Bill and Lauren wanted to become parents, they were more repulsed by the notion of baby-selling and felt strongly that Nikolette had to be rescued from the salesman's clutches. When they got home to Minnesota, they called the FBI and agreed to participate in a sting operation. Three days later, as heavily armed state and federal law-enforcement agents watched through hidden cameras, the couple delivered a satchel filled with money to Kovacs in a New York hotel room.

"Here's the $60,000, just like you asked us for last week. . . . I don't know if you want to count it, or are you satisfied?" Bill asks on the videotape of the encounter, which was aired on NBC's *Dateline*. Cautious entrepreneur that he is, Kovacs starts thumbing through the cash to make sure it's all there. As he does, he suggests he may be able to procure another infant for his customer one day. Bill, who has been coached to draw out as much information as possible, asks for clarification: "There might be another child available?" Kovacs takes the bait. "There will be," he replies. "There is no question. There will be." About twenty minutes later, Kovacs leaves the room and is arrested.

The penalties a nation exacts on citizens who break its rules reveal a great deal about its concerns, its priorities, and its ethos. Jaywalking is a misdemeanor that may result in a small fine, while attempted homicide is a felony that will lead to a long prison term. Proportionality is the key; the more serious the offense, the graver the repercussions. Yet some people in positions of authority apparently believe that searching for your own roots is a more heinous crime than selling babies.

That belief evidently led two U.S. House members, Thomas J. Bliley of Virginia and Christopher H. Smith of New Jersey, to threaten the chances for congressional approval of the most important reform of worldwide adoption practices in history. The changes related to the Hague Convention on Intercountry Adoption, a treaty designed to standardize procedures and improve the treatment of children in need of homes everywhere. The two deeply misguided lawmakers are evidently fans of secrecy and big business. Unfortunately, they also are influential members of committees responsible for drafting legislation to implement the pact, and they tried to use their power to weaken it.

They did that largely by inserting provisions in their legislation, which the Hague treaty itself does not contain, mandating penalties of up to $25,000 for a first offense and $50,000 for each subsequent infraction in two categories: providing adoption services without proper accreditation and violating "privacy statutes." In the first instance, which would have applied to flesh merchants, untrained or uncaring facilitators, and practitioners who don't seek accreditation because they know their procedures are shabby or shady, the punishment was listed as a civil fine. The second classification applied to people who give out information that might identify birth parents, regardless of whether they requested anonymity or even whether the data were needed for medical emergency reasons. This act was deemed "criminal" and violators, in addition to being fined, could have gotten a year in prison.

The legislation, as submitted, not only rejected the child-centered, anticommercial intent of the Hague Convention, but sought to institutionalize negative practices under the guise of rectifying them. It was an outrageous ploy that almost worked. Many adoption businesses supported the measure for various reasons, most because it imposed fewer restrictions on them than the original treaty would—that is, they had a vested financial interest in retaining the status quo; others because they thought any effort to tame the Wild West of intercountry adoption was better than nothing; and a few because they were deliberately misled about what the suggested changes entailed. In the end, independent organizations like the Evan B. Donaldson Adoption Institute and reform groups like the American Adoption Congress voiced strong objections and forced the committees to pull back the measure for redrafting. At this writing, a vastly improved version has passed the House and is awaiting action in the Senate.

Literally and figuratively, selling children today is not a federal offense; it is a misdemeanor listed under individual states' social-service statutes. The only reason Tamas Kovacs received a prison term of up to three years, rather than just being fined, was that he engaged in fraud. He recruited an expatriate American to pose as Nikolette's father, then used the alleged paternity to get phony visa documents, and so forth. Those actions transformed Kovacs's scheme from a relatively minor legal transgression into attempted grand larceny, a financial crime that the law takes very seriously.

A Conspiracy of Silence

Why aren't adoption professionals screaming bloody murder? Why aren't they publicly distancing themselves from the flagrant scammers, or even from their unethical colleagues? Why aren't they demanding strict rules and close monitoring to prevent children from being bought and sold? Why aren't they working diligently to make every adoption as squeaky clean as possible, so that the process can truly become one—and become widely perceived as one—in which everyone's rights and dignity are respected?

Some practitioners are indeed trying to do all that. But it's also true that people who make their living from adoption tend to react to criticism about their field in the same way that members of many other professions, and many families, do: with an informal, undiscussed code of silence. It derives from the same human, defensive sense of us-versus-them that sometimes leads police officers and religious minorities to instinctively circle the wagons when one of their own is accused of improper behavior.

"People assume that adoption is a benevolent, philanthropic response to the needs of orphans, but it's not always. In some ways, it's just another giant industry in which people see a way to get rich. And the shame of it is that it's really the only unregulated industry in the United States," says Maureen Hogan, the president of Adopt America, a national nonprofit organization that finds homes for special-needs children and that helped to derail the defective legislation on the Hague Treaty in Congress.

Maureen is one of the more colorful, controversial activists in the world to which she's devoting her life. She's a onetime liberal Democrat who promotes conservative Republican causes; she's a former private detective who believes in openness; she's a Catholic who is repelled by abortion but is also disgusted by fellow conservatives who maintain that women who are denied anonymity will terminate their pregnancies rather than relinquish their babies for adoption. "It's not true, all the studies show it's not true, people like Bill Pierce [the recently retired president of the National Council for Adoption] know it's not true, and it's horribly disrespectful of the women involved, and dishonest in general, to make emotional arguments like that," she says. "The truth is, they'd say anything to maintain the status quo and protect the business that's served them so well."

Adoption's subterranean existence in the past made it nearly impossible to see what was going on, much less think about how to improve anything. Because they operated in an insular environment with barely any scrutiny or feedback, even the best professionals instituted practices—usually out of the belief that they were proper—that triad members, had they been asked or even observed, would have revealed to be counterproductive and damaging. And the charlatans, people like Georgia Tann in Tennessee, used the cover of adoption's secrecy to obtain children through coercion, theft, and worse, then sold them like hijacked cigarettes unloaded from the back of a truck.

At least some of the adoptive parents who received their hot goods in the dead of night had to suspect something was amiss. Likewise, it's implausible that none of the "legitimate" adoption agencies heard rumblings about the activities going on around them. So, did the people who knew become revolted and blow the whistle? Absolutely not. For all sorts of reasons, many understandable and some reprehensible, an unspoken conspiracy of silence developed among the parties to adoption during the bad old days.

No one plotted it out; it just grew out of everyone acting in what they perceived as their own and society's best interests: Infertile couples kept quiet so as not to jeopardize their chances of getting children; social workers believed concealment improved the adoptive families' prospects for success; baby providers felt they were giving kids better homes or didn't want to endanger their profitable enterprises, or both; nearly everyone thought birth parents had done something so shameful that it should remain forever entombed; and adoptees, when they were told about their origins at all, received unmistakable signals that their status was not a suitable subject for public discussion.

In a dazzling turnabout, today everyone is talking, and the conspiracy is dying from self-inflicted wounds. Except when it comes to money. Some reformers insist that money serves only to corrupt adoption's principals and principles, and therefore needs to be eliminated altogether—as it is in nations like England, where adoption is viewed strictly as a social service. That's a worthy ideal, but it's probably unrealistic in our devoutly capitalistic society. In any event, it overlooks the real costs practitioners incur, from counselors' salaries to subsidies for low-income applicants, from medical assistance for birth mothers to hiring attorneys to ensure that no one's rights are neglected.

So how much should an adoption cost outside the public sector, where the charges are small or nonexistent? The answer is: Less than they do now but, beyond that, its hard to figure because there are so many variables. Some charitable organizations place white babies for under $10,000 but take years to do so, while some lawyers arrange adoptions within months for $50,000. The majority fall between those extremes, but they offer such wildly varying degrees and types of service, and even rent offices in such economically diverse locales, that it's impossible to factor out how much goes to whom or for what.

Even keeping in mind that Americans will always want choices, and politicians will never want to set prices for any enterprise, there are realistic (if difficult) ways to push adoption in more ethical directions and make it less susceptible to financial shenanigans. First, transparency: Legislators, trade groups and triad members, through new laws and public pressure, ought to demand an accounting for where the money goes, a process that would induce practitioners to be more frugal, allow consumers to make more informed decisions, and minimize abuse. Second, state, federal, and international officials need to make vigorous efforts to curtail and punish practices that poison the system; some of these are coercive, others are barely legal and a few wouldn't pass a sinner's morality test. Finally, the preponderance of good people in the adoption industry have to start drawing indelible lines in the sand; they can't allow themselves to cross over to the dark side anymore, and they should report those who do to the nearest sheriff.

The American Academy of Adoption Attorneys, as well as individual lawyers, should be holding press conferences and passing resolutions and demanding disbarment hearings, for example, when their colleagues engage in egregious behavior like paying pregnant women to come to this country, pressuring them to give up their children, and then shipping them home. Adoption agencies should respond in exactly the same way when they learn one of their own has misled a couple about the damage done to their child through institutionalization or has been convicted of transporting children over state lines for sale. Publicly embarrass the bad guys, squeeze the inflationary pressure of their expensive operations out of the system, and show the world whose side you're on.

Here are just a few more examples of activities that no one's yelling about:

- Many agencies hire agents abroad whose job is to find adoptable children and women considering relinquishing their babies. Some of these "spotters" receive set salaries and therefore have less incentive to engage in shadowy activities, while others are monitored by their American employers to prevent abuses. But some are paid for each successful find. The fees—bounties, really—can run as high as $10,000 per child, a huge sum in the poor areas of Eastern Europe, Latin America, and Asia where this is a routine practice. People will do almost anything for that kind of money, and they do.

- Adoption agencies and attorneys regularly tell clients, like the dance teachers in Washington whose journey to Russia is described in Chapter Three, to take $10,000 with them for adoptions. Some explicitly say to hide the money, others just imply it. They specify $10,000 because anything higher legally has to be reported when travelers pass through customs. In fact, many parents-to-be wind up breaking the law by following their practitioners' advice, because they take additional money with them to cover unforeseen purchases, personal expenses, and leisure activities.

- Domestic adoption agencies, particularly ones that operate group homes for pregnant women, typically have those without health insurance sign up for free or subsidized state plans akin to Medicaid. It's a fine practice because it increases the chances that the babies placed for adoption will be healthy, and it's the right thing to do because it promotes the well-being of both the mothers and their children, regardless of whether a relinquishment occurs. Some agencies, however, then turn around and charge prospective parents for the same medical care that their respective birth mothers are already receiving. That adds thousands of dollars to individual costs, and it's fraud.

- It's not just the providers who cheat. To save thousands of dollars on babies' deliveries, a small number of parents-to-be sneak uninsured pregnant women into the hospital using the adoptive mothers' identifications. That's not only against the law, it's coercive since the birth mother feels indebted for the kind deed and may fear she'll be reported to the police if she keeps her child. For their parts, some birth parents, in addition to promising children to multiple couples to obtain numerous payments, use their bait to get expectant adopters to pay moving costs, hotel bills, and other questionable expenses—as Judy and I did for one couple before they disappeared—without any apparent intention of proceeding with a placement.

"I was just shocked at the things that go on," says Danielle Lett, an administrator for a catering firm in New York who was twenty-two in 1997, when she entered a home for pregnant women run by a large Texas-based adoption agency. In the previous couple of months, she'd gotten out of the Army, become pregnant by a boyfriend who prodded her to get an abortion even after she explained that would violate her Catholic beliefs, and been fired from her job as a horse groomer because the owner feared he'd be liable if she got hurt and miscarried. Then Danielle's roommate, a born-again Christian, said she was outraged by the pregnancy and kicked her out of their apartment.

Women from all over the country wind up at the facility in which Danielle sought refuge. The agency that runs it advertises extensively, including on the Internet, beckoning pregnant women to "Come Live with Us." It's an alluring offer for ostracized teens, women down on their luck, or anyone else confronted with a crisis pregnancy. Residents get three meals a day, live in a furnished suite, and receive counseling and prenatal care. They also get to use the swimming pool, fitness center and volleyball court, and can participate in "exciting activities like shopping trips, eating out, sports events, and other special events going on throughout the Dallas-Fort Worth area."

To Danielle, it sounded like a safe haven and a summer camp combined. "I can't begin to tell you how wonderful it felt to go there. It was like a God-send, a chance to think about what to do, to be able to spend time getting my life back together," she says. What she didn't expect was to be subjected to persistent pressure, subtle and explicit, to give up her child. She got counseling on how to cope with the fallout of relinquishment, but almost none about how to handle motherhood if she chose that path, and she and the other pregnant occupants were regularly displayed for visiting prospective parents.

"At every turn, they made us feel that giving up our babies was the only reasonable, responsible decision to make," says Danielle. "When the paying customers came by, it was like we were the products in a meat market, not people making a terrible, permanent decision about our lives. The way we were talked to was always in the context of 'when you relinquish,' and not 'if you relinquish.' After a while, and I really do believe this was the idea, they got you to the point of feeling like you were supposed to give up your baby as the price of admission for all the generous benefits they gave you."

Charitable groups and profit-making firms run shelters like this nationwide, and most function ethically. The key lies not in organizational affiliation but in whether the women are treated with respect and provided with balanced counseling. A few religious groups unabashedly prod unmarried pregnant women in their care to cleanse themselves by ceding the fruits of their sin to righteous couples, while some agencies—though by no means all—pursue their business objectives through gentler means, by generously spreading around their honey to attract as many queen bees as possible.

What's wrong with steering a confused young woman onto a path that will lead to a more stable life for herself and her child? That's certainly what Judy and I hoped the social worker in South Dakota was doing with the young woman carrying "our" child. Betty was estranged from her family and having a tough time. She had a mediocre job but took classes at night, and she seemed determined to improve her lot. A baby was out of the question because it would mean quitting school and work and probably applying for welfare. She told us that one last time just a few days before delivering a boy.

So when I called the social worker from the airport gate seconds before we were to fly to pick up our newborn son, and she told me Betty had changed her mind, I wasn't just shaking with pain. I was dumbfounded. "How could she do this to us? Why did she lead us on this way? How could she make such a bad decision, not just because it hurt us, but for herself?" I asked my wife those questions, over and over, once I felt able to use my vocal cords again. "It's unbelievable," Judy replied. "She's going to ruin her life."

How dare we have assumed we knew what was best for another adult, now and forever? How egocentric to have imposed our expectations on a human being we knew to be bright and sensitive. And how callous to have thought we had been wronged. People change their minds about far less consequential matters without anyone second-guessing their motives or their right to do so. The only positive things I can say about our initial reactions is that they were human responses to a tremendous emotional blow, and they didn't last long. Later, we learned the reason Betty changed her mind was that her mother belatedly offered to help her with money and child care, which meant she didn't have to make the excruciating choice between raising her son and building a better life.

Right until the end, when she contacted a facilitator who found a California couple (with whom she now has an affectionate open adoption), Danielle wasn't sure she'd been fair to the people who took her in when she needed help most. Maybe, she thought, she'd misread their intentions. Maybe, because she'd been at the Texas home for only a month, she'd allowed her emotions to cloud her judgment. Then, as she was leaving for good, an agency official pulled Danielle aside. "We'd like you to reimburse us for your time here," the woman said. "We feel $1,500 would be fair." Danielle couldn't believe her ears. They really did view her as a baby machine and, when she didn't churn one out, they wanted their investment back. She walked out without a word.

Money plays so many villain's roles in adoption that it's dispiriting to even think about it. An empathetic social worker suggests ways for a birth mother to "legitimately" squeeze a few extra thousand dollars out of adoptive parents "because you need it and they can afford it." An established agency leans on clients to simultaneously adopt a child's sibling to avoid splitting them up (the right, virtuous thing to do), then charges $23,000 per adoption even though most of the costs are duplicative. An attorney indicates to an uninformed birth mother that she doesn't need her own counsel, and gives her informal advice as though he's on the woman's side, without disclosing that every word he utters is meant to further the interests of the couple that's paying him a $20,000 fee.

Creating a Privileged Class

Adoption will never become flawless in any way because, like every other social institution, it operates in an imperfect world run by imperfect people. One of our most noble traits, however, is an innate desire to improve children's lives. And that's what practitioners can start doing better tomorrow if they mean a syllable of what they say when they insist they're not in it for the money. It isn't an impossible dream, though the cynics and the free marketers may think so. "This is a capitalist system where the laws of the market work their magic," Bill Pierce, who now works as a consultant to the National Council for Adoption, insists. "People don't seem to believe that $16,000 or $17,000 is too much for a new car. If we're going to have quality service, you're going to have to pay for it."

Unless charges drop precipitously, which no one is predicting anytime soon, at least two troubling quandaries are likely to continue regardless of how principled everyone becomes: A widening socioeconomic chasm between the people who relinquish their offspring and those who receive them, and the progressive exclusion of lower- to middle-income Americans from the pool of potential adopters. Again, since the public system operates by different rules and attracts generally different participants, this refers primarily to the adoption of white babies domestically and of children from overseas.

Both trends obviously stem from a common root, the stunning rise in costs from a few thousand dollars for infant adoptions twenty years ago to tens of thousands of dollars today. Most people who earn less than $40,000 or $50,000 a year simply can't save that kind of money, and they tend to shy away from loans—which are available for adoptions—because repayments can be tough. The Internal Revenue Service and some states offer tax breaks, but they're applicable only after an adoption, so the beneficiaries generally are people who already have financial resources rather than those who need help up front.

Furthermore, adoptions from abroad typically require at least one and sometimes both prospective parents to travel to the child's homeland for as long as several weeks for final legal proceedings, and perhaps for earlier procedures as well. The travelers usually receive little notice of when they'll have to go or for how long they'll have to stay. Practically speaking, all these factors skew the process toward people who can afford to leave work for lengthy periods and get considerable, flexible vacation time.

Adoptions from abroad likely would remain expensive even if U.S. practitioners were to dramatically lower their prices, because most governments have figured out that demand by affluent Americans is so strong that they can charge pretty much whatever they want (currently up to $10,000 per transaction to cover contributions to orphanages, court costs, and other legitimate-sounding fees). It's hard to imagine second- and third-world nations, even those with noble motives, voluntarily giving up such a ready source of income. At the same time, traveling abroad will never be cheap, so lower-income adults will likely have to do their adopting within our borders for the foreseeable future.

They're already finding it harder and harder to do that outside the foster-care system, however, and the process's rising costs aren't the only reason. One of the most disquieting, rarely discussed truths of the new world of American adoption is that birth mothers are systematically widening the economic gap between themselves and the people who adopt their white children, and are contributing significantly to the creation of a privileged class of well-to-do adoptive families. They're doing that, quite simply, by choosing what they perceive as the best possible homes for their children.

Unintended consequences are the scourge of all planners and visionaries, and the reformers who pushed adoption into the light didn't foresee some of the negative effects of openness. They certainly didn't mean for the promise of continued contact to be used as a device for enticing reluctant women to give up their children: "You won't really be losing your baby," some thoughtless and unscrupulous practitioners say reassuringly. "You'll see her all the time." And no one expected women empowered to select adoptive parents to place prosperity so high on their list of criteria. "All things being equal, if I've got a choice of couples who seem secure and loving," a birth mother once asked me, "why wouldn't I pick the one who can give my son the best doctors and toys and schools and the other things money can buy? That's what everyone wants for their kids, ... and so do I."

Ironically, the women and men who choose upper-class homes for their children are among those who suffer the negative consequences. Many find that while they like the people they selected, both as individuals and as parents, their divergent social and economic backgrounds make it hard to form an ongoing relationship—which, after all, is the soul of an open adoption. And the participants sometimes exacerbate their disparities, for instance when birth parents resent the very success that attracted them or when adoptive parents demean their children's creators. These are the kinds of complexities that underscore how different adoptive family life can be, and why people who enter this flourishing world should do so with their eyes wide open and their minds geared for patience, long-range thinking, and, if they want to do themselves a big favor, counseling.

Most people find things work out acceptably if imperfectly, just as they generally do after divorces in which the parties are intent on doing right by their children. In the minority of cases where a relationship among the adults doesn't work, the children may be able to maintain separate connections; if that isn't possible either, the adoptive parents may have to scale back the arrangement or even cut it off altogether. Whatever else they do, they shouldn't make the mistake of thinking any decision lasts forever. Circumstances change. So they should at least keep track of the birth parents' whereabouts so they can resume communications in the future if it's appropriate or, at a minimum, can give the adoptees information with which to make their own judgments when they come of age.

"You never shut the door because ... if you do, you're losing sight of the person it's all for," says Brenda Romanchik, who relinquished her son sixteen years ago and, with the unwavering support of his adoptive parents, has remained an integral part of his life ever since. "Matt has never lost touch with me and I've never lost touch with him, and that's helped both of us work through a lot of stuff over the years. It has also helped his mom and dad deal with issues that could have become big problems for him, but instead were part of normal life," adds Brenda, who is now among the best-known activist/educators in the adoption community. "I'm very grateful that I've been able to do that for my son and his parents. . . . Just because I wasn't ready to be a single mother, and I sure wasn't, doesn't mean I didn't love him or didn't have any responsibility for him."

Brenda is a source of sanity on many topics, but her central concern is helping birth parents understand their place in the rearing of their offspring—that of dependable providers of affection and information.

"People who flit in and out aren't helpful," she says. "Like anything with kids, you have to be consistent and loving and supportive. And you have to be willing to accept that not everything you see in your child's adoption will be perfect and hunky-dory, but you have to support it."

Brenda was wise enough to pursue an open adoption at a time when the concept was still perceived as a fringe experiment. She also was lucky or smart enough to choose a couple whose values allowed them to carry out the idea rather than just give it lip service. But the catalyst that enabled Brenda to make her decisions was the agency she used, Catholic Social Services in Traverse City, Michigan, a pioneer of open adoptions. "Their focus was to encourage you to find someone who is like you, who you could feel comfortable with sitting around the kitchen table," says Brenda. "It isn't about wealth or status; those things don't determine who'll make good parents."

It's hard to envision how the trend toward a privileged class of adoptive parents will abate without the tenacious efforts of practitioners, both by revising their fees to make them more affordable and by educating birth parents about the traits to look for when choosing their children's new mothers and fathers. Some agencies already offer sliding payment scales, but many that do so then try to steer their lower-income applicants toward the children who are more difficult to place. The prize adoptees, white infants, are frequently reserved for the clients who don't get discounts.

Nearly all practitioners charge most for adopting Caucasian babies, and it's common for them to use some of the proceeds to subsidize people who adopt less-sought-after children. That's a reasonable practice with a fine purpose, but here again dollar signs can cloud people's vision. Some practitioners, for instance, explicitly set their rates according to a child's color, age, gender and/or physical condition. A few agencies privately sit down with their clients and show them charts: next to the words "healthy white baby girl" are the highest "fees," followed by slightly lower rates for a healthy white boy, and down the line for children who are minorities, older and/or disabled.

Many needy children presumably wouldn't get families if adopting them became more expensive, and variable fees probably will remain commonplace until our society has achieved color-blindness and economic equality. In the long interim, however, this represents a compelling argument for chiseling every possible unnecessary dollar out of all adoptions—as well as for handling any existing cost differences with utmost compassion and discretion, casting them as the unfortunate means to a desirable end and not as the inevitable consequences of a marketplace driven by supply and demand.

A Businessman's Revolution

When I asked Dave Thomas whether he considered himself a rebel, he shrugged off the question with an amused/bemused "not that I'm aware of" and explained that he was "just a hamburger cook." Which was roughly the equivalent of Apple Computer founder Steve Jobs (also an adoptee who found his birth mother) portraying himself as just a word-processor technician. To be fair, though, the president of Wendy's Old Fashioned Hamburgers seems not to realize his role in the adoption revolution.

The image Mr. Thomas projects in his television commercials, that of a self-effacing regular guy, appears to reflect who he really is. Moreover, he studiously stays away from any topic he views as controversial. So this soft-spoken businessman undoubtedly would be surprised to learn that he's in cahoots with groups like Bastard Nation and the American Adoption Congress in a struggle to change the world. While other agitators engage in high-profile political fights, he is concentrating on two steady grassroots efforts: increasing the number of public adoptions, discussed in Chapter Seven, and persuading U.S. businesses to make it easier for their employees to adopt.

Thomas's work clearly shows how money can be used to enhance rather than depreciate the adoptive process. It also demonstrates, yet again, how far popular attitudes toward adoption have advanced, and how far they still have to go before the practice and its participants achieve parity with families formed by procreation.

Thanks partly to persistent prodding and logistical support from the Dave Thomas Foundation for Adoption, the percentage of U.S. companies offering adoption-related benefits jumped from eleven to thirty percent between 1990 and 1998.[2] The National Adoption Center, which helps develop such corporate plans, says the total has been climbing since then, led by Fortune 500 firms—about sixty-five percent of which now provide adoption benefits. The center estimates the average aid package nationwide consists of $4,000 in reimbursements per adoption, plus one week to several months off with pay, commensurate with the time given to employees who have children by birth.

Most jobholders also are eligible for up to twelve weeks' unpaid leave under the Family and Medical Leave Act of 1993. Like many initiatives during the Clinton administration, that legislation sought to normalize adoption by placing it on a par with biological parenting. It was both an outgrowth of and a contribution to adoption's reformation. But, much the same way as civil rights laws were enacted because equal treatment for all Americans hadn't evolved voluntarily, the fact that the government felt compelled to intervene demonstrates how inadequate and prejudicial most people's thinking about adoption had been—to the extent that they'd thought about it at all.

Just a decade ago, almost no company even considered that infertile personnel were paying into health plans from which they would never derive maternity benefits and which didn't automatically extend coverage to their adopted children. It never occurred to most employers, who routinely gave women time off after a delivery, that new adoptive parents might have deserved similar treatment. And since this was a subject people didn't discuss, much less negotiate about, workers seldom asked for any of those things or even informed their bosses that adopting might require some flexibility for traveling to another country, being interviewed for a home study, or appearing in court for a legal procedure.

The reticence thankfully is ending, so most business owners no longer have the excuse of ignorance, and some have responded with striking generosity. Among the most notable are MBNA America, the bank and credit card corporation, which offers its employees $10,000 toward each adoption plus four weeks' paid leave, and CMP Media, a provider of high-tech information and services, which allots $15,000 that can be used for either an adoption or fertility treatments. You can bet your house that the companies leading this parade had their sensitivities heightened by a triad member or two in their higher echelons, but you can be just as certain that the procession would have come to a grinding halt if its participants had found they were headed in a fiscally painful direction.

What they're learning instead is that providing adoption benefits not only displays social responsibility and an ability to respond to changing conditions, but also makes for more satisfied workers. For most companies, this is also a cheap investment, since only about half of one percent of all employees avail themselves of adoption benefits annually. Some small or struggling enterprises may have trouble incurring any additional expenses, but the hundreds of thousands of solvent firms that could offer adoption benefits, yet don't, could contribute enormously to leveling the playing field for less affluent Americans. If a hamburger chain can stay in the black while offering its workers $4,000 for each adoption and $6,000 if the child has special needs, along with six weeks of paid leave, then most other businesses in this country can probably handle the burden, too.

"It's a no-brainer. For a little investment, it sends a really good message that a company cares and gives an alternative to people who can't have children any other way," Thomas says in a matter-of-fact manner that belies the fervor he clearly feels for his cause. "It should be a regular part of the culture, not a special benefit, but people don't think about that because they don't understand their workers' different lives or how much they could help kids who really need homes. I think they just have to be made aware. Education is so powerful, and . . . all I'm trying to do is to educate people."

Just as nothing about Thomas's voice or demeanor betrays his commitment to radical reform, nothing about his background seems to account for his passion about adoption. If anything, his experience was more negative than most. His adoptive mother, Auleva, died of rheumatic fever when he was five. Rex Thomas was a laborer who traveled often, married three more times, and wasn't the kind to show his son affection.

Dave's unwed mother had given him up just after he was born, but he didn't learn how he'd come into the Thomas family until he was thirteen. His maternal grandmother, the only person who consistently gave him love and attention, decided it was time for the boy to know. He took the news like most adoptees do when they learn they've been deluded all their lives: He was irate, hurt, and distrustful of everyone, except Grandma Minnie. Every day he went to school, and every night he immersed himself in a twelve-hour-a-day restaurant job. Two years and another city later, when Rex announced he was moving again, Dave rented a room at a YMCA in Fort Wayne, Indiana, and said he was staying put.

Other adoptees—or nonadoptees for that matter—might have been embittered by such an upbringing, might have been rendered socially dysfunctional, might have blamed their parents, their bad luck or themselves. At the age of fifteen, Dave Thomas gritted his teeth, somehow achieved the insight to be grateful for having had a family at all, and vowed that other people were no longer going to chart the course of his future. "I had to work myself out of that mess," he says, which he has done, creating a world that is the polar opposite of the one he left behind. He has been married to the same woman for forty-six years, has five children, and has gotten wealthy from the chain he started with a single restaurant in 1969. Having endured a life of bouncing from home to home, Mr. Thomas decided to help other children escape comparable circumstances.

He saw hundreds of thousands of them in the foster-care system, and saw adoption as their salvation. That conclusion may seem paradoxical, given Thomas's personal history. But he grasped that his problem hadn't been adoption but a lack of affection and stability, factors that aren't guaranteed for children raised by their birth parents either. He also retained a belief most Americans clutch while their incomes are relatively modest, but too often relax their grips upon as they approach the upper rungs of the economic ladder: that a lack of money shouldn't impede people from attaining the basics of human existence, such as decent health care, shelter, or family.

Assuming adoption benefits are becoming routine, they promise to accomplish more than just increasing the rate of special-needs adoptions, making the process more equitable and contributing to a greater sense of optimism. In an intensely business-centered culture like ours, the participating companies serve as models for other segments of society to follow suit. And that could throw the normalization of adoption into mainstream America into hyperdrive, with all sorts of direct and tangential implications. Here are just a few not-too-farfetched fantasies:

Insurance firms could realize that they, too, can provide a specialized type of adoption assistance. That is, they could give infertile policyholders a choice between lump-sum subsidies toward an adoption, say $15,000 or $20,000, and their standard coverage for treatments designed to achieve pregnancy, which can easily exceed $50,000 per patient. Many people would snap up such an alternative, and their numbers would grow as this became a routine option and as adoption's image continued to improve.

The combination of financing from employers, insurance firms, and government tax credits would make adoption a viable alternative and even a desirable goal for millions of additional Americans. Since there's no evidence that the supply of white infants would rise commensurately, the heightened demand would lead to a steady upsurge in the ranks of older, disabled and otherwise needy children moving into permanent homes, both within the United States and from institutions abroad.

On a human level, weaving adoption into the regular patterns of life means people would talk about it even more freely, further dispelling the stereotypes, shedding the embarrassments, and addressing the problems. In particular, lifting the stigmas and the shame—if we're really lucky, combined with less money-driven behavior by practitioners—would leave women with crisis pregnancies less susceptible to pressure, making the adoptions that do occur more stable and comfortable for everyone concerned.

Just one last vision, for now, this one for my son and daughter and all their kindred spirits who didn't pick their still-unconventional status or the complications that come with it. When the negative influences of money are excised from the process that replaces children's parents, their feelings toward the people who raise them will never be tainted by questions about their self-worth. When adoption becomes as widely accepted as divorce, which it beats hands-down as a productive social institution, and when birth parents are as widely accepted as in-laws, who also run the gamut from wonderful to worrisome, the only people for whom adoption will become an ignominious subject will be those few wayward politicians and baby traders who still defend phony birth certificates, sealed records, and enforced separations of blood relatives.

And here's why that final dream may come true: The unwitting comrades-in-arms appalled by the status quo don't just consist of rabble-rousers in reform organizations, or even just the growing majority of birth and adoptive parents, researchers, and practitioners whose own experiences have taught them the value of honesty and openness. They also include quietly influential people like Dave Thomas. After all, just because he prefers to stay away from hot topics publicly doesn't mean he has no feelings about them.

"I think everyone has a right to know something about their mother and father. I think it's one of our God-given rights," he told me during an interview that had focused mainly on his efforts to broaden benefits for adoptive parents and provide more homes for children in foster care. After deflecting my initial questions about "controversial" issues like closed records, he evidently decided to finally make his sentiments known. "Those things are controversial for people who have never been adopted, who really don't understand," he said, an edge entering his voice for the first time.

"Everyone should be able to get their birth certificates, their own information. I'd hate to think I couldn't get mine," he continued. Even as he disclosed his previously private thoughts, Mr. Thomas remained in character, urging a conservative approach to prevent any disruption of the adoptive family's life. He suggested that adoptees be legally entitled to obtain their documents when they turn twenty-one, the same age at which he said they should be free to seek out their birth parents. That's how old he was when he found his birth mother, using papers Grandma Minnie gave him.

Too many Americans still operate on the basis of wrong-headed views about adoption. They mean well, but they haven't been told the truth yet.

That's where people like Mary Insulman, the elderly retiree in Oregon, and Bill Troxler, the college president in Maryland, and Dave Thomas come in. They are not hot-headed radicals or callous manipulators who pursue their own interests without regard to the impact on anyone else. Everyone should take heed when they tell their stories, whether the subject is money or unsealing records, because theirs are the voices of reason and impending change.

9

Old Lessons for a New World

Loretta Young was twenty-two when she became pregnant during a tryst with a married man, an up-and-coming movie star named Clark Gable. That was in 1935, when any single woman's reputation would have been irreparably tarnished by the disclosure of either her affair or her subsequent "condition." In this case, it would have taken another toll; actors who strayed from the straight and narrow were sure to be humiliated in the press and, since Hollywood contracts contained morality clauses, they could be fired.

Neither Gable nor Young was about to let a short fling destroy a promising career. Gossip about their liaison swirled for years, but they never said a word publicly. He went back to his wife and proceeded as though nothing had occurred. She waited until her belly began to swell, dropped from sight for a few months, then placed her baby in a San Francisco orphanage. Two years later, she and her new husband, film producer Tom Lewis, quietly adopted the toddler they named Judy.

It wasn't until Judy Lewis was thirty-one, by then a regular on a television soap opera, that she summoned the courage to ask whether the rumors about Gable being her father were true. Her mother told her they were, but swore her to silence. A still famous actress—especially one so devoutly Catholic that people called her "Saint Loretta"—couldn't sully her reputation by admitting she'd once given birth to an illegitimate child. Ms. Lewis, saying she understood, kept their secret for another quarter century, until she decided to divulge it in her 1994 autobiography, *Uncommon Knowledge*.

Ms. Young refused to discuss the book, but her reputation didn't suffer as a result of it because the once-terrorizing shame of unwed parenthood had been ebbing for three decades. Today it would be hard to write a plausible script in which it returns with much force. Adoption's various villains started retreating a bit later in U.S. history, but some are now moving at such a rapid clip that they're disappearing right before our eyes.

Parents lying to their own children comes to mind first, followed by parents lying to themselves. The end of institutionalized secrecy isn't far behind, though the activists pursuing that goal, like true-believers in the midst of any revolution, can't always see the progress through their frustration at not having gotten farther sooner. Unmercifully, the burdens imposed on birth mothers remain the most intractable, but they also are starting to give way as America's acceptance of adoption itself rubs off on all its participants, and as the process continues to open up in ways that will steadily alleviate the necessity for unsealing records, for anguished searches to locate biological relatives, and for Herculean efforts to find permanent homes for the children who need them.

There's no doubt we're bound for a better place; we're already at one now. But society's seemingly endless afflictions are tough to resolve because they're invariably intermeshed with or caused by or lead to additional ailments. Even if we somehow managed to convert the foster-care system from an emergency room into a luxury medical facility, for example, it would still provide better treatment only for the people unfortunate enough to need it. So getting kids into permanent homes more quickly isn't the ultimate answer if they continue flowing into the system unabated, and decreasing the influx would require finding remedies for the poverty, mental illness, racism, drug abuse, and alcoholism that underlie most people's inability to raise their own children.

To date, society hasn't done an exemplary job of resolving those problems. Whatever people's divergent views about a nation's obligations to its citizens, it's a cold fact that even during the greatest economic expansion in our history, even as public adoptions set records, so did the number of children still in foster homes.[1] If there's no serious headway during the best of times, it doesn't augur very well for the future.

Yet positive signs abound. Previous chapters have discussed the benefits of openness for all triad members, but we humans often succumb to our cravings or insecurities rather than do what's best for us. So, ultimately, there are two main reasons the trend toward openness will continue: The pregnant women who make adoption possible want it that way and, as adoptees learn more about themselves, so do they. Ask a parent in a closed adoption how his daughter reacts when she hears that a playmate is in an open adoption, and the invariable answer is: "She wants what her friend has."

In a sense, adoption's revolution is defined by this elemental change: After a long history in which nearly everyone saw the process as involving only adoptive parents and adoptees, we are finally coming to terms with the fact that it also includes a third set of people, whose needs don't depart along with their children. And those people are figuring it out, too. "I don't think birth parents can really be healthy unless they make the choice and are committed to it," says Temple Odom, whose foray into adoption could not have differed more starkly from Loretta Young's if she'd lived on another planet.

Temple's story begins like many others of years past, but it unfolds in ways that vividly demonstrate today's new realities. It was during the hot New Mexican summer of 1989 that she and her high school sweetheart faced the biggest decision of their sixteen years on earth. Jerry said the only thing to do about Temple's pregnancy was get married. Temple's religious beliefs precluded abortion, but beyond that nothing seemed clear to her. And she simply couldn't imagine becoming a wife and mother at her age.

So Temple turned for guidance to the two people she trusted most, her parents, Dean and Betty Sue Mathis. They listened and let her know in no uncertain terms that they disapproved of what she'd done. Her father, a Southern Baptist minister, sought counsel from his own spiritual adviser. Then her parents said they'd support whatever decision she made. "I'm a Christian and I have high moral standards. However, we all make mistakes. There's not a second I've ever regretted giving birth to Daniel, but having sex at sixteen surely was a mistake," says Temple. "But we all also have to make choices, and getting married would have been compounding one mistake with a second one."

The family decided hiding would be wrong, too. So the following Sunday, Pastor Mathis announced to his thousand-member congregation that his teenage daughter was carrying a child. She understood the gravity of her error, but it was time for healing and honesty. "The only power Satan has over us," he intoned, "is when we lie and are deceitful." It wasn't what the pastor expected, but people all over their small community reacted to his sermon by opening up about their own festering secrets and uncomfortable lies. Sometimes they bared their souls to friends and relatives, more often to Temple's father. Whomever they talked to, they invariably began by explaining that if the preacher and his family could tell such a burdensome truth, then so could they.

Temple knew from the start that she "would rather die" than not know where her child would be, whether he was healthy or happy or even alive. Her parents had similarly mixed feelings. The result of Temple's bad behavior was to be their first grandchild, after all, and they hated the idea of losing him. No one felt completely comfortable with any of the alternatives until a friend gave them a book about open adoption. Temple didn't consider an ongoing relationship, but the notion of picking her child's new parents and getting periodic reports on his progress was enough to ease her mind and allow her to proceed. It was the least imperfect solution to a dilemma that defied easy answers.

In a future of diminishing stigmas and ever simpler methods for locating virtually anyone, the adoption of babies in America won't have much of a future without openness. That doesn't mean everyone will want the same level of contact, but it does mean they will have to make clear what they want and don't want; if necessary, they'll have to express their wishes in legal documents that can be amended as circumstances change. Ten states already permit "cooperative adoption" agreements,[2] which can address a wide range of issues, from how often adoptive fathers will send photos to what responsibilities biological parents will have for updating medical information as they age. Most people will prefer to work out their arrangements informally, but these are the sorts of questions triad members, practitioners, and policymakers will have to address.

Shift scenes to a Baptist seminary in Louisiana, where a professor in early 1990 asked his graduate school class to pray for his niece in New Mexico, who had decided to resolve her unintended pregnancy through adoption. Mike Osborne went home that afternoon and told his wife about the teacher's request. Both of them took it to heart because Jennifer had gone through two miscarriages. But she was pregnant again and everything appeared to be going fine; so, for a change, they prayed that night for the well-being of an expectant mother and child other than Jennifer and the baby she was carrying.

Less than two weeks later, Jennifer found herself lying on a couch in the small living room of the couple's apartment. Mike had driven her home a few minutes earlier from the hospital, where she'd recovered overnight from her third miscarriage. This time the trauma had taken a devastating toll: She could never nurture another fetus. Jennifer had stopped crying hours earlier, but she hadn't given up on building a family. She looked up at her husband and said: "Call that professor and ask about his niece."

They subsequently wrote letters and sent pictures to Temple, who was thrilled. The Osbornes were religious, loving, and funny, all the traits she'd hoped for in parents for her baby. (Her father worried whether an aspiring Baptist minister ever would make enough money to adequately care for a family, but he got over it.) And when she asked what they would do if the baby were born with a serious disability, they didn't flinch.

"They said, of course they'd adopt anyway, and that made me feel so confident about them. You want people committed to the baby, as if they had the baby biologically themselves," said Temple, who is now a family therapist studying for her doctorate in Michigan. "It's not about peddling flesh; it's about finding homes for babies. They're not products you should be able to exchange or return, and Mike and Jennifer got that."

Then Temple's mother imposed a final, unexpected demand. The Osbornes had mentioned that they intended to stay at a hotel near the Mathis home after the birth, so everyone could visit easily. But Betty Sue thought that was a terrible plan. "You agree to stay at my house," she said, "or the whole thing's off."

Birth mothers typically want to spend time with their babies, and virtually all mental-health and social-work professionals advise them to do so. Some just hold their children for a few minutes, while others need days or weeks. It's invariably the most excruciating portion of all the parents' journeys because, intuitively, it's nearly impossible to comprehend that anyone could voluntarily hand back this vulnerable, endearing being after calming her cries or feeling his touch. That's why doctors used to drug women and take their newborns away from them immediately, to "protect" them from the ordeal.

Today, research across the spectrum of human behavior shows that people need to face the searing issues in their lives in order to work through them with a minimum of psychic damage. Denial rarely works, and neither does hiding. In the case of adoption, to put it simply, women who say good-bye without first saying hello generally can't fully process their decisions and therefore never come to terms with them. And knowing their children won't vanish into the ether invariably helps them continue to heal over the years.

When other relatives are also involved, particularly female relatives who have borne children themselves, they also have to figure out how to cope. Temple's mother discovered she needed not only to spend some time with her first grandchild, but also wanted to get accustomed to the idea of his being raised by new parents by watching them interact. Our son Zack's paternal grandmother, whom we met briefly, hesitantly asked us whether she could see her first grandchild before we left Colorado with him; our social worker said that would make it harder for the grandmother to let go, and we took her advice. The tears in my eyes right now are a meager apology for our mistake.

It's a whole new world out there, and we all need to do a lot of exploring to learn its boundaries and its resources, not to mention our own.
Judy and I are discovering, to our surprise and delight, that we get ener-
gized by the prospect of ongoing communication with our children's
birth parents. We spend so many evenings now adding to Zack's and
Emmy's life books, and they invariably stop at their mothers' and fathers'
pictures to ask more questions, or just to stare. Their enthusiasm is exciting and contagious.

Most people would have tried to get Temple's mother to retract her ul-
timatum, and many would have backed out. The Osbornes said, "What
the heck," and they've never regretted a second of those awkward, joyous
ten days in the Mathis home. They got to meet the birth father, who has-
n't been in touch since but whose pictures and stories they can now give
Daniel. They received visceral permission to become the boy's parents,
and they became sure they could handle contact with their son's biological family.

"It was so important for me, too," says Temple. "Between my time
alone with Daniel in the hospital and the experience we all had together,
my shame just evaporated. I know it wouldn't be like this for every birth
mother, but I was able to fall in love with my child and know that it
would be all right if I wasn't ready to raise him. I felt grief, but mainly I
repressed it. My mourning didn't really set in until years later. For me—I
think for all of us—we wouldn't trade that time in my parents' house for
a million dollars."

Factoring in the Unobvious

Largely because situations such as Temple's are becoming commonplace,
it's possible to glimpse major aspects of adoption as it likely will exist in
the decades to come. First and foremost, it seems inevitable that it will become the norm for adoptive and birth parents to meet at the start of the
process and for all three sides of the triad to remain connected, or have
the option of doing so, throughout their lives. Some states will continue
undermining the dignity of today's adoptees for only a few more years,
while others will deny them until they die, by keeping records sealed. But
subsequent generations won't have to rely on the whims of poorly informed judges and politicians, because some or all of their parents will
routinely provide identifying documents.

It's a sure bet, too, that a shrinking percentage of future adoptees will
be white or, at least, will be white infants (assuming more parents look to
Eastern Europe and the foster-care system, where the children are older).

The overwhelming reason, of course, is that more unwed adults are choosing to become mothers and fathers. But other social shifts, not typically associated with adoption, are also contributing to the decline.

Most significantly, the teenage birth rate in this country has been steadily falling for a decade—by eighteen percent from 1991 to 1998, according to the latest count by the National Center for Health Statistics. Even if the descent suddenly stopped, which seems unlikely if for no other reason than the growing effectiveness and availability of contraceptives, there would still be fewer young women placing their babies in adoptive homes than there used to be. And all indications are that the trend will continue because, as a matter of social policy, the United States is aggressively encouraging it.

One section of the welfare-overhaul bill signed by President Clinton in 1996, for instance, provides hundreds of millions of dollars to the states for promoting sexual abstinence to students. Largely as a result, by the end of the twentieth century, a third of all schools taught that the only appropriate way to avoid sexually transmitted diseases and unwanted pregnancies is to avoid intercourse altogether. Most of the others implemented "abstinence-plus" courses, which teach young people to always use contraceptives.[3]

Another determinant for adoption's future is the plunge in the number of abortions in America, for reasons including improved contraception and greater social acceptance of single parents, as well as increased restrictions on abortion imposed by predominantly Republican lawmakers,[4] a chilling effect on abortion providers by demonstrations and attacks against them,[5] and a progressively more conservative public sentiment that the procedure should remain legal but should be less accessible and less often used.[6]

The fact that abortions declined until they reached their lowest level in twenty years in 1997,[7] at the same time that adoption in this country was shedding its old ways, seems like prima facie evidence that proponents of closure are mistaken when they assert that more women will abort their babies as the institution becomes increasingly open. Simultaneously, it stands to reason that a continuation of the current patterns will lead an indeterminable number of women to give birth who would have preferred to halt their pregnancies, which in turn presumably means additional babies placed for adoption.

Or not. Political pendulums swing perpetually, so new power brokers might one day lift restrictions and appoint judges who expand abortion rights. Or "morning after" pills could become so readily available that nearly anyone who wants to end a pregnancy will be able to do so regardless of what the politicians or courts tell them. Nearly half a million American women are estimated to have used such "emergency contraception" already. And if pregnant women can get abortions more easily, or feel less shame and social pressure in their pregnancies, not as many babies will be available for adoption.

Then, again, fewer of them will be left in trash cans and on people's porches. No one keeps track of how many children are forsaken like this—an average of a few per state annually, judging from media reports—but the numbers have occasionally soared in a given locale, and particularly shocking incidents have prompted authorities to begin responding. Hospitals in at least two states, Alabama and Minnesota, have established procedures for newborns to remain in the care of medical staff until their mothers decide whether to take them home or place them for adoption. Structured so there's no pressure on the women, that's a potentially workable approach since it can provide for counseling, the recording of extensive information, and legal protection for everyone involved.

On the other hand, a spate of baby desertions in Houston last year triggered a reaction that will do more harm than good. More than a dozen tiny boys and girls had been dumped around the city. Local officials grew so alarmed that they erected billboards pleading: "Don't Abandon Your Baby." The Texas Legislature reflexively took another giant leap; it enacted a statute permitting babies to be left at police stations, fire houses, and emergency rooms, no questions asked. By mid-2000, a handful of other states had followed suit, and bills to legalize similar abandonment were filed in about half the country.[8]

The intent of all these measures may be admirable, but the politicians haven't thought through the implications. Rather than basing a solution on the hospital model, or searching for ways to assist distraught mothers or locate the babies' other relatives, they have created an easy out, perhaps even an incentive, for young women in crisis who obviously aren't thinking clearly. So, while the babies may be dumped in nicer places, there's a huge risk that official permission will lead to more dumping. This approach also guarantees that few of the parents who wind up caring these infants will receive personal or medical data to help them or to share, while the children will never be able to find out about themselves because, just as in China and other nations that have systematized infant abandonment, the law doesn't require that any questions be asked.

The eventual contours of adoption are possible to discern in large part because the roads it is traveling—and building—converge with those being taken in U.S. family life as a whole. In December 1999 Hawaii's Supreme Court declared same-sex marriage violates that state's constitution, then Vermont's justices left that legal door wide open in a ruling several months later.[9] As discussed in Chapter Eight, some states prohibit adoption by homosexuals while others allow it under specific circumstances. The mix changes all the time. Yet all these elements aren't as incompatible as they might seem. When pieced together, they form a consistent picture: that of a once-hidden segment of our population moving inexorably, if circuitously, toward normalization.

Surveys show that most Americans already oppose discrimination based on sexual orientation, and public sentiments about homosexual relationships will continue to shift as they increasingly become a fact of life—and as more gay men and lesbians become parents. In this respect, adoption is playing an essential role in fomenting a fundamental, long-term social transformation. The same-sex marriage cases may get the lion's share of national media attention, but it's the accumulation of less-examined legal changes and rulings around the country that are altering attitudes and practices on the ground.

Not only can homosexuals adopt individually in most places, for instance, but in at least twenty-one states and the District of Columbia they can join their partners in doing so. The process involves one parent adopting first and then the second filing for joint rights, so it's not cheap or easy. But people are doing it every day, and it means the number of officially sanctioned, same-sex, two-parent homes is steadily growing.

Judicial decisions are fueling the transformation, too: A groundbreaking case in Massachusetts in 1999 ended with the state's high court ruling that a lesbian who helped raise her partner's biological son was a "de facto" parent, entitling her to see the boy after the couple broke up. By effectively deeming that the second woman had become an adoptive mother, the justices validated every comparable relationship in the state.

Some Americans will always maintain that the family, as formed and symbolized by the institution of marriage, should consist only of straight couples with rings on their fingers. But developments like single parenting, divorce, and poverty have hammered away at the "ideal" with more force than same-sex couples could ever hope to muster. (Even grandparents are having more of an impact, with one in nine now raising a grandchild at least part-time—an increase of almost twenty percent from a decade ago.)

Given these realities, it seems clear that the critics' main objective isn't to preserve marriage and the family unit, per se, but to save them from a specific group. And there's no question that parenting by homosexuals, whatever its merits or faults and regardless of the strides they have made, is the area in which people retain their strongest prejudices. Many adoption professionals will tell you there are fewer barriers to placing a child interracially or with a disabled person than with a lesbian or, especially, a gay man.

Some of these men and women, who otherwise might have provided homes for needy children, consequently are going the route of insemination and surrogacy. But a steadily rising number are discovering friendly adoption territory. Dottie Finton and Kim Holt are part of the swelling crowd. After five years of living together, they had made an appointment in 1998 for Kim, a loan officer who was thirty-three at the time, to receive a sperm injection at a fertility clinic near their home in Lancaster, Pennsylvania. They canceled the treatment, however, after attending an adoption conference at the suggestion of a friend.

"When we listened to what people there had to say about all the special-needs kids out there," Dottie explains, "we sort of looked at each other and said, 'Let's make a family with someone who really needs it.'" Like most people, they started out wanting as young a child as possible, but as they learned more—and, pointedly, as they saw pictures of and met older children—their hearts began to open to other possibilities. "Once you see their faces, everything changes," says Dottie, a library director who was thirty-one when she and her partner decided they were willing to adopt a child who was blind, deaf, or had other disabilities, a child who was older or of another race, or a group of siblings.

Showing photographs to prospective parents, or introducing the boys and girls themselves, is the most effective method for finding homes for children with special needs. Adults often discover that their stereotypes and fears evaporate when they look into a child's eyes, or leafing through photo albums full of children without families brings home the enormity of the problem and brings out their compassion. Whatever the reasons, the technique is effective, which is why social-service agencies rely on books of pictures, "match parties" at which would-be parents meet available children, and "Sunday's Child" types of appeals in newspapers and on local television stations.

Yet another reality for the Internet to reinvent. Within states and across international borders, tens of thousands of people today see their sons and daughters for the first time on computer screens. Many practitioners are ambivalent about using this technology, aware they're treading a thin line between advocacy and marketing, but they also agree it's the most powerful tool they've ever employed to find parents for children. "Everybody wishes they didn't have to do it, but we also wish the kids didn't have to be in newspapers and on TV," says Carolyn Johnson, executive director of the National Adoption Center, the only organization that lists special-needs children from states across the country. "You do what you have to do for their sake, and the web has really made a dream of mine come true—to let the American public know who these children are."

There seems no limit to the ways in which the World Wide Web is re-configuring adoption's realities, from expediting searches to stimulating creative ideas like the Terminal Illness Emergency Search program, de-vised by Bastard Nation to help adoptees suffering from fatal diseases find their birth relatives to obtain transplants or information that might prolong their lives, or just to meet them once before they die. But the new technology's greatest potential for helping the most people is in its unri-valed ability to disseminate the stories and display the faces of children waiting for homes. "We're still in the infancy stage," says Carolyn Johnson, "but I truly believe it could change the world."

We're certainly not there yet. For half a year, Dottie Finton and Kim Holt filed adoption applications for more than a hundred special-needs children in six states, and they were rejected every time because they did-n't lie; they identified themselves in their home study as a white female couple in a committed relationship. The last straw arrived by way of the U.S. mails in March 1998: An agency wrote to inform them that they would not make "appropriate parents" for a child who was so disturbed that he ate his own feces. In the view of whoever made that judgment, the boy was better off without a family than he would have been with two mothers. They decided to go back to the fertility clinic.

Medical interventions sometimes work better than the body does. Dottie got pregnant, but she lost the baby in a miscarriage during her sec-ond trimester. Within days, they received a mailing from New Jersey about a match party, at which adults could interact with a group of chil-dren aged four to twelve. Kim and Dottie figured they had nothing to lose. About a hundred invitations to prospective parents had gone out, but only four people, other than Kim and Dottie, showed up to see the twenty children at the mansion-like Department of Social Services build-ing in an old section of Newark: a gay black man, a white lesbian, a straight black woman, and a straight Hispanic woman.

Dottie was the first to notice the nine-year-old across the room. She heard him ask someone for help on a project he had begun after Santa Claus handed out presents. Darnell said, "Please." For some reason, his polite tone of voice combined with his shy demeanor sent a chill through Dottie. She whispered excitedly to her partner to look, look at him. When they asked a social worker for more information during lunch, she was amazed. In the four years since Darnell had been taken from his heroin-addicted mother, no one had ever expressed even the mildest interest in him.

Kim recalled that, in the parenting class they'd been required to take the previous year, they were told that black boys over the age of four generally remained under state supervision until they turned eighteen. She thought, "But not Darnell." The two women took a Polaroid picture of the boy home with them. They passed it back and forth in the car, their hands trembling. "We found our son," one would say to the other through her tears. "This is why we went through those hundred kids and the miscarriage and all the frustration," the other would reply. "Because this is the one we were supposed to have."

And this time they had good reason to believe they wouldn't be rejected, because our country is changing far more rapidly than most Americans realize. In December 1997, New Jersey settled a lawsuit in favor of a gay couple who had argued that the state's refusal to allow them to adopt their foster son together, rather than one parent at a time, violated their rights to equal protection under state and federal law.[10] Which means that homosexuals can't get married in this country, and in most places and for most purposes aren't formally recognized as partners, but in one state of the union they can legally, as a couple, become the parents of an adoptive child.

Less than three months after meeting Darnell, Dottie and Kim received permission to adopt him. At the time, Darnell was functioning educationally as a five-year-old because of neurological problems and learning disabilities. (Today he is rapidly catching up to his age level in every respect, thanks to special school classes, solid medical attention, and the persistence of his two mothers.) They visited with him frequently, drove him to their suburban home on weekends, and took him on outings, but his social worker wanted him to remain in the school he was attending until the end of that term, so his new parents didn't move him permanently until that May.

It was hard to wait so long to take him home, partly because Dottie and Kim were anxious to form their family but mostly because they hated leaving him in the apartment where he lived with his single foster mother, five other foster children, plus the woman's granddaughter and the latter's two daughters. They thought the foster mother was kind and hard-working, but the conditions were cramped and drug dealers operated freely in the neighborhood. One Sunday evening, after the two women dropped off their son-to-be after church and dinner, they glanced back for a final look at Darnell. He was standing at a window, his hands clenching the bars that kept him in and the world out, screaming.

Technology Breeds Secrecy

Signe Wilkinson, an editorial cartoonist for the Philadelphia *Daily News*, offered a bizarre, entirely plausible glimpse into the future in a drawing published last January. In each of five frames, a stone-faced judge speaks from an elevated podium to a little boy standing innocently below: "Mondays you see your father. Tuesdays you see your mom's sperm donor. Wednesdays you see your dead father's stepmother. Thursdays you see your great aunt Mattie and . . . Fridays you see your psychiatrist, psychologist and lawyer."

We have an enormous amount to figure out as scientific leaps, shifting attitudes, and legal innovations forever alter family relationships and, in so doing, transform our nation. In ways discussed throughout this book, adoption is both a catalyst for the conversion and a beneficiary of it. But now that it's emerging into the light, where we can explore its history and problems and promise, it can play another vital role as well: that of teacher, because some of the revolutionary changes taking place are so rapid and random that we haven't begun to seriously contemplate how they might play out.

Around the country, for instance, about 200,000 embryos lie frozen in fertility clinics and laboratories. A host of ethical, medical, and legal issues swirl, unresolved and mostly undiscussed, around these minuscule test-tube inhabitants. If their biological parents break up, who can decide if and when the embryos will be transferred into a womb, and whose? What are the implications for everyone involved when the embryos' creators allow clinics to implant their "extras" into other infertile patients? Will there be visitation rights?

How about this: Should it be legal for brokers or owners of human eggs to sell them on the World Wide Web? Or is that an updated form of adoption's baby-selling? Is it ethical for profit-making firms to solicit eggs in newspaper and Web advertisements, without any provisions for counseling or future responsibilities? Or is this a new form of coercion for those women who badly need the money but never conceived of relinquishing a body part and who haven't given a thought to what it might mean to have children out there whose fate they might ponder all their lives or who might one day want to meet them?

Virtually no one is confronting the avalanche of critical questions descending upon us. That's where adoption comes in. It's still an imperfect work in progress, but it offers sharp insights and very close parallels in some instances and, at a minimum, provides a starting point for addressing historic, mind-boggling changes that will further reshape our understanding of what constitutes a "normal" family.

Sperm banks in America, which used to accept only anonymous deposits, began coping with these dilemmas more than a decade ago, as the growing openness about parenthood induced a small number of birth fathers to return to their clinics to ask if they could find out about their offspring; at roughly the same time, men and women started seeking more information about their insemination-fathers after sensational news stories about lovers who discovered they were siblings and doctors who sired dozens of children by injecting their own sperm into patients.[11] Now a growing number of these facilities require identification, and some are compiling files akin to those of adoption agencies.

In the world of new technologies, though, secrecy and ignorance rule. Prospective parents, who if they were considering adoption would get counseling, seek advice on the Internet, or talk to other people who had adopted, often believe that cutting-edge methods will allow them to hide. And that's usually fine with the fertility clinics, which don't pay their medical personnel and technicians to be social workers or psychologists.

It will always be hard to transcend the pain of infertility and the insecurity of rearing children whose blood isn't our own. So many neo-adoptive and pseudo-biological parents, or whatever high-tech mothers and fathers will be called (to their children, I hope, they'll just be mom and dad), will remain the most steadfast members of their nontraditional extended kinship units in their desire for closure, just as a diminishing percentage of adoptive parents are today. Also like their counterparts in adoption, though, they'll eventually figure out that doing the right thing is worthwhile for everyone even if it isn't easy. And they'll get to that point more quickly by learning from adoption's mistakes, from secrecy to severing personal history to affixing price tags to human lives.

But adoption's chronicles contain more than just cautionary tales; they also offer positive messages, instructive guidance, and hope. They affirm that family is about far more than bloodlines, while explaining that ignoring biology helps no one. They show that children are eminently capable of enlarging the circle of those they love without losing affection for the people already there. In probably their most optimistic lesson, they also demonstrate that it's possible to topple even deeply entrenched regimes.

People like Jennifer and Mike Osborne don't see themselves as insurgents, but that's what they were when they invited Temple Odom and her husband to spend a week with them in their Tennessee home in November 1999. (Their son, Daniel—whom they had promised to cherish no matter what, and who has been diagnosed with juvenile diabetes—

was delighted.) They were insurgents, too, when they spent days caring for their second child's birth mother, Susann, while she was having physical problems near the end of her pregnancy. They thought helping a woman they'd gotten to like was the right thing to do regardless of whether she ultimately decided to part with her baby.

Which she did, and one of the things that helped her was the confidence that her daughter would never have to endure the untethered sensation Susann had experienced for most of her own life, though she loved her adoptive parents. As she lay in bed, about to go to the delivery room, Susann talked most to Jennifer about her determination to find the woman from whose body she'd emerged nineteen years earlier. As luck and the flow of adoption's history would have it, that woman had hired a private detective earlier in the year. He found Susann just three months after Susann gave birth to Katie.

Far more astounding than the coincidence of that timing was the fact that, when Susann told Mike the names of her birth parents, he realized he'd grown up with both of them in his small hometown of Danville, Kentucky, and the birth father's mother, Anna, was an old family friend. Mike decided he should contact her. "You won't believe it, Mike," Anna said on the phone, before he even had a chance to say why he'd called. "Susann has contacted us. We have prayed for that girl for eighteen years without knowing if she was dead or alive. It's been misery. Eddie (Susan's birth father) talked to her last night on the phone. She told him she was brought up in a good home and that gives us peace, but then she said she'd just given up her own child for adoption. So we've finally found her and now there's a grandbaby we won't know anything about."

Mike's voice was so choked with emotion that he could hardly hear his own reply: "Anna, that grandbaby is my baby." After a long moment's pause, during which disbelief turned to revelation, Anna began sobbing. "You have just made me the happiest person in the world. I don't care if I ever see her one time," she said. "It's enough just to know that that mystery baby is with people I know and trust." In fact, at the Osbornes' urging, she did subsequently meet Katie, but hasn't asked to do so again.

Relationships ebb and flow in extended families of any sort, so Anna might change her mind one day. Or Katie might initiate contact when she's older. There are no formulas, only the judgments of the adults involved. Mike and Jennifer decided, for instance, to distance themselves from Susann's mother after she visited their home a couple of times. "She never got over having to give up her own baby, which her parents made her do, and it obviously had a terrible, heartbreaking effect on her," explains Mike. "She was getting confused and saying unhealthy things, and it started to scare us. . . . She should have gotten some help a lot earlier, but I sure hope she gets some now."

The Osbornes didn't draw any grand conclusions about open adoption from their disquieting encounters with Katie's maternal grandmother, any more than they did from their warm feelings toward Anna. They simply did what they thought was best for their child, and they could feel secure in doing so because—for all of its imperfections and shifting realities—adoption's custodial boundaries are firmly drawn. The law says that, as long as specific procedures are followed beforehand, the people who adopt children become their permanent parents, with all the authority that implies.

Not so with the new reproductive technologies, which states have barely begun to address. So far, only one bill has been introduced anywhere to specify when a dead man's sperm may be used, and it received minimal interest from New York politicians; the measure would require a man to give written permission before his death and allow only his spouse or "partner" to attempt pregnancy with his sperm. This isn't a fanciful or theoretical matter. A woman in Los Angeles, Gaby Vernoff, had sperm removed from her husband's body about thirty hours after he died, became pregnant with it and, last March, gave birth to a girl. If she'd been a lesbian or needed money or had an infertile friend she wanted to help, could she and should she have given away or sold the sperm?

One final example: The states haven't even begun to deal with the burgeoning practice of embryo storage and transfer, even though the issues involved are morally, ethically, and legally enormous: Who can decide if, when, and into whom one of these lives-in-waiting may be implanted? Are they property that may be given away, abandoned, donated, or sold? Should the gathering of data about the biological parents be mandated, and what rights does the resulting child have to that information?

These aren't hypothetical questions that lawmakers are studying and anxiously waiting to address once they become pertinent. They are everyday occurrences already, and the decisions about them are being made, ad hoc, by fertility clinics, sperm banks, medical researchers, facilitators, and individuals. Bill and Lauren Schneider found that out two days after they returned home to Minnesota from New York in early 1999, after helping to execute a sting operation against a Hungarian baby merchant. Their phone rang. The woman at the other end of the line, in Texas, said she'd just seen a television report about the couple's adventure, which is recounted in Chapter Eight.

"I'd like to talk to you about some embryos I have," she said, explaining that she and her husband had twelve "extras" in addition to the one they'd used to have a child themselves. "They're frozen, and we'd like you to have as many as you think you might need." Before the Schneiders could decide whether to proceed, an opportunity to adopt a little girl came up and they seized it. When they informed the woman in Texas of what they were doing, she sent them a baby gift and e-mailed a final message: "The embryos are still yours if you ever want them."

In late October 1999, the Buffalo *News* ran this glimpse of the future by editorial cartoonist Tom Toles: A man and a woman are gazing lovingly at a swaddled bundle of joy in a crib in front of them. She says, "We chose your sperm from a genius sperm bank." He says, "We chose your egg from a fashion model website." The baby thinks, "Why would I want to have anything to do with you two stupid ugly people?" If America travels as aimlessly into the new procreative universe as it did into the world of adoption, there's no telling where the unintended consequences will begin—or end.

A Plethora of Variables

People involved in adoption know a lot about unintended consequences. They have not only helped to shape the lives of triad members, in some cases so profoundly that they've become revolutionaries, but have also contributed to the reconstruction of the practice itself. Former Soviet President Mikhail Gorbachev's shredding of the Iron Curtain is probably the most spectacular illustration of how events unrelated to adoption have fundamentally altered the institution. But it is the smaller instigators of change that best demonstrate why the prognostication game can be so difficult to play.

- In May 1997, an Arizona couple named Karen and Richard Thorne were charged with abusing the two four-year-old Russian girls they'd just adopted. Passengers and crew members who watched the slapping and screaming on the plane from Moscow to the United States testified against the Thornes; they were found guilty, ordered to receive parental training and therapy, and finally were granted custody of their daughters the next February. The girls spent the intervening months in five different foster homes.

  Such sensational stories are irresistible to the press and the public, but the episode would have received far less attention had it not occurred during a trial in Colorado of another American accused of beating another Russian child. Renee Polreis and her husband, David, had adopted the boy just eight months before he died at the age of two. Mrs. Polreis caused a sensation with her inventive defense: that her son's early life in an orphanage had left him so psychologically damaged that he inflicted the fatal injuries on his own genitalia, buttocks, and belly. A jury deliberated just two hours before finding Mrs. Polreis guilty of child abuse and sentencing her to twenty-two years in prison.

The Thorne and Polreis cases—disturbing as they were—actually did some good. They focused attention on the sometimes devastating effects of institutionalization; raised the level of general understanding about adoption's stresses on parents, particularly with children from orphanages abroad; and induced many agencies to bolster their training of people seeking intercountry adoptions. At the same time, the Thornes' experience in particular—because so many eyewitnesses vividly described the scene before television cameras—also triggered one of the biggest scares in modern adoption history.

Nationalistic members of Parliament in Moscow launched a drive to severely restrict or halt out-of-country adoptions. Reporters barely noted the effort, but it shook the child-welfare and adoption communities, and was serious enough to prompt politicians across the American political spectrum, from then House Speaker Newton Gingrich to Senator Edward M. Kennedy, to appeal to their Russian counterparts to reconsider.

They ultimately did, to a great extent because retaining the children also would have meant devising the programs and spending the money to care for them. For the same reason, I think Russia will end its current moratorium on adoptions soon after reforms in the process are implemented.

- During the 1988 Olympic Games in Seoul, NBC Sports broadcaster Bryant Gumbel told millions of viewers that while South Korea was anxious to show the world many parts of itself, "there are some aspects of their society they'd prefer we'd not examine so closely, and one of those concerns the exportation of Korean orphans for adoption abroad." Gumbel then introduced a report in which these adoptions were described as "embarrassing, perhaps even a national shame" for ordinary Koreans.

  Setting aside his insensitive wording, which turned children into commodities, Gumbel hit a political/emotional bull's-eye. "It was terribly painful and humiliating for the government and many Korean people," says Susan Soon-Keum Cox, who was once a Korean orphan and is now a vice president of Holt International Children's Services, the agency that arranged her adoption by an American couple. "Reforms certainly were needed, but this was presented in a way that helped no one—especially not the children who remained in orphanages instead of getting loving homes."

What officials did—in addition to initiating positive programs to upgrade institutional conditions, promote birth control, and urge more local adoptions—was to announce a ten percent annual reduction of foreign adoptions, leading to a complete halt in 1996. Other factors, including a financial downturn and an inability to find enough parents domestically, have prevented the politicians from implementing their pledge. But, for better or worse, the NBC broadcast rearranged adoption's realities. South Korea, long the biggest source of Americans' adoptions abroad, slashed the flow from a peak of more than 8,000 in 1986 to just over 2,600 by 1990; they haven't reached 2,000 in any year since.[12]

Both the episodes involving Russia and Korea show how fragile a massive social structure can be if it's built without a framework of rules and regulations (state policymakers' lack of oversight of adoption practices comes to mind, as does Congress's struggle to ratify the Hague Treaty). Equally important, these examples clearly demonstrate that closed doors don't only keep occupants in, they prevent information from getting out. So intelligent sportscasters talk about children as though they were television sets, politicians act according to their whims and, what's most troubling, people and whole nations draw broad conclusions from narrow incidents because they never develop any perspective.

• In 1993 a Canadian tabloid newspaper told the world that the singer Joni Mitchell had given birth out of wedlock thirty years earlier and relinquished the baby for adoption. Rather than issue a denial or refuse to comment, Ms. Mitchell for the first time started speaking out about her fear of telling her parents about her pregnancy, how hard it had been to give up her little girl, how she'd never stopped thinking about her. Revealing her secret had a therapeutic effect, and she realized it was time to find her daughter.

As it happens, a young artist in Toronto named Kilauren Gibb had started searching for her birth mother the previous year, soon after her parents finally told her, at the age of twenty-seven, that she'd been adopted. "I had a happy upbringing, which helps all of us know the adoption was the right thing, but finding out so late was devastating," she says. "Things are returning to normal, but it really hurt my relationship with my mom and dad. They only meant to make sure I felt like a real member of the family, but there's no excuse for not telling me something so important about myself for so long."

Kilauren met Joni Mitchell in early 1997, and the two now see each other regularly. Media reports about them have helped Americans, most of whom know little about such reunions, understand that relationships between adoptees and their biological parents can be positive for everyone involved. It is the very fact that such a famous birth mother decided to emerge into the open, though, that has had the greatest impact on the adoption community and on the integration of all its residents into the mainstream.

Just as adoptions by celebrities like actor Jamie Lee Curtis and newscaster Judy Woodruff have raised the institution's visibility and stature for all adoptive parents, and as the successes of adoptees like onetime Beatle John Lennon and skating champion Scott Hamilton have engendered pride in their fellow adoptees, Joni Mitchell's revelation—like those of entertainers Oprah Winfrey and Roseanne, and author Robert Fulghum—have emboldened other birth parents, lifted their spirits, and served as role models by knocking big chunks out of the wall of shame that society has erected around them.

While this book has focused on American adoptions—because this is where the action is, and practices vary so widely around the world—it's important to point out that nearly anything that happens here also has an impact outside our borders. That's not just true because we adopt more children from abroad than any other nation, but also because global communication has become so efficient that people everywhere know what we're doing, while international borders are becoming so porous that people from abroad can easily travel to the United States to get what may not be available to them back home.

A case in point: During the first week of the new century, a wealthy gay couple who had been unable to adopt and weren't legally permitted to hire a surrogate mother in their native England, flew from Los Angeles to London with their newborn twins. The men, Tony Barlow and Barrie Drewitt, had two embryos created with a mix of their sperm and a California woman's eggs, then had them implanted in another woman's womb. After giving birth, the surrogate signed custody over to the two fathers.[13] The transcontinental, homosexual, technological, and presumably very expensive pseudo-adoption was front-page news in Great Britain, where it ignited a firestorm of moral, political, and legal debates. Be certain that this is just the beginning. The decisions we make, or don't make, have enormous consequences, intended and unintended.

Pam Hasegawa, a photographer in New Jersey, certainly never expected to spend twenty-five years of her life looking for a woman she knew almost nothing about. Nor did she foresee, when her father handed her a copy of her hospital bill and the court order for her adoption, that her quest would one day transform her into a revolutionary. She didn't even do anything with the records for more than a decade; he had given them to his eighteen-year-old daughter in 1960 not to instigate a search, after all, but to allow her to prove she wasn't genetically related to her mother, who was clinically paranoid when she died six years earlier. Melvin Quayle just wanted Pam to be able to protect herself against the stigma that existed back then against people who were, or might become, mentally ill.

"This is your life. Take care of these documents," he told her. She did that, but it never occurred to her to do anything more. Until, at the age of thirty, after having married and started a career and borne two children, she picked up *The Search for Anna Fisher,* a seminal book by Florence Fisher about an adoptee's search for her birth mother. Pam read through her tears, then decided she'd denied the missing piece of herself for long enough. She dug out her adoption order and saw her original first name had been Rolande and her mother's was Synge, an Irish spelling. But the spelling on the hospital bill was Scandinavian: Signe. That wasn't much to go on, but she scoured libraries, interviewed family friends, and petitioned a court to get her original birth certificate. It listed her father's name as Peter Hampden and her mother's maiden name as Cunningham.

Hard work didn't get her anywhere, but the fates seemed to be watching over her. Pam had learned, from her parents and during her search, that her birth father died in a plane crash and that her birth mother had studied in Paris to be a musician. So, after a concert by a Scandinavian cellist in New York on a balmy May evening in 1978, Pam decided she had nothing to lose by asking him whether he knew any musicians named Sygne or Signe. Astonishingly, he did: a friend named Signe Sandstrom who had studied in Paris and lived just a couple of blocks from the Quayle family home in Manhattan.

It was almost too easy. Pam was exhilarated and nervous. Three weeks later, after rehearsing and rehearsing what she would say, she tried to keep the phone steady as she softly spoke her first words to the woman she was sure had carried her. "My name is Pam Hasegawa and I was born

Rolande Sygne Hampden on February 7, 1942," she said. "I've been looking for my natural mother for three and one-half years." The voice at the
other end was curt. "What's this got to do with me?" she replied.
"Agencies take care of things like that." This was as close to a confirma-
tion as Pam could have hoped for (next to a warm, inviting "yes"), since
she hadn't even mentioned that she was adopted.

Pam didn't want to impose herself, but she didn't want to lose contact
either. So she began writing to Signe Sandstrom. At the end of every letter, she offered an escape route: "If you are not my birth mother, please
send me a postcard and I will never write to you again." Seven years later,
the seventy-five-year-old woman finally responded with a short note and
a small portrait of herself, on which she'd written the date "1942." She
thanked Pam for sending Christmas presents and letters, but closed with
an ambiguous admonition: "For your own good, I urge you to stop this
search immediately."

Did that mean there was something Pam's mother didn't want her to
find out? Or that she would be disappointed to discover this woman was-
n't her mother after all? It was hard to believe Signe would accept her letters for so long if there was no bond between them, and Pam wasn't
worried about any skeletons she might find. So she kept sending letters,
although less frequently. Every Christmas, she'd send cookies.

On a rainy October night in 1992, Pam Hasegawa finally met Signe
Sandstrom. A housekeeper had found Pam's letters, neatly folded and
stored on a bedroom shelf, and called to ask if she wanted to see her em-
ployer before she died. The hour-long visit was friendly but unsatisfying.
Pam identified herself only as an acquaintance, and the ailing, frail
woman didn't recognize her. Three months later, Pam held Signe's hand
as she lay in a coma. A decade earlier, that might have been enough. Pam
hadn't been looking for another parent to raise her, just more information
about herself and a sense of completion, and now she could have both.
But in an age where nothing is real unless it's scientifically proven, Pam
decided to confirm what she believed was true by getting a DNA test.

A month later, on one of the most baffling days of her life, Pam was told
that she and Signe weren't related. She felt numb at first, then wept through
the night. Even now she shakes her head when she thinks about a lab report
she can't quite accept as accurate. "It felt as though I'd lost my mother a second time," she recalls. "It was a devastating experience, but I had to know. I
really did. We can't not search just because we might not find or because we
might be disappointed. It's a very deep, very basic need."

Pam still tries to track down a clue now and then, but she doesn't hold
out much hope that she'll ever meet her biological mother, who is quite

old now if she's still alive. "It would be great to hear her voice and thank her for my life and tell her everything turned out all right. But I'd be satisfied if I could just see her for a second, just one time." What's become more compelling for Pam than her personal pursuit, however, is working to unseal records and educate people about openness generally, so that future adoptees—and their birth parents—don't have to endure the emptiness and frustrations she's had.

The cadre of adoption activists in America is full of soft-spoken people like Pam, who look more like librarians than revolutionaries; some of the most zealous are deeply religious and staunchly conservative. But that's the transcendently revealing thing about their movement. It isn't fueled by rabble-rousers who feel unfulfilled unless they're trying to change the world, or by selfish personalities who want only to satisfy their own desires. Unlike most of the organizations that oppose them, they also don't stand to make a cent if they prevail. This is an extremely diverse array of people who, by virtue of their experiences, have arrived at a few simple understandings about a very complicated institution. Adoption is at the center of their souls and, except for a small minority who have been most grievously injured, all they want to do is make it better.

Penny Callan Partridge tries to do that in a unique way, with poetry. She is the living, breathing embodiment of the process that provided her with a family at both ends of her life. At fifty-six, the Massachusetts resident is the divorced white mother of an adopted biracial boy named Nathan. From the start, because she knew it was the right thing to do, Penny instigated an open adoption with the woman in Pennsylvania who placed a seven-week-old baby into her arms fourteen years ago.

She knew it was the right thing to do because she'd been adopted as an infant herself, by a wonderful couple in California, so she had a solid sense of what adoptees want and need and dream about. And she knew she didn't want her son to have to undertake a search as wearying as the three-year trek—made possible by her adoptive parents' memories and moral support—that finally led her to her own birth mother. The two women developed a loving bond that remained secure for almost thirteen years, until Catharine Callan died in her Wyoming home in 1989, at the age of eighty-six.

Adoption provides most of the people it touches with a beacon of hope, a second chance, or a family. Or all of the above. It still casts too many shadows on adoptees and their birth parents, but fewer with every day it spends in the light. In the magnificent forms of Zachary Michael and Emilia Kate, it has given Judy and me more sleepless nights and blessed us with more unmitigated happiness, provoked more anxiety and evoked more gratitude for being alive, than we ever could have imagined possible.

A decade ago, adoption gave Penny Partridge something she'd been seeking since she was a quiet little girl who told her fourth-grade teacher that she wanted to be a poet when she grew up: a subject that would consume her and that she could devour. If adoption has a poet laureate, it is Penny (who, while she was married, also adopted her ex-husband's daughter). And she's very good. In a maddeningly small number of words, she's able to evoke what it takes most of us a whole book to try and explain. This selection is called, aptly enough, "My Conclusion."[14]

I am a junk man's daughter,
I have some pipe from his junk yard.
I can see my face in it.
I have his face.
I am an accountant's daughter
I have a ledger he kept.
I can account for his words.
I have his name.
I am a teacher's daughter.
She encouraged her husband to paint.
I have his prize winning painting.
I have her hands.
I am an actress slash housewife's daughter.
I replay her scenes.
I have her mother's pearls.
I have her dreams.
I am from Arkansas
and Philadelphia,
South Dakota
and Pasadena,
Palo Alto and
Shehawken,
San Gabriel and
Massachusetts
I will leave on Earth
two adopted children.
And I will be part
of them.

Adoption Resources

There are hundreds of fine adoption-related resources in addition to the representative sample listed here, including local and statewide support and advisory groups around the country. The easiest way to find them is through the Internet. Virtually every adoption agency, attorney, and facilitator also has a site, as do thousands of triad members.

General Information

National Adoption Information Clearinghouse
P.O. Box 1182, Washington, DC 20013
888–251–0075
www.calib.com/naic

Evan B. Donaldson Adoption Institute
215 East 68th St., New York, NY 10021
212–269–5080
www.adoptioninstitute.org

Internet–Only Sites with Links

www.adopting.com
www.adopting.org
www.adoption.com
www.adoption.org
www.plumsite.com

Foster Care Adoption

North American Council on Adoptable Children
970 Raymond Avenue, St. Paul, MN 55114
612–644–3036
www.nacac.org

Child Welfare League of America
440 First Street, N.W., Washington, DC 20001
202–638–2952
www.cwla.org

Dave Thomas Foundation for Adoption
4288 West Dublin-Granville Road, Dublin, Ohio 43017
614–764–3100
nac.adopt.org/wendy.html

National Adoption Center
1500 Walnut Street, Suite 701, Philadelphia, PA 19102.
215–735–9988
nac.adopt.org/adopt/nac/nac.html

Membership/Advocacy

American Adoption Congress
1025 Connecticut Avenue, N.W. Washington, D.C. 20036
202–483–3399
www.american-adoption-cong.org
For all triad members and professionals

Bastard Nation (adoptees)
21904 Marine View Drive S., Des Moines, WA 98198
415–704–3166
www.bastards.org

Adoptees Liberty Movement Association
P.O. Box 727 Radio City Station, New York, NY 10101
212–581–1568
www.almanet.com

Concerned United Birthparents
2000 Walker Street, Des Moines, IA 50317
800–822–2777
www.webnations.com/cub

National Council for Single Adoptive Parents
P.O. Box 15084, Chevy Chase, MD 20825
202–966-6367
www.adopting.org/ncsapfrm.html

Family Pride Coalition (gay and lesbian)
P.O. Box 34337, San Diego, CA 92163
619–296–0199
www.glpci.org

Business/Professional

American Academy of Adoption Attorneys
P.O. Box 33053, Washington, DC 20033–0053
202–832–2222
www.adoptionattorneys.org

American Association of Open Adoption Agencies
www.openadoption.com

Joint Council on International Children's Services
7 Cheverly Circle, Cheverly, MD 20785
301–322–1906
www.jcics.org

Resolve (infertility and adoption)
1310 Broadway, Somerville MA 02144
617–623–0744
www.resolve.org

National Council for Adoption
1930 17th Street, N.W., Washington, DC 20009
202–328–8072
www.ncfa-usa.org

Search/Support

International Soundex Reunion Registry
P.O. Box 2312, Carson City, NV 89702
775–882–7755
www.plumsite.com/isrr/index.html

Council for Equal Rights in Adoption
356 E. 74th Street, Suite 2, New York, NY 10021
212–988–0110. www.adoptioncrossroads.org

Notes

CHAPTER 1

1. Evan B. Donaldson Adoption Institute [Conducted by Princeton Survey Research Associates], *Benchmark Adoption Survey: Report on Findings* (New York: Evan B. Donaldson Adoption Institute, 1997.

2. B. W. Donnelly and P. Voydanoff "Factors Associated with Releasing for Adoption Among Adolescent Mothers," *Family Relations*, 40 (1991), pp. 404–410.

3. H. D. Grotevant and R. G. McRoy, *Openness in Adoption: Exploring Family Connections* (Thousand Oaks, Calif.: Sage Publications, 1998).

4. B. Z. Sokoloff, "Antecedents of American Adoption," *The Future of Children: Adoption*, 3 (1) (1993), pp. 17–25.

5. Ibid.

6. Ibid.

7. Ibid.

8. Ibid.

9. A. Chandra, J. Abma, P. Maza, and C. Bachrach, "Adoption, Adoption Seeking and Relinquishment for Adoption in the United States," *Advance Data*, 306 (1999), Centers for Disease Control and Prevention/National Center for Health Statistics.

10. W. J. Kim, "International Adoption: A Case Review of Korean Children," *Child Psychiatry and Human Development*, 25 (3), Spring 1995, pp. 141–154.

11. U.S. Department of State, "Immigrant Visas Issued to Orphans Coming to the U.S.," 1999. On-line: http://travel.state.gov/orphan_numbers.html.

12. Ibid.

13. M. Berry and R. P. Barth, "Behavior Problems of Children Adopted When Older, *Child and Youth Services Review*, 11 (1989), pp. 221–238; and A. R. Sharma, M. K. McGue, and P. L. Benson, "The Emotional and Behavioral Adjustment of United States Adopted Adolescents: Part II. Age at Adoption," *Children and Youth Services Review*, 18 (1/2) (1996), pp. 101–114.

14. J. Kroll, "1998 U.S. Adoptions from Foster Care Projected to Exceed 36,000," *Adoptalk* (Winter) 1999, pp. 1–2.

CHAPTER 2

1. J. H. Hollinger, (Rel. 8–11/96) "Introduction to Adoption Law and Practice," pp. 1-1–1-84, in J. H. Hollinger (ed.), *Adoption Law and Practice* (New York: Matthew Bender).

2. J. H. Hollinger, (Rel. 12–5/99), "Aftermath of Adoption: Legal and Social Consequences," pp. 13-1–13-113, in Hollinger, *Adoption Law and Practice.*

3. J. A. Martin, B. L. Smith, T. J. Mathews, and S. J. Ventura, "Births and Deaths: Preliminary Data for 1998," *National Vital Statistics Reports,* 47(25), Oct. 5, 1999, Centers for Disease Control and Prevention. On-line: www.cdc.gov/ nchs/data/nvs47_25.pdf.

4. S. J. Ventura, W. D. Mosher, S. C., Curtin, J. C. Abma, and S. Henshaw, "Trends in Pregnancies and Pregnancy Rates by Outcome: Estimates for the United States, 1976–1996," *National Vital Statistics Reports,* 47(29), Dec. 15, 1999, Centers for Disease Control and Prevention. On-line: www.cdc.gov/ncha/data/nvs47_29.pdf; and Allan Guttmacher Institute, *Abortion Statistics (U.S.)* (1999). On-line: www.agi-usa.org/sections/abortion.html.

5. B. Z. Sokoloff, "Antecedents of American Adoption," *The Future of Children: Adoption,* 3 (1) (1993), pp. 17–25.

6. A. Kadushin, *Child Welfare Services* (New York: Macmillan, 1980).

7. M. Freundlich, *The Market Forces in Adoption* (Washington, D.C.: CWLA Press, 2000).

8. National Adoption Information Clearinghouse, *Adoption Numbers and Trends* (2000). On-line: www.calib.com/naic/adptsear/adoption/research/stats/num-bers.html.

9. B. Z. Sokoloff, "Antecedents of American Adoption," *The Future of Children: Adoption,* 3 (1) (1993), pp. 17–25.

10. M. Allen, "Women Accused of Baby-Selling Used a Friendly Approach," *New York Times,* May 31, 1999, pp. B1, B5.

11. V. A. Zelizer, *Pricing the Priceless Child: The Changing Social Value of Children* (Princeton, N.J.: Princeton University Press, 1985).

12. J. B. Boskey and J. H. Hollinger, (Rel. 13–11/99), "Placing Children for Adoption," pp. 3-1–3-73 In Hollinger, *Adoption Law and Practice.*

13. Ibid.

14. B. Duryea, "'Gray Market' for Adoptions Emerges," *St. Petersburg Times,* May 27, 1996, p. IB.

15. T. O'Neill, "Special Report on Birthfather Rights," *Adoptive Families* (Sept./Oct.) 1994, pp. 8–12.

16. Boskey and Hollinger, "Placing Children for Adoption," in Hollinger *Adoption Law and Practice.*

17. J. H. Hollinger, (Rel. 11–12/98), Appendix 1-A, "State Statutory Provisions Relating to Adoption" (pp. 1A-1–1A-195), in Hollinger, *Adoption Law and Practice.*

18. Ibid.

19. A. S. Rosenman, "Babies Jessica, Richard, and Emily: The Need for Legislative Reform of Adoption Laws," *Chicago-Kent Law Review,* 70 (1995), pp. 1851–1895.

20. Hollinger, "Aftermath of adoption."

21. J. Nast, "Mutual Consent Voluntary Registries: An Exercise in Patience—and Failure," *Adoptive Families* (Jan./Feb., 1999), pp. 30–33, 63.

22. Sokoloff, "Antecedents of American Adoption,"pp. 17–25.

23. E. W. Carp, *Family Matters: Secrecy and Disclosure in the History of Adoption* (Cambridge, Mass.: Harvard University Press, 1998).

24. Evan B. Donaldson Adoption Institute, *Openness in Adoption and Post-Adoption Contact Agreements: A Review of the Empirical Research and Current State Law* (New York: Evan B. Donaldson Adoption Institute, 1999).

25. J. L. Gritter, *The Spirit of Open Adoption* (Washington, D.C.: CWLA Press (1997).

26. L. R. Melina and S. K. Roszia, *The Open Adoption Experience* (New York: HarperCollins, 1993); and J. Gritter, *Adoption Without Fear* (San Antonio, Texas: Corona, 1989).

27. H. D. Grotevant and R. G. McRoy, 1998). *Openness in Adoption: Exploring Family Connections*. Thousand Oaks, Calif.: Sage Publications, 1998); R. P. Barth and M/ Berry, *Adoption and Disruption: Rates, Risks and Responses* (Hawthorne, N.Y.: Aldine de Gruyter, 1988); M. Berry, "The Practice of Open Adoption: Findings from a Study of 1396 Adoptive Families," *Children and Youth Services Review,* 13 (1991), pp. 379–395.

CHAPTER 3

1. Center for the Future of Children, "Adoption overview and major recommendations," *The Future of Children: Adoption,* 3 (1) (Los Altos, Cal.: David and Lucile Packard Foundation, Spring 1993), pp. 4–16.

2. U.S. Department of State, "Immigrant Visas Issued to Orphans Coming to the U.S.," 1999. On-line: http://travel.state.gov/orphan_numbers.html.

3. C. Haub,"Global and U.S. National Population Trends," *Consequences 1* (2), 1995. On-line: www.gcrio.org/CONSEQUENCES/summer95/population.html.

4. S. J. Morison, E. W. Ames, and K. Chisholm, "The Development of Children Adopted from Romanian Orphanages," *Merrill-Palmer Quarterly,* 41 (4) (1995), pp. 411–430.

5. The Joint Council on International Children's Services, "Intercountry Adoptions 1989–1998," *Bulletin of the Joint Council on International Children's Services* (Spring 1999).

6. U.S. Department of State, "Immigrant Visas Issued to Orphans Coming to the U.S.," 1999.

7. Ibid.

CHAPTER 4

1. National Adoption Information Clearinghouse. "Access to Adoption Records" (2000). On-line: www.calib.com/naic/factsheets/acctxt.htm.

2. Oregon Adoptee Rights Initiative, 2000. *Measure 58 Timeline: The Latest*. On-line: www.plumsite.com/oregon.

3. J. H. Neal, "Adopted Children Put Hope on Hold. Intermediaries to Aid Confidential Searches for Birth Parents. Md. Law Takes Effect in '99," *The Sun* (June 1, 1998). On-line: database: Proquest.

4. National Adoption Information Clearinghouse, "Access to Records."

5. See J. M. Pavao, *The Family of Adoption* (Boston: Beacon Press, 1998).

6. T. Lesaca, "Preadoption Risk Factors," *Psychiatric Times* (March 1998). On-line: www.mhsource.com/pt/p980358.html.

7. W. J. Kim, "International Adoption: A Case Review of Korean Children," *Child Psychiatry and Human Development*, 25 (3) (Spring 1995), pp. 141–154.

8. Maine Department of Human Resources, Task Force on Adoption, *Adoption: A Lifelong Process* (Maine: Maine Department of Human Resources, Task Force on Adoption, 1989).

9. National Adoption Information Clearinghouse, "Access to Adoption Records."

10. Abortion rates are lower in open records states (2000). On-line: www.plumsite.com/abortion.htm.

CHAPTER 5

1. National Committee for Adoption, *Adoption Factbook: United States Data, Issues, Regulations and Resources* (Washington, D.C.: National Committee for Adoption, 1989).

2. Ibid.

3. P. Sachdev, "Achieving Openness in Adoption: Some Critical Issues in Policy Formulation," *American Journal of Orthopsychiatry*, 61 (2) (1991), pp. 241–249; R. Avery, *Information Disclosure and Openness in Adoption: State Policy and Empirical Evidence* (Ithaca, N.Y.: Cornell University, 1996); Maine Department of Human Resources, Task Force on Adoption, *Adoption: A Lifelong Process* (Augusta, Maine: Maine Department of Human Resources, Task Force Adoption, 1989).

4. T. O'Neill, "Special Report on Birthfather Rights: How Do We Fairly Respect Everyone's Rights?" *Adoptive Families* (Sept./Oct. 1994), pp. 8–12.

5. National Adoption Information Clearinghouse, *Access to Adoption Records (2000)*. On-line: www.calib.com/naic/factsheets/acctxt.htm.

6. M. Freundlich, "Confidentiality Becomes Political: The New Strategy in Opposition to Open Records," *Decree*, 15 (4) (1997/1998), pp. 1, 3.

CHAPTER 6

1. American Society for Reproductive Medicine, "Fact Sheet: Infertility" (2000). On-line: www.asrm.org/fact/infertility.html.

2. Ibid.

3. Evan B. Donaldson Adoption Institute [Conducted by Princeton Survey Research Associates], *Benchmark Adoption Survey: Report on Findings* (New York: Evan B. Donaldson Adoption Institute, 1997).

4. J. B. Boskey and J. H. Hollinger, (Rel. 13–11/99), "Placing Children for Adoption," in J. H. Hollinger, *Adoption Law and Practice* (New York: Matthew Bender, 1988), pp. 3-1–3-73.

5. Adoption Advocates, "Legislative Alerts: April 25, 1996. Health Insurance Reform" (Adoption Policy Resource Center, 1996). On-line: www.fpsol.com/adoption/alert.html.

6. J. McKenzie, (1993). "Adoption of Children with Special Needs. The Future of Children," *Adoption*, 3 (1), pp. 62–88.

CHAPTER 7

1. U.S. Department of Health and Human Services, *The AFCARS Report: Current Estimates as of March 2000* (Washington, D.C.: Administration for Children and Families, 1999). On-line: www.acf.dhhs.gov/programs/cb/stats/tarreport/rpt0100/ar0100.htm.

2. Adoption and Safe Families Act of 1997. On-line: www.ggw.org/cap/emancipated.html.

3. T. McGuinness, "Mitigating the Effects of Institutionalization," *Adoptive Families* (May/June 1999), pp. 22–25.

4. U.S. Department of Health and Human Services, *The AFCARS Report: Current Estimates as of March 2000*.

5. J. S. Gottman. "Children of Gay and Lesbian Parents," in F. W. Bozztt and M. B. Sussman (eds.), *Homosexuality and Family Relations* (New York: Harrington Park Press, 1990), pp. 177–196).

6. C. Connolly, "The Description of Gay and Lesbian Families in Second-Parent Adoption Cases," *Behavioral Sciences and the Law*, 16 (1998), pp. 225–236.

7. R. P. Barth, J. D. Berrick, M. Courtney, and V. Albert, *From Child Abuse to Permanency Planning* (New York: Aldine De Gruyder, 1994).

8. R. J. Avery, *Public Agency Adoption in New York State, Phase I Report. Foster Care Histories of Children Freed for Adoption in New York State: 1980–1993* (Washington, D.C.: National Institute for Child Health and Human Development, U.S. Department of Health and Human Services, 1998).

9. C. Jenny, et al., "Are Children at Risk for Sexual Abuse by Homosexuals?" *Pediatrics*, 94, (1) (1994); D. Newton, "Homosexual Behavior and Child Molestation: A Review of the Evidence, Adolescence," *Pediatrics*, 13 (49) (1978).

10. P. S. Brucker, B. J. Perry, "American Indians: Presenting Concerns and Considerations for Family Therapists," *American Journal of Family Therapy* (Oct.-Dec. 1998), p. 307.

11. B. J. Jones (Author, *The Indian Child Welfare Act Handbook*), "The Need for a Separate Law." On-line: www.abanet.org/genpractice/compleat/f95child.html.

12. M. Sanchez, "Indians Fear Cultures Will Fade As Tribes Grow," *Kansas City Star*, Sept. 22, 1996, p. A1.

13. P. Wentz, "Why Is a Group That Has Helped Millions of People Trace Their Genealogy Fighting to Keep Oregon Adoptees from Getting Their Original Birth Certificates?" *Williamette Week*, Nov. 23, 1999, p. 14. On-line: www.wweek.com/html/religion112499.html.

14. National Council for Adoption, *Adoption Factbook III* (Washington, D.C.: National Council for Adoption, 1999), Table Three, p. 35.

15. "Views of the Hebrews," from the *Encyclopedia of Mormonism*, Ethan Smith's View of the Hebrews (Poultney, Vt., 1823; second enlarged edition, 1825). On-line: www.new-jerusalem.com/bom-answerman/view-of-hebrews.html.

16. L. Pritchard, "Church Sex Shame; Adoption Probe after Mormon Pedophiles Are Jailed," *Western Daily Press*, Nov. 27, 1999, p. 8; and J. Harding, "New Mormons Probe: Police Fears over Church's Adoptions Agency," *Bristol Evening Post*, Dec. 8, 1999, p. 2.

17. M. Campbell, "More Men Are Raising Children Alone, Census Report Says," *Kansas City Star*, Dec. 10, 1998. On-line: www.kcstar.com/item/pages/home.pat,local/30da970a.c10,.html.

18. U.S. Census Bureau. Statistical Abstract of the United States: 1999, Vital Statistics (Washington, D.C., 1999). On-line: www.census.gov/prod/99pubs/99statab/sec02.pdf; P. J. Smock, "Cohabitation in the United States: An Appraisal of Research Themes, Findings, and Implications," *Annual Review of Sociology*, 26 (2000).

19. E. Cose, "Our New Look: The Colors of Race," *Newsweek*, Jan. 1, 2000, p. 28.

20. F. Chideya, "Shades of the Future: Will Race Provide the Midcentury Crisis?" *Time*, Feb. 1, 1999, p. 54.

21. K. W. Albrecht, 1997–1998 National Transracial Adoptive Families Population Survey. The TransRacial Adoption Group Worldwide, Inc. U.S. House Ways and Means Committee Human Resources Subcommittee testimony (Sept. 15, 1998).

22. J. F. Shireman, "Adoptions by Single Parents," *Marriage and Family Review* 20 (3–4) (1995), pp. 367–388.

23. North American Council on Adoptable Children, "Foster Care and Adoption Assistance Rates" (1998). On-line: www.fpsol.com/adoption/research/fcusda.html.

24. A. Spake, "Adoption Gridlock," *U.S. News & World Report*, June 22, 1998, pp. 30–32, 34, 37.

CHAPTER 8

1. U.S. Department of Commerce, Economics and Statistics Administration, Bureau of the Census. *How We're Changing: Demographic State of the Nation: 1997.* Current Population Reports, Special Studies, Series P23–193 (March 1997). On line: www.census.gov/prod/2/pop/p23/p23–193.pdf.

2. A. Dunkin, "Adopting? You Deserve Benefits, Too," *Business Week*, Feb. 21, 2000, p. 160.

CHAPTER 9

1. U.S. Department of Health and Human Services, *The AFCARS Report: Current Estimates as March 2000* (Washington, D.C.: U.S. Department of Health and Human Services, Administration for Children and Families, 1999). On-line: www.acf.dhhs.gov/ programs/cb.

2. The Evan B. Donaldson Adoption Institute, *Openness in Adoption and Post-Adoption Contact Agreements: A Review of the Empirical Research and Current State Law* (New York: Evan B. Donaldson Adoption Institute, 1999).

3. D. J. Landry, L. Kaeser, and C. L. Richards, "Abstinence Promotion and the Provision of Information About Contraception in Public School District Sexuality Education Policies," *Family Planning Perspectives*, 31(6) (Dec. 1999), pp. 280–286.

4. K. Michelman, "Who Decides? A State-by-State Review of Abortion and Reproductive Rights"(2000). On-line: www.naral.org/publications/press/00jan/011300km.html.

5. Associated Press, "Abortion Clinic Numbers Decline in New York," *New York Times*, Jan. 14, 2000, p. B8.

6. C. Golberg, with J. Elder, "Public Still Backs Legal Abortion but With Conditions Like Limited Access, Poll Says," *New York Times*, Jan. 16, 1998, pp. A1, A16.

7. "U.S. Abortion Rate Is Lowest Since '75," *New York Times*, Jan. 7, 2000, pp. A16.

8. M. Williams, "Babies in the Trash," *Washington Post*, Feb. 4, 2000, p. A31.

9. "Vermont's Momentous Ruling," *New York Times*, Dec. 22, 1999, p. A26.

10. R. Smothers, "Accord Lets Gay Couples Adopt Jointly," *New York Times*, Dec. 22,1999, p. B4.

11. See A. Stone, "VA Doctor Found Guilty in Fertility Fraud," *USA Today*, Mar. 5, 1992, p. A1.

12. Holt International Children's Services, "International Adoption Statistics: Significant Source Countries of Immigrant Orphans 1985–1996" (2000). On-line: www.holtintl.org/insstats.html.

13. "A Better Breed of Dad," *The Guardian*, Jan. 12, 2000. On-line: www.guardianunlimited.co.uk/Archive/Article/0,4273,3949539,00.html.

14. Penelope Callan Partridge, *Pandora's Hope: Poems and Prose About Being Adopted* (Baltimore: Gateway Press, 1995).

Acknowledgments

It would take another chapter (a very long one) to thank the hundreds of people who, by intent or example, have taught me about and continue to guide me through the exhilarating, exasperating world of adoption. They include virtually everyone mentioned in this book and many more who are not: professionals such as Madelyn Freundlich, Joyce Maguire Pavao, and Maureen Hogan, who possess the intelligence to pierce even the densest concepts and the personalities to make learning from them a delight; generations of birth mothers from Sheila Hansen to Donna Asta to Temple Odom, who not only helped me understand the aching complexity of giving up one's offspring but also provided me with life-altering insights into the importance of genetic connections; adoptees including Crystal Lee Hyun Joo Chappell, Bill Troxler, and Mesha Goldsmith, who cemented my views about the essential power of personal roots and eased my insecurities by demonstrating that love truly is expansive rather than exclusionary; and fellow adoptive parents like Jane and David Nast, Carol and Michael Wierzba, Lois and Wallace Hannon, Dottie Finton and Kim Holt, Katherine Creedy and Jim Larson, all of whom showed me that the most fundamental advice we give our children—to treat other people as we would want to be treated—continues to enrich our lives as adults, and all of whom attest by their behavior every day to the basic truth that adoption—international or domestic, public or private, by a couple or an individual—is as wondrous, jubilant, and fulfilling a way to form a family as any other.

My profoundest gratitude also goes to all the adoptees, birth parents, and adoptive parents whose experiences are recounted in this book but whom I did not mention above, as well as to the dozens of triad members, agency officials, organizations, attorneys, searchers, and activists who were generous enough to share their stories and their wisdom but are not mentioned in these pages only because of space limitations. Though their names do not appear, their perceptions and their spirits informed me, shaped my thinking, and are reflected in every paragraph. It is no exaggeration to say that I couldn't have done it without them. In particular, I'd like to thank Susan Caughman for pointing out an embarrassingly obvious fact to me: that some people, in and out of the triad, will take umbrage at my comments on subjects about which they are particularly sensitive or will assume that specific criticisms reveal something intrinsically negative about a given aspect or type of adoption. I can only hope that readers will understand that even my toughest conclusions, and my recounting of even the most outrageous horror stories, are meant only to stimulate improvements in the process and not to denigrate either the institution or its participants (other than those few whose views or practices I explicitly fault).

However readers regard this book, they should know it is a work from the heart, an effort to make life better for all triad members, especially for my children and their fellow adoptees, by stripping away adoption's too numerous misconceptions and stereotypes. Seven people helped me to do that by reading the manuscript in its rawest forms, catching its flaws and suggesting changes that vastly enhanced the final product. They are Judy Baumwoll, my wife, who spent too many late nights poring over every word and applying her remarkable intelligence; Madelyn Freundlich, who not only knows more about adoption than any mortal has a right to, but also possesses one of the keenest minds and most generous souls I have encountered; Fred Greenman, whose devotion to reform is (or should be) intensely appreciated and admired by everyone who cares about adoption; Donald MacGillis, my colleague and friend who honored me with his considerable journalistic skills; Jonathan Kaufman, who proved to be as fine a critic as he is a writer and aficionado of Thai cuisine; Jo Ann Miller, my mercifully proficient editor, whom I cannot thank enough for believing in my notion of an adoption revolution; and Leigh Nowicki, who helped me more than she knows with her research and patience.

I am very grateful to my employers, especially Matthew V. Storin, Gregory Moore, Nils Bruzelius, and my favorite boss of all time, Helen Donovan, for their support of my 1998 series on adoption in the *Boston Globe* and for their cooperation in granting me a leave of absence to expand those newspaper articles into this book. I also want to acknowledge the Century Foundation's selection of *Adoption Nation* for its 1999 Leonard Silk Fellowship; it is a personal honor that I deeply appreciate, but, more significantly, I view it as recognition by a serious, impartial national organization of adoption's emerging prominence, growing acceptance and vital role in American life.

Finally, but most important, I want to express my thanks to the people closest to me for providing emotional support and putting up with my insane single-mindedness during a very long year of research and writing. Judy, Zack, and Emmy gave the most, of course, but I also received invaluable encouragement and understanding from my other family members: my parents, Chaim and Frieda Pertman; my twin brother and his wife, Henry and Patricia Pertman; my sister and brother-in-law, Rita and Walter Abel; my brother and sister-in-law, Allan and Mina Pertman; all of my siblings' spouses, sons and daughters, and grandchildren; and my sister from a previous life, Jane Simon. I love you all more than I have the capacity to express, and I am blessed by your presence in my life. If you weren't my relatives already, I'd want to adopt you.

Index

AAC. *See* American Adoption
  Congress
Abandonment, legalization of, 216
Abortion, 6, 32, 35, 95–96
  and open adoption, 94–95, 115, 193
  and politics, 215–216
Abstinence-plus courses, 215
Abuse, of adoptees, 225–226
Activists, adoption, 19, 231
ACT-Up, 79
Adopt America, 91, 193
Adoptee-rights movement, 79, 82
Adoptees, 5, 6–7, 87, 88–90, 137, 228
  and abuse, 225–226
  and adoptive parents, 133–134
  as adults, stereotype of, 111
  behavior problems of, 24
  and biological parents, 11–12
  and counseling, 85–86
  deportation of, 146
  fantasies of, 97–98, 135
  and health insurance, 145–146
  and health problems, 87–88, 172
  and identity issues, 84–87
  prejudice against, 133.
    See also Roots, search for
Adoptees Liberty Movement Assoc.,
  80
Adoption
  changes in, 4–6
  history of, 6, 15–18
  normalization of, 206, 217
  process of, 24–25, 131–132, 142–143
  promotion of, 106 (*see also* Coercion).
    See also Closed adoption; Open
    adoption

Adoption and Safe Families Act, 176
  and federal assistance, 179–180
Adoption Factbook (NCFA), 169
Adoption law. *See* Regulation
Adoption Triangle: The Effects of the
  Sealed Record on Adoptees, Birth
  Parents, and Adoptive Parents
  (Baran, Pannor, and Sorosky),
  46
Adoption 2002, 176
Adoptive parents, 6, 137
  and adoptees, 133–134
  and bonding, 47–48, 111, 132
  contact with biological parents, 13,
    113, 214
  famous, 228
  fantasies of, 139
  fears of, 142–143
  illegal actions of, 196
  and injuries, emotional, 18
  and open adoption, 115
  and privileged class, 199–203
  profile of, 108
  and searches, 123–124
  stereotype of, 141
Adults with disabilities, 158–160, 163
Africa, 54, 56
African Americans, 158, 168, 178
Age, of adoptees, 24, 92, 164, 202
Agencies, adoption, 10, 41–42, 59–63
Aid to Families with Dependent
  Children, 173
Alabama, 32, 44, 82, 175, 216
Alaska, 32, 95
Albrecht, Scott, 132–133
Alcoholism, 210

American Academy of Adoption
    Attorneys, 105, 195
American Adoption Congress (AAC),
    32, 80, 110, 114, 117, 192, 203
American Greetings company, 19–20
Americans with Disabilities Act, 160
Apple Computer, 203
Arizona, 162
Arkansas, 162
Asia, 54, 56, 196
Asta, Donna, 9–11, 48–49
Austin, Patricia, 124, 144

Baby boomers, 34–35, 129–130, 186
Baby Jessica case, 105, 118, 120, 122
Baby Richard case, 8, 118, 120, 122
Baby-selling, 29, 38–39, 60, 187–189,
    193–194, 194–195, 199
    and birth parents, 188–189
    and the Internet, 187–192
    penalties for, 191–192.
    See also Profiteering
Balinalik, Steve and Linda, 68–72
Baran, Annette, 46
Barlow, Tony, 228
Barr, Roseanne, 5, 228
Barth, Richard, 164
Bastard Nation, 79, 80, 117, 203, 219
Benefits, adoption-related, 203–206
Biological parents
    contact with adoptive parents, 13,
        113, 214
    and social stigma, 10 *See also* Birth
        fathers; Birth mothers; Birth
        parents
Birth certificates, access to, 31–33,
    78–82, 143–145
    See also Closed adoption; Open
        adoption; Records, access to;
        Registries
Birth fathers, 106, 118–120
    and custody, 122–123
    rights of, 44, 121–123
    stereotype of, 118
    See also Birth parents
Birth mothers, 137. 200-201
    advertising to find, 108
    attitudes toward, 9
    and change of mind, 109

and coercion, 105, 197–198
and confidentiality, 33–34, 80–81,
    94–95, 115, 123, 143–145
healing process for, 11
and injuries, emotional, 12, 110–111
and loss, 112
and regaining custody, 103–105
and relinquishment, 10
stereotype of, 10, 111, 141
    See also Birth parents
Birth parents, 6, 12, 137
    and adoptive parents, economic
        disparity between, 201
    adoptive parents' fantasies about,
        139
    and baby-selling, 188–189
    emotional and injuries, 18
    illegal actions of, 196
    influence on adoptive parents, 135
    and searches, 123–124
    stereotype of, 138
    See also Birth mothers; Birth fathers
    views on adoption process, 132
    Birth fathers
Black Child Welfare Acts, 169
Black market, 57, 73
Bliley, Thomas J., 191–192
Blood relatives, 80
Bolivia, 177
Bonding, 35, 47–48, 111, 132
Bounties, 195–196
Brace, Rev. Charles Loring, 17
Burkette, Mike and Rita, 180–182

Callan, Catharine, 231
Canada, 68, 227
Cannon, Alfred O., 83, 135
Caribbean, 56
Catholic Charities adoption agency, 10
Catholic Social Services, 202
Ceausescu, Elana, 72
Ceausescu, Nicolae, 55–56, 72
Central America, 54, 56, 57
Chappell, Crystal Lee Hyun Joo,
    52–53, 174
Chappell, Garnet and Michael,
    173–175
Child placement, 41–42, 43, 149
    regulation, 162–163, 167–168

Children, trafficking in, 185–186
  See also Baby-selling
  Profiteering
Children with special needs, 92, 138,
  218–220
  and adoption costs, 149
  and adoption-related benefits, 206
  and institutionalization, 153,
    160–162
  and international adoption, 151–154
  and nontraditional parents, 163–164
Children's Action Network, 159
Children's Aid Society, 17
Children's Bureau, 36
Child-selling, 187
  See also Baby-selling
China, 15, 21–22, 23, 55, 57–58, 63, 64,
  65, 163, 186, 216
Chosen Angel Adoption, 185
Chung, Connie, 143–145
Church of Jesus Christ of Latter-Day
  Saints. *See* Mormons
Clinton, Bill, 176, 215
Clinton administration, 25, 203
Closed adoption, 12, 32, 210
CMP Media, 204
Coercion, 105, 197–198, 221
  See also Adoption: promotion of
Colombia, 151
Colonists, 16
Colorado, 41, 82, 175
Committee on Women, Family, and
  Youth Affairs, 65
Companies, U.S., 203–206
Computer searches, 79–80, 81. *See also*
  Internet
Concerned United Birthparents (CUB),
  105, 117, 125
Confidentiality, 12
and birth mothers, 33–34, 80–81,
  94–95, 115, 123, 143–145
  See also Privacy, invasion of
Congress, U.S., 82, 146, 189
  and baby- selling, penalties for,
    191–192
  and Hague Treaty, 66, 191–192, 193,
    227
Connecticut, 41
Consent, revocation of, 43–44

Contact between biological and
  adoptive parents, 13, 113, 214
  benefits for adoptees, 11–12
  conflicts about, 138–139
  and economic gap, 201–202
  effects of, 136–138
  and international adoption, 146–148,
    173–174
  See also Open adoption
Contraception, 215
Cooperative adoption agreements, 47,
  212
Co-parenting, 48
Correia, Susan and Russell, 20–22, 58
Costs, 20, 28–29, 33, 73, 149, 154, 195
  effect on adoptees, 25
  and independent adoption, 36
  and international adoption, 22,
    67–72
  laws governing, 39
  medical and living, 42
  and physical condition of adoptees,
    202
  and profiteering, 38–39
  and surrogacy, 163. *See also* Money
Counseling, 48, 85–86, 197, 222
  post-placement, 149
Cox, Susan Soon-Keum, 227
Creedy, Kathryn, 176–178
Crosby, David, 5
Cruise, Tom, 5
CUB. *See* Concerned United
  Birthparents
Culture, 19
Curtis, Jamie Lee, 228
Custody
  and birth fathers, 122
  and birth mothers, 103–105

Dances With Wolves (movie), 168
Dave Thomas Foundation for
  Adoption, 159, 179, 203
Delaware, 32, 41, 82, 123
Department of Health and Human
  Services, U.S., 159
Discrimination, 145–146, 162–163, 167,
  217–218
Divorce, 14, 171–172
DNA testing, 230

Drewitt, Barrie, 228
Drug abuse, 210

East, Caprice, 82
Eastern Europe, 55, 57, 92, 151, 196, 214
Education about heritage, 57–58
  and relinquishment, 10
Egg donors, 21, 224
Embryos, frozen, 221, 224–225
England, 15–16, 194, 228–229
English, P. C., 16
English common law, 15
Estonia, 62
Ethnicity, 92, 158
Ettore, James, 108
Europe, 54
Evan B. Donaldson Adoption
  Institute, 7–8, 36, 114, 121,
  132–133, 192
Evans, Maureen, 57

Facilities, transitional, 157
Families, nontraditional, 49, 89, 175,
  222–224
  proliferation of, 14
  teaching about, 14–15, 172
Families, traditional, 171
Family and Medical Leave Act,
  203–204
Family of Adoption, The (Pavao), 100
Family reunification, 24
Family trees, 14, 33
Fantasies: of adoptees, 97–98, 135
  of adoptive parents, 139
Fathers. *See* Birth fathers; Single
  fathers
Federal assistance, 178–180
Ferguson, Joseph, 122
Fertility treatments, 130, 131
Finton, Dottie, 218, 219–220
Fisher, Florence, 80, 229
Florida, 42, 43, 162, 163, 175
Ford, Gerald, 5
Fortune 500 firms, 203
Foster care, 6, 158, 167, 179, 210
  and adoption process, 24–25
  See also Public sector

Foster-care system, 5, 149, 150–151,
  180–182, 200, 214
  reformation of, 157–161, 164
Foundling homes, 17, 45
Franklin, Lisa, 124, 144
Fraud, 187, 195–196
Frederick, Harold and Melissa, 28–29,
  41–43
Freundlich, Madelyn, 36, 121
Friedman, Herbert, 41, 120
Fulghum, Robert, 228

Gable, Clark, 209
Gates, Bill, 39
Gaul, John, 146
Gay parents, 158, 162
  stereotype of, 166
  See also Nontraditional parents
Gender of adoptees, 31, 164
  and adoption costs, 202
Genealogy, 33
Georgia (U.S. state), 39
Georgia (republic), 64, 65
Germany, 54
Gibb, Kilauren, 227–228
Gillman, Sally, 59–60
Gilpatrick, Gail, 97–100
Gingrich, Newton, 226
Goldberg, Mesha, 90–92
Goldsmith, Carol, 91, 159–160
Goodman, Ellen, 134–135
Gorbachev, Mikhail, 225
Government regulation, 37, 39
Graessle, William, 124
Grandparents, 217
Greece, 54
Greenman, Fred, 118–119
Grotevant, Harold, 48
Guatemala, 57, 59, 64, 176
Gumbel, Bryant, 226–227

Hague Treaty, 66–68, 191–192, 193, 227
Hamilton, Scott, 228
Hampden, Peter, 229
Hannon, Lois and Wallace, 151–154
Hansen, Sheila, 3–4, 94
Hasegawa, Pam, 229–231
Hawaii, 216–217

Health-care system, 186
Health insurance, 196
    and adoptees, 145–146
    and infertility, 204, 205
Health problems of adoptees, 172
"Herman" (cartoon), 19
Hicks, Thomas Jugarthy, 39
Hill, Helen, 79
Hogan, Maureen, 193
Holt, Bertha and Harry, 55
Holt, Kim, 218, 219–220
Holt International, 55, 146, 227
Holton, Barbara, 158
Homes, for unwed mothers, 196–197
    and promotion of adoption, 106
Home study, 42
Homophobia, 175–176, 192
Homosexual parents, 158, 162–163,
    172, 217–220
    and surrogacy, 228–229
    See also Gay parents; Lesbian
    parents
Humphreys, Joan, 108

Idaho, 163
Identity
    and adoptees, 84–87
    and language, 88–90
    and open adoption, 92–93
    and physical traits, 90
    search for, 77
    and transracial adoption, 90–92
Illegal activities, 195–196
Immigration and Naturalization Act,
    146
Immigration and Naturalization
    Service (INS), 23, 37, 57
Independent adoption, 36–37
India, 54
Indiana, 162
Indian Child Welfare Act, 167,
    168–169, 171
Industrial Revolution, 16
Infants: adoptions of Caucasians, 22,
    37, 202
Infertility, 15
    and baby boomers, 129–130
    and health insurance, 204, 205

medical interventions for, 21, 186
    stereotype of infertile couples,
    130–131
Injuries, emotional
    and adoptive and birth parents, 18
    to birth mothers, 12, 110–111
INS. *See* Immigration and
    Naturalization Service
Insemination, 218
Institute for Black Parenting, 179
Institutionalization of children, 60–63,
    153, 160–162
    effects of, 150–151, 226
    problems with, 86–87
Insulman, Mary, 27, 32, 33, 87–88, 208
Insurance firms: and adoption-related
    benefits, 206
Intercountry adoption, 53–58, 92, 159,
    176–178, 191–192
    See also International adoption
Internal Revenue Service, 199–200
International adoption, 21–23, 146–148,
    151–154, 173–174, 200, 226–227
    ethics of, 59–74
    ongoing changes in, 64–72
    See also Intercountry adoption;
    Transracial adoption
Internet, 32, 37, 79–80, 81, 186, 108,
    218–219, 222
    and baby-selling, 187–192
    and circumvention of regulation,
    162
    and computer searches, 127. *See also*
    Computer searches; World Wide
    Web
    and profiteering, 148
    registries, 190
    and roots, search for, 13
    and trafficking in children, 185
Interstate Compact on the Placement
    of Children, 43

Japan, 54
Jobs, Steve, 5, 203
Johnson, Carolyn, 218–219
Joint Council on International
    Children's Services, 57
Journey of the Adopted Self (Lifton), 10

Kansas, 17, 32, 43, 95
Katz, Jeffrey, 25
Kaufman Adoption, 185
Kaye, Jeffrey, 105
Kelly, Charlene, 107–109, 113
Kennedy, Edward M., 146, 226
Kentucky, 43
Kinship care, 178, 179
Konkol, Daniel, 132–133
Korea, 57, 65, 73, 163
Korean War, 23, 46, 52–53, 55
Kovacs, Tamas, 189–191, 192

Language, impact of: on adoptees,
    88–90
  ignorant use of, 88–90
La Raza Child Welfare Acts, 169
Larson, Jim, 165–166
Lastick, Jerald and Rhea, 62
Latin America, 23, 177, 196
Lawsuits
  and invasion of privacy, 144–145
  and wrongful adoption, 61–63
Learning Channel, The, 97
Leavitt, David Keene, 122–123
Legal guardianship, 36
Legislation. *See* Regulation
Leigh, Mike, 33
Lennon, John, 228
Lesbian parents, 158, 162. *See also*
    Nontraditional parents
Lett, Danielle, 196–197, 198
Levin, Carl, 116
Lewis, Barbara, 126
Lewis, Judy and Tom, 209
Lewis, Tom, 209
Lifton, Betty Jean, 110
Loans for adoption, 199
Lyons, Champs, 175
Mancinelli, Gary and Joan, 62
Marianna State Prison, 126
Marriage, 171–172
  same-sex, 216–217
Maryland, 82, 176
Massachusetts, 16–17, 28–29, 41–42,
    61–62, 105, 217

Matching of adoptees and prospective
    adoptive parents, 30, 31, 218
Mathis, Dean and Betty Sue, 211
MBNA America, 204
McCain, John, 116
McRoy, Ruth, 48
Media, 8, 161, 227–228
  and abuse stories, 225–226, 226–227
  examinations of adoption, 144–146
  effect on adoption, 97
  and perpetuating stereotypes,
    143–146
Medicaid, 188, 196
Medical interventions: for infertility,
    21, 186
Mental illness, 210
Michigan, 162
Middle East, 176
Minnesota, 216
Minnesota Act of 1917, 30
Minorities, 58
  adoption among, 22
  legal protections for, 172
Mitchell, Joni, 5, 227–228
Money
  influence on adoption, 141, 148
  See also Baby-selling; Costs;
    Profiteering
Montana, 82
Morgan, Brenda and David, 185
Morgan, Ron, 135
Mormons
  adoption practices 170–171
  resistance to open adoption, 115
Morning-after pills, 215–216
Moskowitz, Barbara, 125–126
Mothers. *See* Birth mothers; Single
    mothers; Unwed mothers
Mothers' Pensions, 172
Multiethnic parents, 53, 56, 57–58
Multiethnic Placement Act, 176,
    178–179
Musser, Sandy, 125–127, 128
Musser Foundation, 125–126
Mutual consent registries, 44, 80, 116
"My Conclusion" (Partridge), 232

Nast, Jane, 117
National Adoption Center, 203, 218–219
National Center for Health Statistics, 215
National Center for Social Statistics, 36
National Council for Adoption (NCFA), 94, 95, 167, 193, 199
    deceptive actions by, 169–171
    resistance to open adoption, 114–116
Native Americans, 166–171
NCFA. *See* National Council for Adoption
Nebraska, 17
New Jersey, 220
New York state, 164
Nickles, Don, 146
Nontraditional parents, 158–159, 163–164, 171
    See also Homosexual parents; Multiethnic parents
North American Council for Adoptable Children, 159, 179
Northern Ireland, 176

Odom, Temple, 211–214, 223
O'Donnell, Rosie, 5
Ohio, 82
Oklahoma, 122, 162
One Church, One Child, 179
Open adoption, 33–34, 211–214, 222
    and abortion, 94–95, 115, 193
    and adoptive parents, 115
    benefits of, 11–14, 19, 207–208, 210–211
    and cooperative adoption agreements, 47, 212
    and custodial boundaries, 224
    future trends, 214–217
    guidelines, 47–48
    history, 45–46
    and identity issues, 92–93
    negative effects, 12, 200–201
    resistance to, 114–117

stereotype of, 116
    See also Birth certificates, access to; Closed adoption; Records, access to
Openness movement, 37
Oregon, 27–28, 32, 79–82, 94, 163, 169
Organ transplants, 87, 219
Orphan train movement, 17–18
Osborne, Jennifer and Mike, 212–214, 223–224
Out-of-home care, 158

Palmer, Jim, 5
Pannor, Reuben, 46
Parenting classes, 149, 165, 220
Parent Network for the Post-Institutionalized Child, 153
Parents. *See* Adoptive parents; Biological parents; Birth parents; Multiethnic parents; Nontraditional parents; Single parents
Partridge, Penny Callan, 231–232
Pavao, Joyce, 89, 98, 100, 139
Pediatrics (journal), 16
Pennsylvania, 42–43, 81, 125
Personality conflicts among triad members, 48
Physical traits, 31, 90
Pierce, William, 95, 115–116, 169, 171, 193, 199
Placement. *See* Child placement
Politics of abortion, 215–216
Polreis, Renee and David, 226
Post-placement counseling, 149
Poverty, 166, 210
Prejudice against triad members, 88–90
    against adoptees, 133
Privacy, invasion of, 144–145
    See also Confidentiality
Profiteering, 38–39, 107
    and the Internet, 148
    See also Baby-selling; Children, trafficking in

Putative-father registries, 44, 120
Putin, Vladimir, 65

Quayle, Melvin, 229

Race, 19, 92, 164
    and adoption costs, 202
    of children in foster care, 158
Racial intermarriage, 172
Racism, 210
Rape victims, 9
Records, access to, 27–28, 30–33, 44–45,
    141, 169–171, 214
    See also Birth certificates, access to;
    Open adoption; Roots, search for
Reform groups: and open adoption,
    114–117
Registries, 44–45, 80, 115, 116, 120, 127,
    169, 190
Regulation, 16–17, 18, 39, 158, 216
    and access to records, 141
    and birth certificates, access to,
        31–33
    child placement, 162–163, 167–168
    circumvention of, 162–163
    closed adoption, 32
    and embryo storage, 224–225
    and homosexual parents, 217–218
    inconsistencies in, 40–44
    and intercountry adoption, 55
    and placement, 41–42
    and search for roots, 115, 125
    and unlawful searches, 126–127
Religious conservatives, 32, 94, 106,
    115
Religious groups, 197
Relinquishment, 10, 22, 29–30
Reproductive technology: and
    custodial boundaries, 224
Republicans, 215
Reunion (television program), 97
Rhode Island, 43
Rhode Island Adoption Exchange,
    25
Right to Life, 10
Romanchik, Brenda, 201–202

Romania, 55–56, 57, 61, 62, 68–74,
    151–154, 177
Rome, 15
Roosevelt, Theodore, 172
Roots, search for, 13, 15, 112, 115,
    125–128, 136, 191, 227–231
    See also Birth records, access to;
    Records, access to; Searches
Roots, 33
Roseanne (Roseanne Barr), 5, 228
Rosen, Benjamin, 188
Russia, 23, 55, 57, 59, 65–66, 68–72,
    186, 226, 227

Salaverri, Georgia, 131–132
Same-sex marriage, 216–217
Sandstrom, Signe, 229–230
Savely, Jim, 34
Schneider, Lauren and Bill, 189–191,
    225
Schools
    and abstinence-plus courses, 215
    and verbal ignorance, 88–89
Scrivens, Linda, 103–105
Search and consent procedures, 44, 80
Searchers, 125–128
Searches, 97–101, 123–124, 126–127
    See also Computer searches;
    Internet; Registries; Roots, search
    for; World Wide Web
Search for Anna Fisher, The (Fisher),
    229
Search Institute (Minnesota), 86
Secrecy, 7, 30, 210, 222
Secrets and Lies (movie), 33
Sexual abstinence, 215
Sexual orientation, 217
Shelters, 197
Shevardnadze, Eduard, 64
Shevardnadze, Nanuli, 64, 65
Single fathers, 33
    and social stigma, 119–120
    See also Birth fathers
Single mothers, 33, 35
    See also Biological mothers; Birth
    mothers

Single parents, 158–159, 178, 186,
 215
  See also Biological parents; Birth
  parents
Small World Adoptions, 34
Smith, Christopher H., 191–192
Smith, Lamar, 146
Social stigma, 3–4, 8, 10, 30–31,
  106–107, 119–120, 206, 212
Sorosky, Arthur D., 46
South America, 56
South Korea, 23, 151, 226–227
Soviet bloc, 92, 151
Soviet Union, 23, 56
Sperm banks, 222
Sperm donors, 21, 224
Spielberg, Steven, 5, 159
Spotters, of babies and pregnant
  women, 195
Stapf, Rita, 126
Stereotypes, 8, 19–20, 40, 116, 206
  of adoptees as adults, 111
  of adoptive parents, 141
  of birth parents, 10, 111, 118, 138,
  141
  of children with special needs, 218
  of gay parents, 166
  of infertile people, 130–131
  and the media, 143–146
Sunday's Child appeals, 218
Supreme Court, U.S.
  and access tobirth certificates, 79
  and granting custody to birth
  fathers, 122–123
Surrogacy, 21, 163, 218, 228–229
Synder, Virginia, 124

Tann, Georgia, 38–39, 194
Tax breaks, 200
Tax credits, 39, 189, 206
Technology, reproductive, 224, 225
Tennessee, 32, 34, 82, 94, 95, 123, 169,
  171
Tennessee Children's Home Society,
  38
Tepper, Thais, 153

Terminal Illness Emergency Search
  program, 219
Texas, 42, 162, 216
Theft of infants, 39
Thomas, Dave, 203, 205–206, 207, 208
Thomas, Rex, 205
Thorne, Karen and Richard, 225–226
Toles, Tom, 225
Training courses. *See* Parenting classes
Transitional facilities, 157
Transplants, 87, 219
Transracial adoption, 23, 52–53, 56,
  90–92, 159, 176
  and behavior problems, 53
  and federal assistance, 178–180
  and foster care, 180–182
  recruitment efforts for, 180–181
  See also International adoption
Tressler Lutheran Services, 158
Triad members. *See* Adoptive parents;
  Biological parents; Birth parents
Troxler, Bill, 77, 81–82, 83–84, 135–136,
  208
20/20 (television show), 143–145

Uncommon Knowledge (Lewis), 209–210
Unconventional families. *See* Families,
  nontraditional
Unethical behavior, 195-196
  and international adoption, 59–74
United States, 15–18, 51, 58, 68
  adoption statistics, 7, 29, 35–36
  obstacles to adoption, 23–24
  relinquishment and seeking, 22
Unwed mothers, 196–198
  laws protecting, 43, 44
  and secrecy, 210
  and social stigma, 3–4, 30–31,
  106–107
Ussery, Kimberly, 185
Utah, 162, 163
Vermont, 82, 217
Vernoff, Gaby, 224
Vietnam, 59
Virginia, 176
Washington, 163

Wendy's Old Fashioned Hamburgers, 203, 204–206
West Virginia, 44
White House Conference on the Care of Dependent Children, 172
Wierzba, Carol and Michael, 11, 48–49, 139–140
Wilkinson, Signe, 221

Winfrey, Oprah, 228
Wisconsin, 175
Woodruff, Judy, 228
World Wide Web, 33, 79, 108, 221
    registries on, 127. *See also* Internet
Wrongful adoption lawsuits, 61–63

Young, Loretta, 209–210, 211

About the Author

Adam Pertman is a staff reporter for the *Boston Globe*. He was nominated for a Pulitzer Prize for a series of articles on adoption published by the *Globe* and has been awarded the Century Foundation's Leonard Silk Journalism Fellowship for *Adoption Nation*. He and his wife, Judy Baumwoll, live with their two adopted children in Newton, Massachusetts.

For more information about *Adoption Nation*, the author, and adoption in general, visit Adam Pertman's web site, www.adoptionnation.com.